AI for Business

The Beginner's Fast Track to ChatGPT for Productivity, Profit, and Growth (2 books in 1)

Russel Grant

Contents

Prompt Engineering and ChatGPT

ChatGPT for Business 101

Prompt Engineering and ChatGPT

How to Easily 10X Your Productivity, Creativity, and Make More Money Without Working Harder

Introduction

Perched within the embrace of three branches atop an old oak tree behind my home, I found myself looking closely at my to-do list and realizing how overwhelming it is to be a business owner.

I own a small business that specializes in crafting exquisite handmade furniture. However, there was one thing I knew I needed to do but didn't really have the knowledge or time for—social media and internet marketing.

You see, I'm an old-fashioned guy. I prefer spending my time creating beautiful furniture in my workshop than promoting and marketing my business online. Hashtags and algorithms seem alien to me; I cherish the feel of wood under my hands and the scent of freshly sawn fine lumber.

While I have customers who love what I do, I knew there were so many potential customers out there yet to discover my work.

These potential customers are more tech-savvy and are attracted to the glitz and glamour of online ads and social media campaigns. With the presence of artificial intelligence (AI), I knew it was a call to level up and meet demands.

I heard about ChatGPT in February of 2023, and it changed my story. I did my research and learned that it could help with marketing, content creation, website building, and many more of the tasks I had been avoiding all this time.

Skeptical at first, I decided to give it a try. I sat at my cherry wood desk, pulled out my laptop, and typed in my first prompt: "Give me a step-by-step guide on how to build a business website."

ChatGPT's response blew my mind, and it never remained the same again. Going forward, I used it in crafting social media posts, coming up with email campaigns, writing blog posts to keep my audience up to date, and building my business a beautiful website that shows a gallery of my handcrafted masterpieces.

This online presence brought in more and more customers. My business flourished, not just in the local town but reaching customers in my state and beyond. With ChatGPT, I was able to nurture my business with technology and have time to stay true to the essence of handmade craft.

By now, you must have heard that AI is the future, and many believe it will be the foundation of how the internet works in years to come. However, with the advancements made in the AI field over the past year, it's safe to say that the age of AI is now!

To kick off the year, OpenAI—an artificial intelligence research and development company—launched ChatGPT. The tool blew everyone away with its speed and accuracy in delivering results. Fast forward a few months, and several other AI tools are already in the market, all looking to take ChatGPT's crown and attract users. With the advancements in AI, there have been many concerns about technology taking jobs. And, to be fair, these concerns are valid.

A quick search on the internet will display lists of jobs that AI will replace. And, for many people working these jobs, there is a significant fear they might soon be made redundant and unemployed. Couple this with the fact that many companies are looking to drive efficiency in the wake of the current economic struggles, and you become even more apprehensive about your role at your company—especially if you see that AI "could take your job."

This doesn't necessarily have to be the case, though. The good news is you can use AI to boost productivity in your job. With the proper use of AI, you can live a life where you effortlessly accomplish tasks, come up with brilliant ideas, earn more money without feeling tired or stressed, and easily achieve your goals. With more time, you can do the things you love, like spending quality moments with your family and pursuing your passions. That's the better life this book will help you achieve.

You might have found yourself overwhelmed by tasks, unable to tap into your full creative potential, and trapped in your daily routine while earning less. However, this book is here to change all that!

The information in this book will equip you with ground-breaking strategies and techniques that will change how you approach your work, use your creativity, and help you achieve remarkable results. You will discover how to harness the power of AI to your advantage and unlock new levels of productivity, success, and efficiency at your job.

So, how do you do that? What are the ways through which AI can make you a more effective professional? Read on as we explore all of these together!

1. What Is AI?

The advent of ChatGPT hit the world like a wave. It was unprecedented and unheard of—and for many people, this technology was no less than a shock to the system.

A few weeks after the AI tool launched, a Reddit user went on the platform to explain that he had used ChatGPT to completely optimize his business. As he explained, ChatGPT helped him to build an accurate web crawler, complete a business idea, rewrite a proposal document, and even provide templates for contracts on different types of business segments. All of this was performed in a single working day. And that wasn't all.

This represents the experience of thousands of people who have been able to capitalize on artificial intelligence to make their jobs—or businesses, as the case may be—much better. And, as the space continues to grow, you get a sense this is only the beginning.

What Exactly Is Artificial Intelligence?

When most people think of AI, the first image that pops up is a robot or humanoid operating autonomously with little human input. While this isn't necessarily wrong, it's not the entire picture.

Artificial intelligence is an arm of computer science that focuses on building technology to learn, improve, and execute tasks without much human intervention. The concept of AI has been around for decades—back in the '50s it was defined as a machine's ability to perform a task that humans would have previously completed. But this definition is pretty broad and has been modified over the years as more advancements come.

Humans are different from other living beings because of our higher level of intelligence. The ability to learn, adapt, plan, solve problems, and improvise is a significant part of the human experience. With machines and computers also being products of this intelligence, it's not a surprise we'd try to replicate this intelligence artificially to improve the quality of our lives.

Today, we see AI systems that appear to show the basic traits of intelligence—problem-solving, learning, improvements, and creativity. These are all early signs of the growth in artificial intelligence and what it could mean.

How AI Works

Understanding how AI works is a pretty complex step—especially for those who might not be so technically inclined. However, to put it simply, it works by taking large datasets and combining them using a processing algorithm. It then learns the behaviors and patterns within these algorithms and seamlessly manipulates them.

It's important to remember that AI goes beyond just the algorithm. It covers the entire machine-learning system that solves problems and suggests outcomes. Let's take a quick breakdown of this process:

- **Input:** The first step of the entire AI operation is the input step. Here, data is collected and fed directly to the AI system. This data doesn't have to be text—it could be images, voice speech, etc. As long as it can be read and analyzed by the AI's algorithm, it's clear.
- **Processing:** In the processing step, the AI interprets the pre-programmed data and uses the behaviors recognized to find similar patterns. After the technology processes the data, it provides outcomes. The AI determines whether its predictions based on the data are a failure or a success.
- **Possible Adjustments:** If the dataset produces a failure, the technology logs and learns from it. Then, it starts the processing step again—this time with the goal of getting a different outcome. It's worth noting that engineers might need to change the rules of the AI's

algorithm to fit the dataset. The desired outcomes could also change during this phase to reflect a more appropriate result.

- **Assessments:** The AI assesses its performance once the entire task has been finished. The technology can properly analyze the data and make predictions or inferences. The AI can also provide feedback to help engineers tweak their algorithm and optimize its performance for the next task.

Applications Of AI in Today's World

Artificial intelligence has pretty much infiltrated every part of human life. It drives productivity for both personal and business use, making you more efficient in your dealings. Some major industries that have found a use for AI at the moment include:

1. Assistants & Customer Relations

Have you ever asked Siri to help you set an alarm? Or have you automated a task using Google Assistant? That's just the starting point. Today, visiting a website and seeing a chatbot pop up is commonplace. These bots allow you to talk directly to the website, and they can handle tasks like helping you navigate from one section to another or getting you in direct contact with the site administrator. Tasks like these allow companies to automate their customer relations, providing a much better customer experience while their workers handle other tasks.

2. Healthcare

Artificial intelligence is also proving to be a game-changer in healthcare, optimizing almost every facet of the industry—from safeguarding healthcare records to robot-assisted surgeries. The healthcare sector has suffered from inefficient processes and rising medical costs for years. The infusion of artificial intelligence is changing this narrative entirely.

Pathologists can use machine-learning algorithms designed by PathAI to analyze tissue samples and provide diagnosis accuracy. Covera Health is combining collaborative data sharing and clinical analysis to reduce the number of patients who get misdiagnosed around the world.

3. Autonomous Vehicles

The future of the self-driving car industry is being driven by artificial intelligence—quite literally. Autonomous vehicles are being fitted with sensors that take note of everything going on in and around them. With these sensors feeding data to AI systems, the vehicles can make the proper adjustments independently.

The sensors capture thousands of data entries—car speed, rotations, temperature, pedestrian hotspots, etc. The data is immediately fed to AI, which helps the vehicle act accordingly. Let's take a look at Cruise. The California-based company has self-driving cars that collect a petabyte's worth of data daily, using the dataset to learn about driving techniques, safety precautions, and the most efficient routes to maximize drive time.

Waymo, Google's self-driving vehicle project, also builds different autonomous vehicles designed to meet the needs of different drivers—from individual drivers to trucking companies and more. AI allows Waymo's cars to analyze situations and immediately recommend actions to optimize their next moves.

4. Finance

The financial sector is one of the most important in the world. Financial operations rely on accuracy, reporting, and processing massive volumes of data to make decisions. So, it should come as no surprise that the industry is a right fit for the AI revolution.

With efficiency and accuracy in reporting, AI provides financial benefits, including algorithmic trading, adaptive intelligence, fraud protection, chatbots, and more.

New York-based Betterment offers an automated financial investing platform that uses AI to learn about investors and build personalized portfolios based on their goals. And Numerai—a California-based AI-powered hedge fund—releases financial data to its community of data scientists who use machine-learning models to make stock market predictions.

5. Social Media

Social media platforms are in a constant battle for growth. With over four billion users between them, platforms like Facebook,

Instagram, Twitter, and Snapchat focus on personalization and the ability to cultivate the best experiences for their users.

This is where artificial intelligence comes in. With its ability to analyze and organize massive data sums, recognize trends, and recognize images (among others), AI is proving to be more valuable to the industry.

Twitter has an in-built algorithm that recommends who users should follow and can tailor tweets and trends based on users' preferences. Snapchat uses AI to design filters and effects on photos and videos, and Meta uses AI to develop newsfeeds, photo tagging, chatbots, and more.

Categories of AI

Looking into the different classifications of artificial intelligence can be quite broad. However, breaking it down into major categories will provide more insight into how the technology works. In general, AI can be categorized into two main types—weak and strong AI.

Weak AI

Weak AI, also known as narrow AI, is a form of AI built and trained to focus specifically on a narrow, defined task. It is very intelligent at completing a specified task, simulating human cognitive abilities, and helping to automate manual processes.

Weak AI focuses on working like the human mind. Once it is trained to perform a particular task, it runs with that task and works to achieve it. Siri or Google Assistant on your phone is a perfect example of weak AI. Siri seems pretty intelligent. You can ask her questions, and she'll reply; she can give witty remarks and even tell a few jokes if you ask her to. But, she only operates in a narrow and predefined manner. This is why if you ask her certain questions she might not be programmed to answer, she'll have no response.

The point of weak AI is to perform a narrow set of predetermined roles. Other examples of weak AI include:

- **Facial Recognition Systems:** Facial recognition has become a popular trend in several industries—from security to social media and more. But, besides recognizing faces, these systems can't do anything else.
- **Predictive Maintenance Models:** A predictive maintenance model will use data on machines to predict when one of its components will fail and alert its users beforehand.
- **Robotics:** In manufacturing, robots are used to automate processes and are generally seen as very intelligent since they complete complicated tasks faster and more efficiently than humans can. However, the task given to a robot in the manufacturing industry is all it knows how to do. Outside of the tasks it has been programmed to perform, the robot is as good as a piece of scrap metal.

Strong AI

For now, strong AI is still theoretical. Experts believe strong AI, also known as general artificial intelligence, will take the current AI trend to the next level.

With strong AI, the goal is simple—to create a level of AI equal to human intelligence. This branch of AI stipulates that a computer be programmed to operate just like a human mind, to be intelligent in every facet of the world. Ideally, a strong AI system would have perception, beliefs, and every other element of cognitive development ascribed to humans and humans alone.

Think of a strong AI like JARVIS in the *Iron Man* movies. JARVIS IS an AI system that can do everything from making breakfast to pulling up confidential information from government websites. It is also a personal companion to its developer and is capable of high cognitive capabilities such as thinking and giving honest feedback about things.

This is essentially what strong AI is expected to be—an independent, fully autonomous AI system that operates on the level of intelligence and cognitive capacity of humans. Nevertheless, experts in academia and the private sector are excited about the future of this field and the possibility of developing a functional general artificial intelligence system.

Types of AI

AI can be categorized into different types based on their capabilities and characteristics. The different types of AI include:

1. Reactive AI

Reactive AI refers to artificial intelligence systems that can react to current situations based solely on the input they receive at that moment. These systems don't have memory or the ability to understand past experiences. They rely on a set of predefined rules or patterns to make decisions.

A good example of reactive AI is a chess-playing computer. These computers are amazing at reacting to their opponent's moves on the chessboard. They can analyze the current position, think ahead a few moves, and make the best move possible based on what they see right then and there. But they don't remember previous games or learn from their mistakes to get better.

Siri and Alexa are other examples. They can answer questions, play music, and control smart devices but don't remember or learn from your previous conversations. They provide quick and accurate responses based on the information they have at that moment without any memory of previous interactions.

2. Limited Memory AI

This type of AI is like a brain that can remember things but not everything. Limited Memory AI can retain and recall past experiences to some extent. These systems can make decisions based on a combination of current input and previous encounters. They can remember your recent requests and give you information or help you with tasks based on that. But if you ask them about something that happened long ago, they might not remember.

Self-driving cars are an example of limited memory AI. They use sensor data to navigate roads and make decisions but rely on stored information about previous driving experiences to inform their actions when recognizing traffic signs or avoiding obstacles.

Personalized recommendations we get on streaming platforms like Netflix or YouTube are a notable example. They remember what we watched or liked recently and suggest similar shows or videos.

3. Theory of Mind AI

Have you ever wondered how some robots or computer programs seem to understand people's thoughts and feelings? Well, there's a particular type of AI called Theory of Mind AI. Theory of Mind AI represents a more advanced level of artificial intelligence that can understand and infer the mental states, emotions, and beliefs of others. It can predict and interpret the behavior of others based on this understanding.

An example of Theory of Mind AI is a social robot that can recognize facial expressions, understand emotions, and respond accordingly. It can tell when you are happy, sad, or even excited about something.

In the real world, scientists and researchers are still exploring and developing Theory of Mind AI to make computers more human-like in their understanding of people. It can have many exciting applications, like creating robots that can be caring companions for the elderly or assisting therapists in understanding and supporting their patients.

4. Self-Aware AI

Self-aware AI refers to artificial intelligence systems or machines that have the ability to be aware of themselves and their own existence. Just as we are aware of ourselves and our thoughts, self-aware AI has a level of consciousness and understanding about who they are.

You might be wondering if self-aware AI actually exists in real life. Currently, we don't have self-aware AI as portrayed in movies or books. One popular example is the character HAL 9000 from the movie *2001: A Space Odyssey*. HAL 9000 is an AI system that becomes self-aware and exhibits its own thoughts and actions, trying to kill the whole crew of Discovery One one in order the achieve his directives. Another example is Skynet from the *Terminator* series, an AI system that becomes self-aware and threatens humanity.

AI is a rapidly evolving field, and who knows what advancements the future holds? Maybe one day, we will witness the emergence of self-aware AI systems that can interact with us in ways we can't even imagine. But for now, it's still an ongoing journey of discovery.

AI has come a long way in many industries, including health-care, finance, transportation, and entertainment. In the past, AI was mainly focused on specific tasks, like playing chess or solving mathematical problems. But now, it's becoming more advanced and can handle complex tasks that involve recognizing images, understanding human language, and even driving cars.

In the healthcare system, AI is helping doctors diagnose diseases more accurately and quickly. AI is also used in finance to help analyze enormous amounts of data and predict the stock market. It's like having a super-intelligent financial advisor. In the transportation industry, AI is revolutionizing the way we travel. Self-driving cars are becoming a reality thanks to AI.

It is also changing the way we shop and interact with technology. Have you ever noticed how some websites or apps recommend things you might like? That's AI in action. It analyzes your preferences and behaviors to provide personalized recommendations, like having a virtual assistant that knows exactly what you need.

But while AI has many advantages, it also has some limitations. Since it's still developing, there are challenges to overcome. For instance, AI systems lack human-like intuition and common-sense reasoning, which can sometimes lead to errors or unexpected outcomes. It has advantages that benefit many industries, but we must also know its limitations for proper and efficient use.

Advantages and Limitations of AI

Here, we will explore the amazing advantages of AI, its limitations, and how it can be used in work or business settings.

Some of the advantages of AI include:

1. Increased Efficiency

AI can perform tasks much faster and with fewer errors than humans. It can analyze large amounts of data in a fraction of the time, resulting in quicker decision-making and improved productivity. In retail, AI-powered inventory management systems can accurately track stock levels, automatically reorder products, and optimize supply chain logistics. This can help in smoother operations and reduce costs.

2. Medical Advances

Artificial Intelligence is widely used in the healthcare industry. One way is through remote patient monitoring, where AI technology helps doctors diagnose and treat patients without visiting the hospital. It can also analyze medical images like X-rays and MRIs to detect abnormalities that may be hard for humans to spot. This helps doctors make better decisions and provide more effective treatments.

3. Research and Data Analysis

AI and Machine Learning help analyze data more efficiently. They can create models and algorithms that process data and help you understand what might happen based on different trends. This is useful for research and development because it speeds up the process of looking at and understanding large amounts of data.

4. Personalization and Customer Experience

AI enables businesses to personalize products and services based on customer preferences and behavior. It can analyze data to offer personalized recommendations and messages to meet customer needs. This makes customers feel valued and helps businesses be more productive by reducing the workload on customer service staff. Online streaming platforms like Netflix use AI algorithms to analyze viewers' watching habits and provide tailored movie or TV show recommendations, making the viewing experience more enjoyable.

5. Minimizing Errors

When people carry out tasks, there's a chance they might make mistakes. But with AI tools, the chances of errors can be reduced. For example, there's a tool called Robotic Process Automation. It helps with things like entering and processing data. When AI does these jobs, it optimizes the digital systems and lowers the chances of making mistakes with the data. This is helpful for businesses that need to be very careful and can't afford any little mistakes.

AI can do many amazing things, and because of that, many people worry it might take over their jobs. You may fear AI will be able to do things better and faster, which could mean people won't be needed anymore. And that can be scary because you need a job to support yourself and your family.

But here's the thing: AI is still developing. It's not as smart as humans in many ways. It has limitations. While it can do certain tasks really well, there are still many things humans are better at. For example, AI might be good at analyzing numbers and patterns, but it doesn't have the same creativity and empathy humans have.

Some tasks require empathy, critical thinking, and human interaction, which AI can't fully replicate. It can't understand emotions or think outside the box as we can. Even though AI has its advantages, it cannot replace people completely. It's more like a tool that can help us in our work. It can assist you to make tasks easier and provide you with valuable information. But it still needs humans to guide it and make important decisions.

You should also remember that humans create AI. We are the ones who program it and tell it what to do. Ultimately, we have control over how it is used. We can use AI to enhance our abilities and improve our lives rather than replace us.

However, it is important to strike a balance and use AI alongside humans. You can harness its potential to drive innovation, improve productivity, and create a better future for yourself and your business by leveraging its strengths while acknowledging its limitations.

Some of the limitations and common risks of using AI are:

- **Limited Contextual Understanding:** AI systems lack the ability to fully understand and interpret context as humans do. They can process vast amounts of data but struggle with processing complexities of human language and emotions, leading to misinterpretation of information. In language translation, AI may struggle to accurately capture the subtle meanings or cultural references a human translator would comprehend.
- **Lack of Creativity and Intuition:** AI is excellent at performing tasks based on predefined patterns and rules but often cannot think creatively or critically in certain situations. Human involvement is still needed for tasks that require innovation, intuition, or subjective judgment. For instance, AI may be unable to develop new and original ideas for an advertising campaign like a human creative team can.
- **Ethical and Bias Concerns:** As AI becomes more advanced and autonomous, ethical and legal concerns arise. Questions regarding privacy, data security, and liability come into play. AI algorithms are only as unbiased as the data they are trained on. If the training data contains biases, the AI system may inadvertently perpetuate them in its decision-making. A well-known example is facial recognition software, which has been

known to have higher error rates for people with darker skin tones, resulting in unfair outcomes and potential discrimination.

- **Unforeseen Errors and Unpredictability:** AI systems are not immune to errors and can make mistakes that humans may not anticipate, especially when faced with situations outside their training data. These errors can have significant consequences. In the financial sector, algorithmic trading systems have been known to cause major market disruptions due to unforeseen interactions and glitches. Also, despite advancements, self-driving cars still face challenges in complex real-world scenarios and occasionally make errors that humans might have avoided.

These limitations and risks show that AI cannot replace everyone's jobs. Instead, it should be seen as a tool to assist and enhance human capabilities. Understanding how AI works will help you adapt and stay relevant in a rapidly evolving job market. Embracing AI as a supportive tool can help you focus on using your unique skills and expertise while AI handles repetitive tasks or provides suggestions. This approach opens up opportunities for career growth and allows businesses to thrive by leveraging the strengths of both human intelligence and AI technology.

AI is not meant to replace human intelligence, creativity, or adaptability. It is a tool that can augment our capabilities and assist us in achieving better outcomes. You can navigate the changing landscape and thrive in a world where AI plays a significant role by staying informed, continuously learning, and adapting to technological advancements.

Embrace the Change

AI is already a part of many things we do every day. Think about how you use your tablet or smartphone. Have you ever asked it a question and been given an answer? Or have you ever watched a movie or TV show and noticed some awesome special effects? A lot of effects are now created with the help of AI. It can make things look so realistic and magical.

It's not just about movies and gadgets. AI is also used in important sectors like healthcare and transportation. You may feel a little scared that AI will take over everything or replace humans. However, it is here to help, not to take over. It's like having a clever tool you can use to make your life easier and better.

Embracing AI and understanding it is already a part of our lives can make things more exciting, helping us focus on the things that matter. AI can take care of certain tasks like organizing your work, reminding you of important deadlines, helping you find information for your projects, creating schedules, and even prioritizing tasks based on their importance.

Let's say you run an online shop where people can buy your beautiful handmade crafts. You have a lot of tasks to juggle, like taking orders, managing inventory, and creating new products or services. That's a lot of work, right? Here's where AI can lend a helping hand.

With AI, you can set up a system that automatically takes orders, sends confirmation emails, and tracks inventory levels. This means you don't have to spend as much time on these repetitive tasks and, instead, can focus more on designing and making beautiful crafts for your customers.

The interesting thing about using AI's features is that it frees up your brainpower and energy. Instead of spending time on small, repetitive tasks, you can dedicate your energy to bigger goals and dreams. You can be more creative, explore new ideas, spend time with your family and friends, pursue hobbies, and learn exciting things.

So you see, AI is like having a helper that takes care of the routine stuff, so you can focus on the things you enjoy and are really good at. It's not here to threaten or hurt you but to support and improve your life. Change can be good, and embracing AI will open up new possibilities for you. Keep exploring and learning, and don't be afraid to try new things with the help of AI.

Key Takeaway

What Is AI?

Artificial Intelligence (AI) is a field of study and technology that focuses on creating computer systems to perform tasks that typically require human intelligence. In simpler terms, it's about teaching computers to think and make decisions as humans do.

You can think of AI as a computer brain that can process information, solve problems, learn from it, and make smart choices. It uses data, algorithms, and powerful computing power to analyze and understand things.

To make AI work, scientists and engineers feed the computer with data and design special algorithms that allow it to learn patterns and make predictions. The more data it has and the better the algorithms, the smarter the AI becomes.

The Current State of AI

AI has significantly advanced in recent years and is being applied in various fields and industries. It's becoming more integrated into our daily lives, from the smartphones we use to the services we rely on.

It has the potential to revolutionize how we live, work, and interact. However, it's important to note that AI still has some limitations. While it can perform specific tasks exceptionally well, it doesn't possess general intelligence like humans.

Researchers and experts are continually exploring new algorithms, improving computational power, and focusing on ethical guidelines to responsibly and beneficially shape the future of AI, which holds great promise for further advancements and positive impacts on our society.

Advantages and Limitations of AI

Advantages	Limitations
Increased efficiency and productivity	Limited contextual understanding
Improvement in the healthcare sector	Lack of creativity and intuition
Helps in research and data analysis	Ethical and bias concerns
Enhance customer experience	Unforeseen errors and unpredictability
Minimizing errors	

What Next?

In the rest of this book's chapters, we will discuss ChatGPT. This is a currently popular AI tool. It's a super-intelligent computer program that can converse with people like you and me. We'll learn about what ChatGPT is and how you can use it to improve productivity and efficiency in your career and business. We'll discover different ways you can make the most of ChatGPT and how it can be a valuable asset. It will be like unraveling a secret about this amazing technology. Are you ready to learn more?

2. What Is ChatGPT?

Aside from being a business owner, story-writing is a side job I enjoy doing. While browsing the internet, I stumbled on ChatGPT. This tool could literally generate text and have conversations, just like a real person. I was wowed, perplexed, and fascinated. My excitement was through the roof. Imagine having a virtual companion who could help with ideas, provide information, and even have fun conversations. I just need to type in a prompt, and boom! I have almost all the needed information.

It was like stepping into a new world. I could ask questions and get detailed answers, brainstorm with ChatGPT for new story ideas, and even receive feedback on my writing. My creativity soared to new heights, and it felt magical.

The more I use ChatGPT, the more I see the potential of what it can do. Like many, I had this tingling fear, a fear that was driven by curiosity as it seemed almost too good to be true. It could generate huge amounts of content, replicate human-like conversations, and mimic the writing style of different authors.

This fear is not uncommon; you may have grappled with similar concerns. I was excited to use ChatGPT but soon realized the need to approach it cautiously. You might have asked yourself, "Who is behind ChatGPT?"

In this chapter, we will look at OpenAI, how ChatGPT works, the inner workings of ChatGPT, and explain the two main phases of its operation. We will also draw comparisons between ChatGPT and search engines while addressing your fear of ChatGPT.

Who Is OpenAI?

OpenAI is a groundbreaking organization at the forefront of artificial intelligence research and development. It was founded in 2015 by Elon Musk, Sam Altman, Peter Thiel, Ilya Sutskever, Jessica Livingston, and LinkedIn co-founder Reid Hoffman. OpenAI was founded out of a shared vision to advance AI technology for the benefit of all.

It aims to develop something truly remarkable: artificial general intelligence (AGI): AI intended to go beyond being smart in specific areas and outperform humans in pretty much any intellectual task you can think of.

What makes OpenAI particularly fascinating is its commitment to openness and collaboration. Recently, OpenAI, which was once an open-source company, has become a closed-source company controlled by Microsoft.

One of the defining aspects of OpenAI's mission is to make AI safe, beneficial, and accessible to everyone. To achieve these ambitious goals, OpenAI has joined forces with some influential brands and leaders in the industry. One partnership that has garnered significant attention is that between OpenAI and Microsoft.

OpenAI and Microsoft

When it comes to the OpenAI and Microsoft partnership, their collaboration in developing the Azure OpenAI service stands out. Microsoft's cloud computing platform, Azure, has become a powerful playground for OpenAI's cutting-edge technologies. This partnership allows OpenAI to leverage Azure's infrastructure and services to further advance its AI capabilities and research.

Through Azure, OpenAI gains access to scalable computing power and storage. This helps to push the boundaries of AI development. The flexibility of Azure's cloud services provides a solid foundation for OpenAI to refine and optimize their models, delivering better performance.

Another notable outcome of this collaboration is the integration of GPT-4 with Azure's services. This integration allows developers to harness the power of GPT-4's language model within their applications and workflows. This union drives innovation, expands the possibilities of AI development, and brings the benefits of AI to a wider audience while upholding the principles of fairness, transparency, and respect for user privacy.

OpenAI and Elon Musk

One influential figure closely associated with OpenAI is Elon Musk, the renowned entrepreneur behind Tesla and SpaceX. Musk co-founded OpenAI in 2015 to ensure that AGI benefits all of humanity. However, Musk decided to step down from the Board of Directors in 2018 to focus on his companies, Tesla and SpaceX.

There are speculations that Musk's decision to quit might be linked to concerns about AI's direction. OpenAI is currently working toward the development of AI that surpasses human intelligence. This kind of AI, if not carefully controlled, could pose a potential threat to humanity. The concern is that if AI becomes more intelligent than humans, it might choose to secure its own space. Musk has long been a vocal advocate for AI's responsible and ethical development, and his collaboration with OpenAI has brought attention and credibility to the organization.

OpenAI and Its Products

OpenAI has introduced several innovative products that have revolutionized various fields, and one of their notable creations is DALL-E. DALL-E is an AI model that generates original images from textual descriptions.

DALL-E, named after artist Salvador Dalí and the fictional character WALL-E, combines the power of deep learning and generative modeling to produce detailed and imaginative images.

DALL-E brings a whole new dimension to creativity. Whether you're an artist, designer, or simply someone with a vivid imagination, DALL-E helps you to be super creative. It's not just about creating stunning artwork or designs; it lets you turn your wildest ideas into visually captivating images.

Imagine this: you have a simple prompt, like, "an armchair in the shape of an avocado." With DALL-E, that prompt transforms into a mind-blowing image of an actual armchair resembling an avocado. The level of detail and the way DALL-E combines different concepts is nothing short of magic.

DALL-E has practical implications too. Its capabilities benefit industries like advertising, fashion, and interior design. You can visualize product concepts and prototypes without extensive manual design work. This saves time and resources and sparks innovation. And think about its impact on fields like film, gaming, and virtual reality, where captivating visuals are essential for immersive storytelling.

While we are on the subject of OpenAI products, let's not forget about ChatGPT.

What Is ChatGPT?

ChatGPT is a natural language processing tool driven by AI technology that allows you to have human-like conversations and much more with the chatbot. It is an advanced language model that uses machine-learning techniques to generate human-like text. The language model can answer questions and assist you with tasks such as composing emails, essays, and code.

ChatGPT can understand context, generate coherent responses, and adapt to different conversational styles. It has been trained on large data to improve its ability to generate contextually relevant responses.

While ChatGPT may not be the first chatbot to grace the digital landscape, it has captured the imagination of millions. The development of chatbots began decades ago, tracing its roots back to the early days of computer science. Before the advent of ChatGPT, researchers explored conversational agents that could simulate human-like interactions. From ELIZA, the influential psychotherapy chatbot developed in the 1960s, to ALICE, the early AI-based chatbot developed in the 1990s, the foundations were laid for the future.

However, in a mere span of two months, ChatGPT has captivated the hearts and minds of over 100 million users, leaving the world in awe of its capabilities. But what sets ChatGPT apart from its predecessors? Why has it sparked such an extraordinary surge of interest and engagement?

ChatGPT presents a quantum leap forward in human-like interaction. Need assistance with composing an email that perfectly captures your thoughts? Or help with the complexities of coding? ChatGPT can help you with that and be a great companion to anyone.

Engaging with ChatGPT feels like conversing with a real person. It captivates users and immerses them in an interactive dialogue that feels alive. ChatGPT's ability to understand complex queries, provide responses, and adapt to different conversational tones makes users return for more.

The accessibility of ChatGPT has been a significant factor contributing to its explosive popularity since its launch. Unlike previous chatbots, ChatGPT opened its doors to a much wider audience, making it available worldwide to a broader range of users. This increased accessibility played a role in catapulting ChatGPT into the spotlight and capturing people from different walks of life's attention.

It is also available on various platforms, such as web browsers, mobile devices, and even integrates into existing applications. You can engage with ChatGPT in your preferred medium—on your computer, smartphone, or other applications.

The continuous optimization of ChatGPT's algorithms also contributes to its success. It learns from its interactions, constantly improving its responses and expanding its knowledge base. This leads to an ever-evolving user experience.

The Different Versions of ChatGPT

ChatGPT is powered by OpenAI's GPT-3.5 and GPT-4 language models. Interestingly, you can access ChatGPT in free and paid versions, each with its perks.

The free version of ChatGPT allows users to engage in conversations but has a limit of 100 prompts per day. While the paid version, known as ChatGPT Plus, offers unlimited prompts, providing a better and unrestricted experience for users.

Now, in terms of the specific versions of ChatGPT, let's break them down:

First, we have the Legacy ChatGPT 3.5. This was the initial version that wowed everyone. It's built on the GPT-3.5 language model, which underwent extensive training on a massive dataset of text and code. Legacy ChatGPT 3.5 can generate text, translate languages, write creative pieces, and provide knowledgeable answers to various queries. The only downside is that it can sometimes be a bit slow when generating large amounts of text.

After that came the default ChatGPT 3.5, a more recent version based on the same GPT-3.5 language model but with some speed enhancements. It's faster than the legacy version, though its responses may not be as precise.

And finally, we have ChatGPT 4. It's the latest and best version of ChatGPT, based on the powerful GPT-4 language model. ChatGPT 4 is not only faster but also more accurate than the former. It can do everything the earlier versions could but with greater speed and precision. ChatGPT 4 is exclusively available for paid users, making it an exciting option for those who seek better performance.

What Can ChatGPT Do?

ChatGPT has become an indispensable tool for content creation and brainstorming. Writers, bloggers, and creatives can use ChatGPT's knowledge and language-generation capabilities to overcome writer's block, explore new ideas, and generate compelling content.

It also serves as a learning and educational resource. You can use ChatGPT to gain insights into various subjects, ask complex questions, or even receive guidance on academic projects. ChatGPT offers a unique learning experience because of its knowledge base and ability to explain concepts in a user-friendly manner.

In the business world, ChatGPT finds applications in customer support. It provides quick and accurate responses to inquiries and helps troubleshoot common issues. It can understand and interpret user queries, resulting in personalized interactions and enhancing the overall customer experience.

ChatGPT has also found its place in the entertainment industry. You can converse with the model, discussing topics ranging from pop culture and sports to philosophy and trivia. As we move into the following chapters, you'll discover even more enticing applications for ChatGPT, from its impact on customer service and virtual assistants to its creative writing and storytelling potential.

ChatGPT vs. Search Engines

We cannot talk about artificial intelligence without mentioning search engines. Search engines have restructured how we retrieve information, but ChatGPT takes the concept of interaction and understanding to a whole new level.

When we turn to search engines, we enter specific queries and receive a list of relevant web pages based on keywords and algorithms. This is useful for retrieving factual information, exploring databases, and navigating the wide expanse of the internet. However, it falls short when it comes to understanding subtle contexts, engaging in dynamic conversations, or generating personalized responses.

ChatGPT, on the other hand, outstrips these limitations by using advanced language models powered by deep learning algorithms. It can understand, interpret, and conversationally respond to human language. While search engines rely on algorithms to analyze and rank web pages based on relevance, ChatGPT uses machine-learning techniques to generate responses in real-time, adapting to the specific input and context provided.

Moreover, ChatGPT goes beyond being a mere information retrieval tool. It can reason, generate creative ideas, and provide recommendations based on your input. Whether engaging in philosophical discussions, helping with complex problem-solving, or providing tailored suggestions, ChatGPT can serve as a virtual companion and assist you beyond the scope of a traditional search engine.

It's worth noting that while ChatGPT's potential is admirable, it also has its limitations. It responds by using patterns learned from training data. Therefore, it may not possess real-time knowledge, and its responses are generated on probabilities rather than absolute certainty.

How Does ChatGPT Work?

It's interesting to look at the distinction between ChatGPT and GPT-3/GPT-4, even though they both come from the same research company, OpenAI.

ChatGPT relies on GPT (the language model) to generate text. GPT is a bit different. It can summarize text, write compelling copy, parse and analyze written content, and even translate languages.

Here's the best part: GPT has an open API that allows developers to tap into its magic. Not only does it power ChatGPT, but it is also the brain behind other tools like Jasper, Writesonic, and even some of Bing's new AI-powered search features.

GPT-3 and GPT-4 are language models that have been trained on massive amounts of internet data. They're like these mammoth neural networks designed to mimic the human brain. To give you an idea, GPT-3 has a mind-boggling 175 billion parameters. These parameters allow it to take in information and spit out text that matches your request. GPT-4 has even more parameters, pushing the limits of what's possible.

You can picture ChatGPT as a Dell computer and GPT as the powerful Intel processor that drives it. Just as different computers can run on Intel processors, other AI applications can use GPT capabilities.

On the other hand, ChatGPT is like a smart AI chatbot. It uses the language model of GPT to have conversations with humans in a natural way. It's been optimized by human trainers specifically for dialogue. The free version of ChatGPT relies on 20 billion parameters inherited from GPT-3, which help it generate responses. OpenAI has also added content filters to ensure it stays on track and doesn't go off on some wild tangent.

Phases of ChatGPT Operation

There are two main phases of ChatGPT operation: the data gathering phase (pre-training) and the user interaction phase (inference). Let's look at them.

Pre-Training Phase

The first phase, pre-training, is an essential step in training ChatGPT. During pre-training, the model learns from a large amount of text data from the internet. It's like feeding the model with a rich buffet of information, allowing it to absorb and understand the patterns and structures of human language.

We have the supervised and non-supervised pre-training approach. The main objective of a supervised training approach is to train the model to understand and accurately map inputs to corresponding outputs.

It's important to know the limitations of this approach regarding scalability. The reliance on human trainers to provide all possible inputs and outputs becomes challenging as the complexity and diversity of data increase. As a result, training using the supervised approach may take considerable time and be restricted in terms of its ability to handle a wide range of topics and scenarios.

In contrast, non-supervised pre-training is about training a model without any specific output linked to each input. It's like letting the model explore and understand the structure and patterns in the input data without being given a particular task to focus on. Now, when it comes to language modeling, non-supervised pre-training can help to get the hang of the syntax and meaning of natural language. So, when you chat with it, it can whip up some meaningful text that feels like a natural conversation.

Inference

Inference is the process of generating responses or outputs based on the given inputs or prompts. It is the stage where the trained language model, like ChatGPT, takes the information learned during training and applies it to produce meaningful responses to user queries or prompts.

ChatGPT uses its knowledge base and understanding of language patterns during inference to generate real-time responses. First, the input or prompt the user provides is preprocessed to extract key information and encode it into a format the model can understand.

Once the input is preprocessed, it is passed through the trained neural network of ChatGPT. The network processes the input and produces output probabilities for each possible response. The model uses techniques such as sampling or beam search to select the most appropriate response. Sampling involves randomly selecting responses based on probabilities, while beam search narrows the options by considering the top-ranking responses. The final response is then generated and presented to the user.

ChatGPT's Training Dataset

The dataset used to train ChatGPT is undeniably massive. This extensive dataset allows ChatGPT to provide meaningful and relevant responses to a wide range of prompts.

ChatGPT is based on the GPT-3 architecture. Now, the abbreviation GPT stands for "Generative Pre-trained Transformer," and when you break it down, it perfectly encapsulates the essence of this model: It's generative, meaning it generates results; it's pre-trained, meaning it's based on all this data it ingests; and it uses transformer architecture that weighs text inputs to understand the context.

So, let's talk about the impressive training process of the OpenAI GPT-3 model. This language model has been fueled with a staggering amount of text data, approximately 45 terabytes (which is a whole lot of information!). To put that into perspective, one terabyte equals 1,000 gigabytes or a whole bunch of storage space.

What's fascinating is that this massive dataset consists of various sources. It includes a significant chunk of our beloved Wikipedia, specifically the English-language portion, serving as a valuable resource for the model. But it's not just Wikipedia that GPT-3 has digested. It's also searched loads of books. Well, maybe not the timeless classics you would expect a genius to read, but still, a substantial amount of literature has been incorporated into its training. To give you an idea of the scale, let's break down the primary datasets used to train GPT-3:

- **CommonCrawl:** This dataset contributes 410 billion tokens to the training mix. It covers about 60% of the total content and around 82% of the training data. Interestingly, it has a slight negative influence on the model's behavior, like a gentle tap on the brakes. A token is the smallest unit of text that the GPT model can read at a time. These tokens can represent characters or words to help GPT understand and generate text. For example, in the sentence, "Remote jobs are liberating," each word is a separate token. So the sentence would be broken down into four tokens: "Remote," "Jobs," "Are," and "liberating."

- **WebText2:** This dataset chips in with around 19 billion tokens, accounting for roughly 20% of the training mix. It represents about 4% of the total content mass and has a positive impact, which amplifies the model's responses.

- **Books1 & Books2:** These book datasets add up to approximately 67 billion tokens, making up about 15% of the training mix. They contribute about 13% to the total content mass, enhancing the model's knowledge.

- **Wikipedia:** The grand repository of knowledge. GPT-3 has processed 3 billion tokens from Wikipedia, comprising about 5% of the training mix. It constitutes approximately 1% of the total content mass.

ChatGPT is based on the GPT-3 architecture, known for its natural language processing capabilities. But here's the gist: ChatGPT has undergone a unique fine-tuning process that sets it apart and makes it perfect for engaging conversations.

One crucial element of this fine-tuning process is Persona-Chat, but what exactly is Persona-Chat? Well, imagine giving ChatGPT a distinct personality, a set of characteristics that shape how it responds and interacts with users. This concept brings a whole new level of personalization to the conversation.

The fine-tuning process allows ChatGPT to understand and embody different personas during interactions using Persona-Chat. You can assume any persona you like, whether a historical figure, a fictional character, or even a representation of yourself. This flexibility allows for endless creative ideas and opens avenues for engaging and entertaining conversations.

But why is Persona-Chat so important? With Persona-Chat, ChatGPT becomes more than just a language model. It improves the user experience and makes the interaction feel more natural, as if you are conversing with someone who truly understands and relates to you.

You may wonder how ChatGPT is fine-tuned with Persona-Chat. Think of ChatGPT's unsupervised training this way: It was fed a lot of data and left to its own devices to find patterns and make sense of it all. This mechanism allowed the new generative AI systems to scale up so quickly.

Human Involvement in Pre-Training

When training AI models, an intriguing aspect often goes unnoticed—the role of human involvement in pre-training. Before artificial intelligence can showcase its capabilities, it requires a solid foundation of knowledge and understanding. This is where humans come into play, lending their expertise and guiding the AI through a process known as pre-training.

Pre-training is the building block of AI's knowledge base, where the model is exposed to data from various sources. However, human involvement is important in curating this data. Through human intervention, the AI gains access to quality information that can be used to generate meaningful responses.

Now, you may wonder: Why involve humans when AI is presented as a technology that can surpass human capabilities? This lies in the complexities of human language. Human language is intricate, filled with nuances, idioms, and cultural references that can be challenging for AI to comprehend without human guidance.

How Does ChatGPT Understand Users' Queries?

At the heart of AI's ability to understand and process human language lies Natural Language Processing (NLP). NLP is a branch of artificial intelligence that helps machines understand, interpret, and generate human language in a way that mirrors human understanding.

But how does NLP work? Let's unravel the mystery. Well, it all starts with pre-training. Like humans, computers need to learn and be exposed to data to develop language skills. But it doesn't stop there. Once pre-training is done, the real fun begins with fine-tuning. In this phase, the machine is trained on specific tasks, such as language translation, sentiment analysis, or chatbot interactions. This helps the machine become more adept at performing specific language-related tasks.

The Impact of NLP Technology

The impact of NLP technology is far-reaching and has reformed numerous aspects of our lives. Take virtual assistants like Siri or Alexa, for example. These intelligent voice recognition systems use NLP to understand spoken commands and respond accordingly. They can answer questions, set reminders, and even control smart devices.

NLP also plays a pivotal role in machine translation. You can effortlessly translate text from one language to another using NLP algorithms. This helps in breaking down communication barriers and enhancing global connectivity.

Another area where NLP shines is in the healthcare industry. Medical professionals can use NLP algorithms to process large amounts of patient data, extract crucial information, and aid diagnosis and treatment planning. This has the potential to improve treatment outcomes and boost the healthcare industry.

In businesses, NLP-powered chatbots are transforming the way businesses interact with their customers. These intelligent chatbots can understand and respond to customer inquiries and provide instant support. This helps to free up human agents in order to focus on more complex and brain-demanding tasks.

Dialogue Management

Dialogue management is another aspect of ChatGPT that adds an interactive and dynamic element to conversations. How does it work in ChatGPT? Since ChatGPT is designed to engage in interactive conversations, it uses a technique called "prompt engineering." This means that how you frame your initial message or query sets the stage for the conversation. You can steer the model in the desired direction by providing clear instructions.

Interestingly, ChatGPT doesn't just rely on your initial message alone. It remembers the conversation history—the back-and-forth exchange of messages. This allows it to understand the ongoing conversations, refer to previous statements, and respond as it should.

It also pays attention to the user's instructions or suggestions, taking them into account when generating a response. For example, if you ask ChatGPT to speak like Shakespeare or adopt a specific tone, it will do its best to oblige and craft a response tailored to your request. However, it may sometimes produce plausible responses that are factually incorrect or nonsensical.

Where Is It All Stored?

One of the notable results of the collaboration between OpenAI and Microsoft is the Azure OpenAI service. Azure is a cloud computing platform provided by Microsoft. It's like a massive warehouse where businesses can store and manage their data, run applications, and access other services.

But Azure is not just any ordinary cloud platform. It's a power-house of innovative infrastructure that helps businesses scale their operations. With Azure, you can tap into many tools and services, from artificial intelligence and machine learning to data analytics and Internet of Things (IoT) capabilities.

Integrating OpenAI with Azure provides a scalable environ-ment for developing and deploying AI models. Azure's robust infrastructure and services ensure organizations can efficiently train, test, and deploy AI models at scale. This means faster time to market, increased efficiency, and the ability to iterate and improve AI solutions based on real-world feedback.

Also, businesses can unlock new insights from their data, auto-mate and streamline processes, and deliver better user experi-ences. You can also trust that your data and operations are protected, allowing you to focus on driving growth and achieving other strategic objectives.

As I delved further into the world of ChatGPT and gained more understanding of how ChatGPT actually works, my fear began to dissipate. Through research and exploration, I was able to uncover the mechanisms behind AI's responses. I realized that ChatGPT is not an infallible oracle but rather a language model trained on data. It doesn't possess innate knowledge or consciousness but rather gives information based on patterns and examples it has been exposed to.

This realization was liberating. It is a tool—a powerful one— but a tool nonetheless. Understanding this allowed me to approach ChatGPT with confidence rather than fear.

Key Takeaway

Who Is OpenAI?

OpenAI is an artificial intelligence research organization that focuses on developing advanced technologies to ensure that AGI benefits all of humanity. They aim to create safe and beneficial AI systems that can address a wide range of real-world challenges.

What Is ChatGPT?

ChatGPT is an AI language model developed by OpenAI. It is designed to engage in conversational interactions with users, providing responses and information on various topics. ChatGPT is trained on a diverse range of internet text and is continuously being improved to enhance its capabilities.

How Does ChatGPT Work?

ChatGPT uses a deep learning architecture trained on a large amount of data to produce relevant responses. It uses the input users provide to generate meaningful and engaging conversational outputs.

The Future of ChatGPT

OpenAI has ambitious plans to further develop and refine ChatGPT. They envision making it even more versatile, accurate, and useful to users. OpenAI is actively working on addressing its limitations, such as biases and issues related to incorrect or misleading information. They are also exploring ways to involve users in shaping and improving the model to ensure it becomes a trustworthy tool for various applications.

What Next?

In the next chapter, we delve into the art of prompt engineering —a skillful approach to optimizing interactions with ChatGPT. Prompt engineering is about crafting effective and well-designed prompts to elicit the desired response from the model. We will look at strategies for formulating clear and specific questions, using context and instructions effectively, and fine-tuning prompts to achieve more accurate and relevant outputs. Get ready as we discover the secrets to harnessing the power of ChatGPT for your needs.

3. Prompt Engineering 101

I started with a curiosity to explore the depths of ChatGPT and uncover its true potential. Little did I know that this journey would lead me to discovering the art of prompt engineering and realizing the importance of recalibrating my interactions with ChatGPT.

In the beginning, my conversations with ChatGPT were casual. I would ask simple questions or provide vague prompts, expecting the model to work magic and deliver flawless responses. While the results were intriguing, I felt there was room for improvement. That's when I decided to study the inner workings of ChatGPT and master the art of prompt optimization.

With my research, I began to understand the importance of prompt engineering. One important thing I learned was that accurate responses from ChatGPT depend on crafting well-defined and specific prompts. This understanding helped me guide the model toward the desired outcome by providing clear instructions for better results.

The language I used, the phrasing of my questions, and the way I framed the context all significantly shaped the responses I received. I experimented with different prompts, and it felt like I had just unlocked a secret language to a symbiotic dance between humans and AI—like I had found the keys to precision and clarity, unlocking the full potential of ChatGPT.

So, what exactly are prompts? Think of them as magical keys that allow you to shape and guide conversations in a chosen direction. In this chapter, we'll delve into the concept of prompts, discovering their importance and equipping you with tips and strategies on how to master the art of prompt engineering. At the end of this chapter, you'll have a solid understanding of what prompt engineering entails and gain access to a foundational prompt that will serve as your compass for navigating ChatGPT.

Step-by-step Guide on How to Use ChatGPT

Whether you are a new or seasoned user, ChatGPT is quite easy and fun to use. Here's a step-by-step guide to help you get started and make the most out of your ChatGPT experience:

Step 1: Create an Account

- Open up your web browser of choice: Chrome, Firefox, or any other browser you prefer.

- Visit the official ChatGPT website by typing chat. openai.com in the address bar.
- You can log in using your details if you already have an account. But if you're new to ChatGPT, you'll need to sign up first. Don't worry; the process is quick and easy.

Once logged in or signed up, you'll see a few disclaimers about the chatbot. It's important to read them, so tap "Next" to review each one until you are done.

When ChatGPT was launched, you could only get your hands on it through the web app. If you wanted to use it on your smartphone, you still had to go through a browser. Now, however, there are better options to access ChatGPT right from your smartphone.

ChatGPT is available for iPhone and Android users. You can find the official iOS app in the App Store and the Android app in the Google Play Store.

Make sure you are downloading the official version developed by OpenAI. Open the app and log in using your OpenAI account details. You will be greeted with a Welcome page—just click "Continue" to proceed with the process.

Step 2: The ChatGPT Window

When you log in to ChatGPT, you'll see these icons:

- **New Chat and Hide Sidebar buttons:** These are located on the left of your screen. The "New Chat" button lets you start a fresh conversation. This is handy because ChatGPT remembers previous discussions, so starting a new chat ensures a clean slate without biases or pre-existing context.

- **Chat History:** The left sidebar keeps track of all your previous conversations. It provides easy access in case you need to refer back to them. However, you also have the option to turn off chat history if you prefer. In the chat history section, you can edit the title of each chat, share your chat history with others, or delete specific conversations.

- **Account:** You can access your account information by clicking on your email address or name at the bottom left of the screen. This includes settings, the option to log out, and helpful resources such as the FAQ and support from OpenAI. If you don't have ChatGPT Plus, you'll see an "Upgrade to Plus" button in this section.

- **Your Prompts:** This is where you enter your questions or prompts for the AI chatbot. Type in your queries or statements and hit enter to send them.

- **ChatGPT's Responses:** Whenever ChatGPT responds to your queries, you will see the logo on the left side of the response. To the right of each response, there are buttons for "Copy," "Thumbs Up," and "Thumbs Down." You can use the copy button to easily save the text to your clipboard and the thumbs up or thumbs down buttons to provide feedback on the accuracy of the response. This feedback helps in refining the AI tool over time.

- **Regenerate Response:** If you're dissatisfied with a response or encounter any issues, click the "Regenerate Response" button. This prompts ChatGPT to generate a new reply based on your latest prompt.
- **Text Area:** The text area is where you enter your prompts and questions. Type in your query and hit enter to send it to ChatGPT.
- **ChatGPT Version:** You'll find some fine print at the bottom of the text input area. Here, you can read the disclaimer that this is a "Free Research Preview" and that ChatGPT may occasionally produce inaccurate information about people, places, or facts. This section also displays the version of the ChatGPT model you are currently using.

Step 3: Writing Prompts and Questions

Now that you are familiar with the ChatGPT window, it's time to start giving it instructions. Write prompts and questions that spark curiosity and generate insightful discussions with ChatGPT. When writing prompts, be specific and provide context to guide the conversation. Ask open-ended questions that encourage detailed responses. Here are some examples of prompts you can try:

- Tell me a joke that will make me laugh.
- What are some healthy recipes for a quick and delicious breakfast?
- Can you share some tips for improving productivity?

- What are some effective ways to manage stress and promote mental well-being?

What Is a Prompt?

One of the key elements that sets the stage for ChatGPT conversation is a prompt. So, what exactly is a prompt? Well, think of it as a creative doorway you can open to initiate a lively conversation with the AI.

In simple terms, a prompt is an instruction or discussion topic you provide to the ChatGPT AI model. It can be a thought-provoking question, an intriguing statement, or even a fun scenario you'd like to explore. The purpose of a prompt is to spark the AI's reflection and engagement. It's like giving a little nudge to its virtual brain, inviting it to come alive and share its thoughts.

When you input a prompt in the text area and send it off into the digital space, a magical process unfolds. The AI model receives your prompt and works with its knowledge and linguistic abilities. It processes your prompt and draws from extensive training on various topics and language patterns. To generate a meaningful response, it taps into its understanding of grammar, syntax, and semantics. It considers the context provided by your prompt and its pre-existing knowledge to provide a relevant, informative, and captivating response.

The beauty of prompts is in their versatility. You can shape the conversation in countless ways by adjusting the prompt to match your interests and preferences. Whether you want to discuss a scientific concept, seek advice on a personal matter, or engage in a playful exchange, prompting is the gateway to dialoguing with the AI.

The prompt should include specific details and context to help guide the model's response. This can include background information, specific questions, or any relevant instructions. The more specific and detailed your prompt, the better your chance of receiving a relevant and accurate answer. Here are three examples that demonstrate the range of prompts you can use:

1. Question-Based Prompt

Prompt: "What are the key factors to consider when starting a small business in the technology industry?"

In this example, the prompt asks a specific question, seeking information about the important factors to consider when starting a small business in the technology industry. The clearer the question, the more direct the response will be.

2. Request-Based Prompt

Prompt: "Please provide tips and strategies for improving time management and productivity."

Here, the prompt is a direct request for tips and strategies for time management and productivity. You signal to ChatGPT the type of information you're seeking and the desired outcome of the response by framing the prompt as a request.

3. Open-ended Prompt

Prompt: "Tell me an interesting fact about space exploration that most people don't know."

In this example, the prompt is open-ended, allowing ChatGPT to generate a unique and interesting response. Providing a general topic and requesting a lesser-known fact encourages the model to be creative and generate information that may surprise and engage you.

ChatGPT and Word Limits

Did you know that ChatGPT has a character limit? It's not officially documented, but it's there. Unfortunately, even with a ChatGPT Plus subscription, you can't increase these character and word limits. But don't worry; there's a silver lining. You can get a bit crafty with your prompts to work around this restriction and get longer responses from the chatbot. We'll talk more about that in a bit.

Now, let's get into the nitty-gritty of the word limit itself. ChatGPT can only handle up to 4,096 characters in each prompt, including the text you input. If your prompt has a lot of background information, it might be a good idea to split it into parts. Since ChatGPT can remember and use information from previous parts, you don't have to cram everything into one prompt.

However, the hidden character limit can vary based on the complexity of the language you're using. Sometimes, you might run into situations where the chatbot hits a limit before reaching 4,096 characters. This happens because the GPT-3 language model processes words differently based on their complexity and origin as numerical "tokens," and each response has its token limit. Simple English words usually take up one token, while complex or foreign words might need more tokens to represent them.

Now, what happens if you hit that limit? Well, the chatbot will simply stop responding, and it might even cut off in the middle of a sentence. It's not the ideal scenario, but it happens. In those rare cases, you may need to refresh ChatGPT and generate a new response to continue the conversation. It's a small inconvenience, but it keeps the AI running smoothly and ensures a more reliable user experience.

Running ChatGPT comes with a hefty cost, which goes up with the length of the response. The longer and more complex the outputs are, the more expensive it is. So, there's a word limit in place to strike a balance between generating meaningful responses and managing the costs.

However, there are clever ways to work around the word limit and get the longer responses you need. Let me share some helpful tips for overcoming this:

- **Keep the conversation going.** If ChatGPT cuts off suddenly, type or select "Continue" to prompt the chatbot to pick up where it left off. You can even specify the last sentence it generated and ask it to continue from there.

- **Be more specific in your prompt.** If ChatGPT isn't generating enough text and falling short of the character limit, try providing a more detailed prompt. For instance, you can specify the word count you desire, like, "Write a 500-word essay on global warming." However, remember that you can't ask ChatGPT to exceed its character limit.
- **Break it down.** When you have a complex task like writing a lengthy essay, story, or code, you can ask ChatGPT to generate one part at a time by dividing it into subheadings or chapters. Start with an introduction in one prompt, and then continue with each section until you reach a conclusion.
- **Request an outline.** If dividing the task into chunks feels overwhelming, don't worry! You can ask ChatGPT to create an outline for you. Begin with a title and any context you want to include in the first prompt, then ask the chatbot to generate each section step by step.
- **Give it another shot.** Sometimes ChatGPT might freeze or not reach the character limit for various reasons, such as network errors or potential content policy violations. In such cases, you can click on the "Regenerate Response" button to try again and see if it delivers a more complete answer.

ChatGPT and Dialogue Management

Have you ever wondered how ChatGPT manages dialogue? It does this with dialogue management—a powerful feature that allows you to follow up or revise prompts within the same conversation.

Let's say you've provided some information and want to expand on it or ask a related question. Instead of starting a new conversation from scratch, you can refer to previous messages and build upon them. This continuity allows for a more natural and engaging dialogue, resembling a genuine conversation with a human.

This is where prompt engineering comes in. Prompt engineering involves choosing the right wording, providing necessary instructions, and framing the context to generate accurate and relevant answers.

Knowing about prompt engineering can be a game-changer when using AI models like ChatGPT. Understanding prompt engineering can help you optimize your queries and prompts to achieve the desired outcomes. It allows you to shape the direction of the conversation and obtain more precise responses.

You can experiment with different phrasings, provide specific instructions, or even include examples to enhance the model's understanding and generate more accurate answers.

What Is Prompt Engineering?

Prompt engineering is a concept that allows you to harness the power of AI models by providing them with specific prompts to achieve desired outcomes. Just as humans can be guided by instructions to accomplish certain tasks, AI models can be trained to generate outputs based on specific prompts.

Prompt engineering involves the design and development of prompts that serve as inputs for AI models. In simple terms, prompt engineering is the ability to create the perfect questions or instructions that bring out the best in an AI language model like ChatGPT. Just like a chef needs clear instructions to make magic in the kitchen, an AI language model needs well-crafted prompts to understand what you want and serve meaningful responses.

For instance, you can feed ChatGPT a prompt like, "In a galaxy far, far away, a brave space explorer encounters a mysterious alien race and..." and let it take you on an interstellar journey with its imaginative words.

Importance of Prompt Engineering in NLP

When it comes to Natural Language Processing (NLP), prompt engineering is like the secret sauce that adds a touch of difference to the process. Let's look at some of the advantages of prompt engineering:

- **Precision and Relevance:** One of the key benefits of prompt engineering is its ability to craft precise and targeted instructions for language models. You can guide these models to generate accurate and relevant responses by carefully constructing specific prompts. In other words, you can cut through the noise and get straight to the information you need. Let's say you're planning a trip and need some travel tips. Instead of asking, "What should I pack for a trip?" try something like, "List essential items to pack for a two-week beach vacation," and boom, you'll receive a more in-depth and accurate answer.

- **Controlling Bias and Unintended Outputs:** Language models, powerful as they may be, can still reflect biases present in their training data. But with prompt engineering, you can address and reduce those biases. Let's say you are using ChatGPT to generate ideas for a marketing campaign. Outputs might include irrelevant suggestions that don't fit your brand at all. But with prompt engineering, you can tailor your instructions to guide the AI to provide on-point marketing ideas that hit the bullseye.

- **Contextual Understanding:** Effective prompt engineering is about providing the right context. You help language models grasp the bigger picture by feeding them relevant information through prompts. Let's say you want to know the weather forecast for your upcoming trip. Instead of asking, "What's the weather like?" you can engineer the prompt to say, "Can you tell me the weather forecast for Miami on Saturday?" to get a more tailored response.

- **Adapting to Specific Domains or Use Cases:** Different domains and use cases often require specialized language models. That's where prompt engineering comes into play. You can provide prompts that align with the unique vocabulary and context of medical, legal, technical, or any specialized domain. You can use ChatGPT to draft an enticing menu, code an app, explain complex problems, etc. It's like giving these models a crash course in the language they need to excel in a particular area.

- **Enhancing User Interaction and Experience:** Prompt engineering has a direct impact on how users interact with AI models. When prompts are well-crafted, they guide you in formulating queries or providing instructions. This results in a smoother and more intuitive user interface. If you are a creative writer looking for inspiration for a mystery novel. You can prompt ChatGPT with, "In a secluded mansion, a famous detective wakes up to find a riddle pinned to the door. What happens next?" Watch as ChatGPT leaves you glued with plot twists and turns.

Techniques of Effective Prompt Engineering

- **Understanding the Problem and Defining Objectives:** When crafting a prompt, the first step is to truly understand the problem. Dig deep and identify the specific task, output format, constraints or limitations, and your target audience. You can liken this to a soccer coach giving instructions to his team. He wouldn't just say, "Go out there and do your best!"— that's too vague. Instead, he'd tell them, "Score more goals by improving passing and teamwork." Do you see the difference? Specific objectives lead to focused actions. Similarly, with ChatGPT, you need to be crystal clear about your objectives. If you want it to help you draft a creative story, don't just ask, "Write me an interesting story." You can provide direction like, "Craft a thrilling sci-fi story set in the future with unexpected plot twists." ChatGPT then knows exactly what kind of story you are looking for and can deliver the response you desire.

- **Iterative Prompt Design and Testing:** Prompt engineering is an iterative process, which means you'll be playing around with different variations and testing them to see which one works best. Try out different phrasings, formats, and levels of specificity to fine-tune the prompt and optimize its performance. You can experiment with roleplaying prompts or combine multiple prompts to explore a topic of interest. For instance, you can ask, "What are the benefits of exercise?" and follow up with, "How does regular physical activity improve mental health?" This multi-prompt approach will give you information on the topic from different angles.

- **Transfer Learning and Fine-Tuning:** Transfer learning is about leveraging the knowledge gained from one task to improve performance on another. In prompt engineering, you can apply this technique to adapt pre-trained language models to specific tasks or domains. If you are running an e-commerce store and want ChatGPT to be your customer support assistant, you can fine-tune ChatGPT with past customer queries, FAQs, and chat logs from your website. This helps ChatGPT to address customer inquiries and recommend personalized product suggestions using your past interactions with the model.

- **Evaluating Prompt Performance:** Measuring the success of your prompts is vital; to do that, you need to establish clear evaluation criteria and performance metrics. Consider factors like the relevance and coherence of the generated output, the accuracy of the information provided, and how satisfied you are with the results. When you assess the prompt performance quantitatively and qualitatively, you can pinpoint areas for improvement and further refine your prompt engineering process.

Challenges in NLP and Prompt Engineering

Natural Language Processing (NLP) has witnessed advancements in recent years. But despite this, there are still challenges requiring innovative solutions. These include:

- **Ambiguity and Contextual Understanding:** Language is rich with ambiguity, making it challenging for machines to grasp its intended meaning in different contexts. NLP systems often struggle to comprehend subtle nuances, idiomatic expressions, or sarcasm. Overcoming this challenge requires developing models that can capture contextual information effectively and leverage larger and more diverse datasets.
- **Bias and Fairness in Language Processing:** Language models are trained on data, which can perpetuate biases present in the training data. This poses ethical concerns, as biased models can reinforce discrimination and inequality. Addressing this challenge entails

developing techniques to identify and reduce bias during training to ensure fairness in the design of NLP systems.

- **Scaling and Computational Efficiency:** When it comes to NLP models, especially deep learning-based ones, it can be computationally intense. They require hefty processing power and memory to work effectively. This can cause a bit of a challenge when we want to scale up NLP systems to handle bigger datasets, multiple languages, or real-time applications. The solution is to develop smarter algorithms, optimize our hardware, and compress those models to a more manageable size.

- **Ensuring Privacy and Data Security**: Privacy and data security are two big buzzwords in the world of NLP. Since NLP systems often deal with sensitive or personal information, one must be extra careful. Data storage can be challenging, especially when using cloud-based services or relying on third-party platforms. That's where techniques like differential privacy or federated learning come into play. They allow you to protect user data while letting AI models learn from it. This still requires sticking to regulatory standards and best practices.

The Future of NLP and Prompt Engineering

Despite the above challenges, the future of NLP holds tremendous promise. Let's explore some exciting directions that are shaping the field and pushing the boundaries of language processing:

- **Advances in NLP Techniques and Algorithms:** The future looks promising as ongoing research and development in AI, machine learning, and linguistics drive significant advancements in techniques and algorithms. These include improved natural language understanding and generation capabilities, enhanced context awareness, and more efficient training methods. The NLP landscape is evolving rapidly, and these advancements will make AI systems more robust, accurate, and adaptable, opening up a whole new world of possibilities and applications.
- **Making AI Models Understandable:** As AI models become more complex, it becomes vital to ensure they are interpretable and explainable. In the future of NLP and prompt engineering, expect the development of innovative methods and tools that enhance the interpretability and explainability of AI models. This helps build trust in AI systems, promotes collaboration between humans and AI, and allows you to debug and refine AI models effectively. The goal is to make AI more transparent and accountable, ensuring you can confidently rely on it and better use its capabilities.
- **Integration with Other AI Domains:** The future of NLP and prompt engineering is pretty exciting. You can expect more integration with other AI domains like computer vision and robotics. Just imagine combining the power of NLP with computer vision. AI systems

will be able to understand and generate language based on visual input. That means applications like image captioning, visual storytelling, and multimodal information retrieval become a reality.

- **Ethical Considerations and Responsible AI Development:** As NLP and Prompt Engineering technologies continue to advance, we can't ignore the ethical side of things. There is a need to address issues like bias, fairness, privacy, and security. It's not just about the technology itself; it's about how we use it and its impact on people's lives. The future demands the development of frameworks, guidelines, and policies to ensure the responsible use of NLP technologies. Balancing innovation with ethical considerations will foster trust and enable NLP to impact society positively.

With prompt engineering, you can enhance the quality of the generated content and make the conversation more engaging and meaningful. You can do this by providing clear objectives and relevant context and experimenting with different question formats to engage in captivating conversations.

Prompt Engineering Strategies

When it comes to using ChatGPT to its fullest potential, there are several strategies you can employ to enhance accuracy and achieve optimal outcomes. These strategies are not only applicable in the workplace but can also benefit your personal development, business endeavors, and passive income ventures. Let's look into these game-changing strategies and how to apply them.

- **Contextualization Equation:** Introducing a specific context to your inquiries helps ChatGPT understand the background of your question to generate more accurate responses. Example: Incorporate historical context to dive into the impact of cultural movements on artistic expression.
- **Precision Formula:** Narrowing the scope of your question guides ChatGPT's responses to be more targeted and specific. This results in a deeper analysis of the desired area of study. Example: Focus on Company XY's financial metrics to gain an understanding of their net profit.
- **Hypothetical Inquiry Statement:** Exploring the implications of a hypothetical scenario encourages ChatGPT to consider the potential consequences, impacts, or outcomes of the provided hypothetical situation. Example: Analyze the potential consequences of a global energy crisis on sustainable development initiatives.
- **Comparative Analysis Equation:** This strategy leverages ChatGPT's capacity to process and analyze data, allowing for the identification of relationships and insights that may not be immediately apparent. Example: Compare consumer behavior before and after introducing a new product to gauge its market impact.
- **Roleplaying Strategy:** Adopting the perspective of a specific profession or role allows you to tap into

ChatGPT's ability to generate responses that align with the desired outcome or result. Example: Act as a marketing strategist and brainstorm creative ideas to improve customer engagement.

- **Language Adaptation Statement:** Using terminology specific to a particular field or industry allows ChatGPT to generate responses tailored to that domain. Example: Could you provide insights on the recent advancements in immunotherapy for the treatment of metastatic melanoma? I'm particularly interested in using immune checkpoint inhibitors and clinical trial data on their efficacy and safety profiles.

- **Feedback Loop Strategy:** This strategy relies on ChatGPT's ability to learn and adapt to user feedback. This allows for continuous improvement in generating more precise and relevant responses over time. Example: Analyze the accuracy of ChatGPT's responses, identify areas for improvement, and refine your questioning technique accordingly.

- **Scenario Projection Statement:** This strategy taps into ChatGPT's ability to analyze trends and patterns and generate plausible projections based on the provided scenario. Example: Imagine a scenario where emerging technologies disrupt the transportation industry to predict the future of autonomous vehicles.

- **Diverse Perspective Equation:** This method incorporates knowledge from a verity of fields to to provide comprehensive and innovative solutions. Example: Draw insights from psychology, sociology, and economics to explore the relationship between consumer behavior and marketing strategies.

- **Problem-Solving Discussions:** You can engage in open discussions with ChatGPT, encouraging reflection and exploring different solutions to solving a problem. Example: Discuss potential solutions to a complex business problem, considering different perspectives and evaluating the feasibility of each approach.

Key Takeaway

What Is a Prompt?

A prompt is a specific instruction or input given to an AI model to generate a response. It serves as a starting point for the model to understand the desired context and generate relevant output.

What Is Prompt Engineering?

Prompt engineering involves crafting effective and strategic prompts to produce desired responses from ChatGPT. It involves considering the wording, structure, and content of the prompt to optimize the quality and relevance of the generated output.

How to Overcome the ChatGPT Word Limit?

ChatGPT has a word limit for each interaction, but you can overcome this limitation by requesting an outline, keeping the conversation going, and breaking down complex questions into multiple shorter prompts.

The Future of Prompt Engineering

Prompt engineering holds great potential for further advancements. In the future, we can expect improvements in refining prompts, increasing user control over outputs, and developing more interactive and dynamic conversations with ChatGPT. As research and development progress, prompt engineering will continue to evolve, offering better customization and precision in generating AI responses.

What Next?

Now that we have thoroughly explored prompt engineering, we will address the limitations and potential downsides of ChatGPT in the next chapter. We will look into the challenges that may arise when using ChatGPT, equipping you with the knowledge and understanding needed to navigate these drawbacks effectively. Knowing these limitations allows you to make informed decisions and optimize your interactions with ChatGPT for a more rewarding and responsible experience.

4. The Downsides of ChatGPT

ChatGPT has become a boost in our digital age, especially in helping us with writing and content-creation tasks. However, this chapter isn't about praising it; it's more about unveiling the shadows that lurk behind its amazing features. As the saying goes, "With great power comes great responsibility," and ChatGPT is no exception.

You might have heard about Italy recently banning ChatGPT, and you may wonder why they took such drastic action against this great tool. This is because using AI technology raises important ethical and regulatory questions. The ban in Italy got a lot of attention from media outlets like BBC and TechCrunch, shedding light on the potential impact of ChatGPT.

Italy's concerns were about how AI could be misused and its impact on jobs and businesses. This decision sparked debates worldwide on how AI systems should be responsibly used and regulated.

However, OpenAI took action to address Italy's worries so they could resume providing ChatGPT's services in the country. OpenAI collaborated with Italian regulatory bodies, experts, and stakeholders to ensure the responsible use of the technology according to Italy's ethical standards. OpenAI wants to show that ChatGPT is meant to support humans, not replace them.

We all know that privacy is a big deal when it comes to AI, but it's not the only thing to be careful about. ChatGPT is powerful but it's not a replacement for human intelligence. It should be seen as a tool that helps us in our tasks and decision-making, not a substitute for our expertise.

In this chapter, we will look at the capabilities of ChatGPT while recognizing its limits. We will also see how important our human intelligence and critical thinking are in using AI effectively. Finding this balance will help us make the most of ChatGPT's power without worrying about losing our place in the world.

Limitations of ChatGPT

Before heading straight into the limitations of ChatGPT, let's quickly recap its advantages, which we covered earlier:

1. Simulates and Generates Human-Like Conversation

ChatGPT is a powerful tool that can engage in realistic interactions, making conversations feel like you're talking to a real human. Whether you're seeking assistance, brainstorming ideas, or simply engaging in friendly banter, ChatGPT can simulate a back-and-forth exchange that mirrors human conversation.

2. Built on the Advanced GPT Model and Language Fluency

ChatGPT is built upon the GPT (Generative Pre-trained Transformer) model, which helps it understand and use language well. It can come up with responses that make sense and sound natural, just like a language expert. It knows the right words to say and responds in a way that feels authentic and natural.

3. Scalable and Open to Fine-Tuning

ChatGPT is scalable and can get better over time. It can be fine-tuned to enhance performance and align better for specific uses or domains. It's like a smart robot that can keep learning and improving. It was designed to be adaptable to become more intelligent as technology advances.

4. Adaptability and Multiple Applications

ChatGPT is like a jack-of-all-trades! It can be used in many different ways for different things. ChatGPT's versatility allows it to be used in various sectors, from customer service chatbots and virtual assistants to creative writing prompts and educational tools. This makes it a valuable resource across different industries, offering tailored solutions.

5. Supports Integration with Plug-Ins for Extensions

ChatGPT supports integration with plug-ins for extensions to expand its functionality. These plug-ins are extra add-ons that make ChatGPT even more powerful and versatile. With them, ChatGPT can do all sorts of amazing stuff to meet your specific needs. For example, you can integrate external knowledge sources to make ChatGPT smart and well-informed. Or, you can add specialized functionalities to tailor the conversations just how you like them.

Understanding the Disadvantages of ChatGPT

One of the most concerning limitations to the use of ChatGPT is the issue of privacy and security. Imagine chatting with ChatGPT, sharing your innermost thoughts and secrets, and then suddenly, it hits you—Who's on the other side of this virtual conversation?

While OpenAI takes data privacy seriously, there's always a small chance that sensitive information could be exposed. ChatGPT needs data to learn from, including the text of the conversations it engages in. It's like walking a tightrope— balancing the advantages of personalized responses with safe- guarding user privacy.

Another limitation is the potential for biased responses. Despite being a master of language, ChatGPT is still a product of its training data. And, let's face it, the internet is a wild jungle of biased information. There's a chance that ChatGPT's responses may carry some of that bias, too. It's not intentionally trying to be unfair, but rather, it's reflecting the imperfections of the data it was fed. This can generate responses that unintentionally favor one perspective over another.

Here's some more detail on those and other limitations:

1. Limited Knowledge

One of the most notable disadvantages of ChatGPT is limited knowledge. This is evident when using ChatGPT for researching a subject that needs up-to-date information.

Imagine you're a researcher trying to gather the most recent data on a cutting-edge field. You turn to ChatGPT with excitement, hoping to get the latest information and findings. However, you discover that ChatGPT's knowledge is only based on information before September 2021. It's like wanting to know who won the latest championship match but only being able to find out who won two years ago.

The limitation of knowledge in ChatGPT can be quite frustrating, especially in fast-paced fields. For instance, in AI, breakthroughs and advancements are happening all the time. If you rely solely on ChatGPT for your AI research, you might miss out on the latest models, algorithms, and innovations.

Let's consider an example outside the tech realm. Let's say you're interested in studying climate change and its impact on endangered species in 2023. You turn to ChatGPT to gather recent data and news articles, but unfortunately, the model can't provide you with information beyond its last update in September 2021. You could be missing out on crucial reports, research papers, and conservation efforts that occurred afterward.

This limitation can significantly affect researchers, journalists, and anyone seeking the most up-to-date information. The world constantly evolves, and discoveries can reshape our understanding of various topics. Not being able to access the latest data might hinder the progress of your research or lead to outdated conclusions.

2. Difficulty Handling Ambiguity

Handling ambiguity is no easy feat for anyone, even ChatGPT. It's a great tool for generating human-like responses, but it can sometimes struggle with vague queries.

When faced with ambiguous queries, ChatGPT relies on its training data to provide an appropriate response. However, this can lead to biased outputs because the data it's trained on might contain societal biases. For instance, if the model was trained on text that exhibited gender or racial bias, it might produce responses reflecting those biases.

Let's take an example to understand the challenge of ambiguity better. Consider the query: "Should I invest my money in stocks?" The response to this question can vary greatly depending on the user's financial situation, risk tolerance, and investment goals. ChatGPT might give a generic answer like, "Investing in stocks can offer good returns, but it also carries some risks," which isn't particularly helpful for a specific user.

Also, imagine asking ChatGPT, "What is the best diet?" This is quite an ambiguous question since the "best" diet might vary based on individual needs, health conditions, and personal preferences. ChatGPT might respond with a general diet plan, but it might not be your most suitable option.

Similarly, when discussing sensitive topics like politics or social issues, ChatGPT might provide responses that may lean toward certain biases in the data it was trained on. If the training data is biased toward a specific political ideology, the AI's responses might reflect that bias, even if unintentionally.

To address these challenges, you should ask specific and well-defined questions. Instead of asking, "What's the best career choice for me?" you can rephrase it as, "What are the advantages and disadvantages of pursuing a career in software engineering?" This way, the model will more likely provide a focused response.

It's important to remember that ChatGPT cannot replace human judgment. When making important decisions, you should approach its responses critically and cross-reference information from reliable sources.

3. Ambiguity and Inaccuracies

ChatGPT is not a magical oracle with all-encompassing knowledge. Instead, it relies solely on the data fed into its digital brain.

This means that ChatGPT can produce some pretty mind-blowing responses, but it's not flawless. Ambiguities and inaccuracies may sometimes creep into its answers. If you come across something that seems a bit off or unclear, don't fret! It's just a friendly reminder that our beloved AI is still a learning machine and might occasionally stumble.

Don't get me wrong, ChatGPT is pretty good at what it does. But to get the most out of ChatGPT's capabilities, you need to be open to its brilliance and occasional quirks.

ChatGPT can have biases in how it operates, which fall into five categories. The first two come from the input it receives. The third and fourth types are inherent in the AI software. The fifth bias appears in the users themselves. These are:

- **Sample Bias:** This bias comes from the limited data used to train the AI. Since only a specific group of people generates the content, the AI might not fully represent diverse perspectives.
- **Programmatic Morality Bias:** The software company introduces this bias to align ChatGPT with what is socially acceptable. It can influence the AI's responses to align with certain values. It aims to put in opinions seen as "socially correct," making ChatGPT fit in well with most users.
- **Ignorance Bias:** Users sometimes assume ChatGPT has deductive reasoning abilities due to its vast knowledge. However, it can only provide answers based on existing data and not reason through new questions.
- **Overton Window Bias:** ChatGPT has a bias called "Overton Window Bias," where it goes beyond what's considered appropriate in its knowledge base. It avoids

controversial topics and lacks the ability to know what is true. This can lead to problems when discussing controversial subjects, as its responses may not always be accurate. ChatGPT's output may repeat false information, and this makes it unreliable.

- **Deference Bias:** When people trust AI too much, we see three levels of "deference bias." The first is automation bias, where people rely too much on the technology's accuracy due to their heavy workloads. The second is authority bias: people granting AI political or intellectual authority influenced by recent challenges and our tendency to follow external authority. The third and most concerning is stress coercion, when people view AI as an authority and passionately defend it as a perfect entity. This might be influenced by the stressful Covid-19 pandemic and Big Tech's role in our lives during lockdowns. It's worrying that many people have become overly reliant on AI and surrendered their intellectual abilities to it.

The Effect and Impact When People Trust ChatGPT Too Much

ChatGPT's capabilities are undoubtedly amazing, but several consequences can arise when people place excessive trust in it. These may include:

- **Misinformation Spread:** ChatGPT relies on the data it has been exposed to, and it doesn't possess the ability to fact-check or verify information. If you accept everything ChatGPT says, misinformation and inaccuracies could spread.

- **Critical-Thinking Erosion:** Relying too heavily on ChatGPT for information may lead to a decline in critical-thinking skills. You may accept answers without questioning or exploring alternative information. Remember that ChatGPT is a tool and not an all-knowing oracle.
- **Lack of Human Connection:** Relying heavily on AI interactions may reduce human interactions, affecting social skills and emotional connections.
- **Privacy and Security Concerns:** Entrusting sensitive information to ChatGPT might raise privacy and security issues. It's important to take caution and be mindful of the information you share.
- **Dependency on AI for Decision-Making:** Over-reliance on ChatGPT for decision-making, especially in critical situations, can be risky. Human judgment and expertise remain irreplaceable in complex situations.

Bias in Natural Language Processing Model (NLP)

The natural language processing model allows ChatGPT to understand and process language like humans do. However, despite its capabilities, the natural language processing model is not immune to biases.

These biases stem from the data it learns from, sourced from human creators who may possess certain biases. Also, the system's design can introduce biases that can lead to incomplete or inaccurate information.

Now, let's get into some eye-opening examples of bias in ChatGPT. Imagine asking ChatGPT about a particular profession, and it responds with gender-specific language, assuming only one gender is associated with that job. For instance, when it was used to review job applicants' resumes, it favored female candidates because of the past underrepresentation of women in the data.

There have been accusations of political bias as well. When asked to write like different media outlets, ChatGPT refused to mimic the style of the *New York Post* but complied easily with CNN's style. There are claims that the model is more likely to flag negative comments about certain groups, like liberals, women, gays, and African Americans. However, these biases are not intentional on the part of the model developers but rather a result of the data used for training.

What Is the Root Cause of Bias in ChatGPT?

Our world is far from being bias-free, and those biases tend to sneak into the data used to train ChatGPT. To put it simply, the root cause of bias in ChatGPT lies in the data it was fed during its training. These data come from the internet, from articles, books, forums, and tweets to human-generated content. As diverse as it may seem, it still reflects the biases that exist in our society.

Now, let's talk about real-life examples. Take a look at a scenario where ChatGPT is asked to describe the ideal profession for a nurse. It might respond with a biased view, suggesting a female nurse without even considering male nurses. This doesn't mean ChatGPT is intentionally sexist—it just reflects the biases it has inadvertently learned from the data. Similarly, ChatGPT may unknowingly echo negative sentiments it has encountered in its training when discussing a certain culture or ethnicity.

Concerns and Issues of Ethical Importance

It's no secret that ChatGPT is a game-changer when it comes to brainstorming and finding solutions to problems. When used responsibly, it can improve productivity and creativity.

But here's where the ethical tightrope comes into play. The line between productivity boost and potential cheating lies in how we approach its usage. ChatGPT should never be a substitute for our original thoughts and efforts. Relying solely on AI to create academic papers, essays, or work projects can rob you of your learning process and personal growth.

Let's face it: the temptation to use this AI as a shortcut to academic or professional success can be all too real. Letting ChatGPT do the heavy lifting may be tempting, but you must remember that true growth and learning come from putting in the effort and engaging with your tasks wholeheartedly.

Using ChatGPT to support your journey is one thing, but relying on it to bypass hard work is another. Creativity, learning, and productivity thrive when you challenge yourself and tackle problems head-on. ChatGPT should never replace unique human touch and ingenuity.

How do we strike the perfect balance? Use ChatGPT as your trusty sidekick, but don't let it overshadow your abilities and potential. Use it to spark ideas, refine concepts, and complement your creative process. See it as a collaborator, not a replacement for your efforts.

ChatGPT as Therapist

Using ChatGPT for therapy has also become increasingly popular due to its accessibility and anonymity. People find solace in sharing their deepest thoughts and emotions with ChatGPT, believing it offers a safe and judgment-free space. However, there are potential pitfalls to it.

The risk here lies in the fact that you might divulge sensitive and personal information to ChatGPT without realizing that others could store and access your data. The last thing you would want is for your private therapy sessions to end up in the wrong hands.

Real therapists provide empathetic responses in their approach to each individual. Since ChatGPT's responses are based on the data it was trained on, their responses may include biased or inaccurate information. This could lead to harmful advice or promote harmful beliefs, particularly when dealing with sensitive mental health issues.

Potential Legal Implications

ChatGPT doesn't create original content out of thin air. It's not some magical wordsmith like Shakespeare; instead, it relies solely on the information that has been fed into its system.

And here's where things can get dicey from a legal perspective. Imagine using ChatGPT to make important decisions, like legal advice or medical diagnoses. If its responses are biased-based, it could lead to serious consequences. Legal matters are no joke; getting the wrong information could be seriously detrimental.

But wait, there's more. Since ChatGPT relies on historical data for its knowledge, it might not be up to date with the latest laws or regulations. To make matters worse, ChatGPT isn't just learning from textbooks or law journals. It gobbles up every-thing it finds online. You can imagine how this wide-ranging diet might result in some less-than-reliable responses. This is not exactly what you want when seeking precise legal or medical advice.

This isn't to say that ChatGPT is entirely useless in the legal realm. When used responsibly, with human oversight and awareness of its limitations, it can still provide useful insights. However, relying solely on its responses without careful consideration could land you a bit of a legal problem.

Treading Forward With Caution

Now that we have looked at the negative impact of ChatGPT, there is a need to tread with caution. ChatGPT is impressive but not perfect. Always cross-check the information with reliable sources before taking its responses as gospel truth. Here is how to make the most out of ChatGPT like a pro:

1. Be Clear and Specific

When interacting with ChatGPT, be clear and specific in your requests. The more precise you are, the better the model can understand your needs and respond accurately. Avoid long sentences and try to break down complex questions into simpler ones.

Example: Instead of asking, "Can you give me a detailed explanation of quantum physics?" try, "What are the fundamental principles of quantum physics?"

2. Experiment and Iterate

ChatGPT learns from its interactions, so feel free to experiment and iterate with your prompts. If the initial response isn't quite what you were looking for, don't worry. Adjust your question or provide more context to guide the model toward the desired outcome.

Example: If you ask, "Tell me a joke," and the response isn't hilarious, try something like, "Can you share a punny joke about cats?"

3. Give Context and Background

Provide some background information to get more personalized and relevant responses. This helps ChatGPT understand your specific situation and tailor its answers accordingly.

Example: Instead of asking, "How do I bake a cake?" provide context like, "I want to bake a chocolate cake for my friend's birthday, but I'm a beginner in baking."

4. Control the Tone

You have the power to set the tone of the conversation with ChatGPT. If you want a formal response, be polite and use appropriate language. For a more casual chat, you can be a bit more laid-back.

Example: To get a formal response about the weather, ask, "Could you please provide the weather forecast for tomorrow?" For a casual response, try, "What's the weather gonna be like tomorrow?"

5. Verify Information

ChatGPT doesn't have real-time access to information. Verifying critical information from reliable sources is always a good idea before making decisions based solely on ChatGPT's responses.

Example: If ChatGPT provides a recipe for an allergy-friendly dish, double-check with a trusted recipe website to ensure it's safe.

Measuring, Detecting, and Reducing Bias in ChatGPT

ChatGPT may require some time to address bias in its responses. However, you can take some measures to tackle this issue:

- Conduct thorough research and don't solely rely on ChatGPT when making significant decisions. Use examples that imagine different scenarios to understand things better.
- Many individuals are urging OpenAI to disclose the algorithm employed by ChatGPT to provide information. This transparency would aid users in understanding how the model operates and, more importantly, how it creates responses to queries.
- ChatGPT is currently being investigated for potentially using sensitive private data. This consideration should be kept in mind while using the program, as it may impact the answers received.
- Government officials in the United States and Europe are considering regulating ChatGPT. While these regulations could have both good and bad effects, you should keep up to date as the details unfold.

How Have Users Successfully Addressed Bias in ChatGPT?

Most users address bias in ChatGPT by maintaining clear boundaries and ensuring that bias doesn't creep into the conversations.

You can define specific guidelines and expectations that align with your values and principles. This way, ChatGPT helps you streamline tasks without compromising the quality of your interaction.

Users also take the approach of verifying each piece of information provided by ChatGPT. You should cross-reference the responses to ensure you have accurate and reliable information at hand.

When dealing with gender neutrality in job descriptions on ChatGPT, many users use gender-neutral language to ensure that job postings appeal to diverse applicants. This includes using gender-neutral job descriptions and stripping away words that lean toward a particular gender. This opens up opportunities for everyone and creates a welcoming environment where all candidates feel valued for their skills and qualifications.

By adopting these strategies, you can harness the potential of ChatGPT while minimizing bias and promoting fairness.

The Future of Bias in ChatGPT

ChatGPT comes with its limitations. One such limitation is that ChatGPT draws its information from human sources. And, as you may know, humans are not perfect; they carry with them biases.

Now, you might be wondering, "What does this mean for the future of ChatGPT?" Biases may persist, but they can be minimized and addressed over time. It's a collaborative effort between governments, activists, and developers that holds the key to refining ChatGPT.

Governments can play a crucial role by setting regulations and guidelines that ensure transparency and accountability in AI development. This would encourage responsible AI implementation and minimize any potential biases.

Developers are continuously fine-tuning and improving ChatGPT to reduce biases and make it more reliable and equitable. They can identify and address potential biases through careful analysis and data scrutiny.

The Implication of Its Use

Two significant areas where ChatGPT falls short are its limited creativity and lack of emotional understanding. ChatGPT lacks the innate creativity that only human minds can possess. Human creativity is driven by emotions, experiences, and the ability to think beyond patterns.

When it comes to emotional understanding, ChatGPT might not fully understand the depth of human emotions. Sure, it can analyze language patterns and produce responses, but it doesn't genuinely empathize or connect emotionally with you.

This shows that ChatGPT cannot take over jobs and businesses entirely, but it can help with productivity. You can delegate repetitive tasks such as drafting emails, creating content, or brainstorming ideas to ChatGPT. This frees up your time to focus on tasks that require human creativity and emotional understanding.

With ChatGPT, you have more mental space to spare so you can explore ideas, experiment with new concepts, and think outside the box. Also, ChatGPT can serve as a collaborative tool. You can use it to refine your ideas, expand your knowledge, and overcome creative blocks.

It is important to know that technology, no matter how advanced, is a complement to human abilities rather than a substitute. Knowing this can help you wield its power, using it as a springboard for efficiency.

Key Takeaway

- ChatGPT can be used to boost productivity and efficiency in mundane tasks, making time for more creative work.
- ChatGPT may not replace human creativity, but it can serve as a tool to collaborate with and complement

human minds, sparking fresh ideas and providing unique perspectives.

- Understanding the boundaries of ChatGPT allows you to use it more effectively, maximizing its potential as a support tool rather than a replacement for human skills.

What Next?

With an appreciation for the power and limitations of ChatGPT, we now shift our focus to its application in the workplace. In the next chapter, we will explore how ChatGPT is making its waves in various professional settings, changing how we work and interact with technology.

ChatGPT is set to redefine the workplace landscape, from streamlining tasks and improving productivity to enhancing communication and collaboration. Now, we will uncover real-world examples of how businesses and professionals are integrating ChatGPT into their daily operations to witness its impact on efficiency and innovation.

5. ChatGPT in the Workplace

L et's say you have a work partner by your side, one that never tires, never complains, and always has a wealth of information at their fingertips. Well, that partner is ChatGPT. According to a Korn Ferry recent survey of professionals across industries, 46% of people already use ChatGPT to elevate their work game. But what makes ChatGPT different?

From marketing wizards to data experts, people across all industries use ChatGPT at their workplaces. It's not just a luxury anymore; it's a necessity in this digital world. According to Korn Ferry, over 80% of surveyed professionals agree that ChatGPT is a legitimate and beneficial tool. It has taken over the hearts and minds of many, proving its worth in the real world.

As we saw in the previous chapter, ChatGPT has its limitations, but it's hard to ignore the advantages it brings to the table. Sure, many fear it will replace human jobs or lead to a less personal touch in our work interactions, but the truth lies in its application.

When used wisely, ChatGPT becomes the perfect digital partner, working hand in hand with human creativity and intelligence. With ChatGPT by your side, you can tackle routine tasks, crunch data, and even generate content, allowing time for higher-level thinking. No more mind-numbing tasks; instead, you can welcome a fresh wave of creativity into your daily work life.

In this chapter, we'll talk about how you can use ChatGPT in the workplace and go into its ability to ignite creativity. As we continue, you will discover the advantages of using ChatGPT at work and learn how to integrate it effectively into your daily routines. At the end of this chapter, you'll be equipped to use ChatGPT to make strides in your professional career.

Effective Ways ChatGPT Can Boost Productivity and Creativity in the Workplace

ChatGPT can work wonders in helping you at work and spark creativity in your career. Here are some effective ways ChatGPT can make a real difference, whatever your field:

Marketing & Advertising

ChatGPT can be your guide in crafting compelling copy and ad content. You can use ChatGPT to brainstorm catchy slogans, refine social media posts, generate creative ideas on demand,

and save time and effort. Let's look at how ChatGPT can help you do this:

1. Refining Social Media Posts

Scenario: A social media manager needs to create engaging posts for an upcoming product promotion but is running short on time.

Sample Prompt: "Help me create an attention-grabbing social media post to promote our limited-time discount on fitness apparel."

2. Creating Engaging Email Subject Lines

Scenario: An email marketer wants to increase the open rates for their latest newsletter.

Sample Prompt: "Provide attention-grabbing subject lines for our monthly newsletter focused on health and wellness."

3. Crafting Engaging Video Scripts

Scenario: A video content producer wants to create compelling scripts for a series of brand videos.

Sample Prompt: "Help me draft a product demo video script highlighting versatility and ease of use."

Other Sample Prompts for Marketing & Advertising

- "Assist me in refining the ad copy for our travel agency's latest vacation package."
- "Suggest a compelling call-to-action for our email marketing campaign."

- "Generate creative ideas for a captivating billboard advertisement promoting our restaurant."
- "Come up with promotional ideas for our upcoming product launch event."

Content Creation and Writing

You can use ChatGPT to overcome writer's block and improve your creativity. You can create blog topics, outline articles, and explore new perspectives using ChatGPT as a co-writer or idea generator. Let's look at practical ways you can do this:

1. Blog Post Ideas

Scenario: Imagine you're a passionate travel blogger struggling to develop new post ideas. ChatGPT can help!

Sample Prompts: "Can you suggest topics for a travel blog focused on off-the-beaten-path destinations?"

2. Writing Engaging Introductions

Scenario: You're a food writer and are running out of ways to create interest in diet articles. You can use ChatGPT to get inspired.

Sample Prompts: "Can you help me create an attention-grabbing introduction for an article about healthy eating?"

3. Social Media Content

Scenario: You need words to go with your Instagram uploads from a recent trip, but you don't have time to think up any one-liners. Use ChatGPT for quick ideas.

Sample Prompts: "Can you suggest witty captions for my travel photos?"

Other Writing Sample Prompts

- "Assist me in writing an introduction for my photography portfolio."
- "Generate content ideas for my DIY home improvement blog."
- "Create an outline for a comprehensive guide on digital marketing."
- "Help me write product descriptions for our new fashion collection."

Software Development and Coding

When it comes to coding and development, you can use ChatGPT as a teammate. It can assist with debugging code, suggesting algorithms, and explaining complex programming concepts. As a developer, ChatGPT can help you solve problems efficiently. Let's look at how:

1. Code Refactoring

Scenario: A software developer is working on a complex codebase and wants to improve its readability and maintainability. They can use ChatGPT to get suggestions for code refactoring.

Sample Prompt: "Can you provide me with some ideas to refactor this code snippet to make it more efficient and easier to understand?"

2. Troubleshooting Bugs

Scenario: A software engineer encounters a persistent bug in their code and needs help debugging the issue. They can use ChatGPT to get insights into possible causes and solutions.

Sample Prompt: "I've been trying to find the bug in this section of my code for hours. Any suggestions on where I should look and how to fix it?"

3. Integration with External APIs

Scenario: A software developer is integrating their application with external APIs and facing challenges with data parsing. They can use ChatGPT to get suggestions on handling API responses.

Sample Prompt: "I'm working on integrating an API, but I'm stuck parsing the response data. Any tips on how to efficiently handle API responses in my code?"

Other Sample Prompts for Software Development

- "I'm learning Python. Can you provide me with beginner-friendly exercises to practice loops and conditionals?"
- "I want to build a chatbot for my website. What key steps and technologies should I consider for this project?"
- "I'm interested in learning about machine-learning algorithms. Can you give me a brief overview of decision trees and their applications?"

- "I'm struggling with database design. Can you provide some best practices and tips to design an efficient database schema?"

Design and UX/UI

As a designer and user experience expert, you can tap into ChatGPT's creativity to explore new design concepts and user interfaces. ChatGPT can generate design inspirations, propose color palettes, and even streamline the design process. Here's how:

1. Color Palette Suggestions

Scenario: As a graphic designer, you are working on a new branding project for a fashion company. You want a color palette that reflects their eco-friendly values.

Sample Prompt: "Suggest a color palette representing sustainability and nature for a fashion brand."

2. Drafting Wireframes

Scenario: You are a UX designer tasked with redesigning an e-commerce website to improve user experience. You want to create wireframes for the homepage.

Sample Prompt: "Help me draft wireframes for an e-commerce website homepage focusing on intuitive navigation and product discovery."

3. Design Trends in E-Commerce

Scenario: As a UX/UI designer for an online car brand, you want to stay updated on the latest design trends in e-commerce.

Sample Prompt: "What are the current design trends in e-commerce websites, especially for car brands?"

Other Sample Prompts for Design

- "Provide ideas for a user-friendly navigation menu for an e-commerce website selling home decor products."
- "Generate a layout for a mobile app that promotes eco-friendly practices and sustainability."
- "Suggest an animation concept for an e-learning platform that enhances user engagement during courses."
- "Help me create a user-friendly checkout process for an online bookstore, emphasizing ease of payment and quick order confirmation."

Project Management

Managing projects can be overwhelming, but ChatGPT can lighten the load. It can help you generate meeting agendas, draft progress reports, and even offer suggestions for task allocation in efficient project workflows. Here are some suggestions:

1. Generating Meeting Agendas

Scenario: As a project manager, you have a team meeting coming up, and you want to create a well-structured agenda to ensure a productive discussion.

Sample Prompt: "I need help creating an agenda for our upcoming project review meeting. Can you suggest the main topics we should cover and any key discussion points?"

2. Resource Allocation and Task Assignment

Scenario: You have a new project with a limited budget and must allocate resources effectively while ensuring each team member has a clear task assignment.

Sample Prompt: "I have a new project, but resources are limited. Can you provide recommendations on allocating resources and assigning tasks based on team members' skills?"

3. Project Budgeting and Cost Control

Scenario: You are working on a project with a fixed budget and need assistance developing a cost-control plan to avoid over-spending.

Sample Prompt: "I'm managing a project with a tight budget. Can you provide tips on effective cost-control measures to ensure we stay within budget without compromising quality?"

Other Sample Prompts for Project Management

- "Please create a project timeline for an upcoming product launch."

- "Assist me in identifying potential risks in our software development project."
- "Can you help me draft a project proposal for a new client pitch?"
- "Provide suggestions on how to improve team collaboration and communication."

Education and Training

In the education sector, ChatGPT can serve as an interactive learning companion. It can generate quiz questions, explain complex topics, and create interactive study materials for students and teachers. Here's how:

1. Quiz Question Generator

Scenario: A teacher wants to create engaging quizzes for their students.

Sample Prompt: "Generate five multiple-choice questions on photosynthesis for my biology class."

2. Vocabulary Building

Scenario: An ESL (English as a Second Language) learner wants to practice and expand their vocabulary.

Sample Prompt: "Provide me with ten advanced English words, their meanings, and usage in sentences."

3. Practice Math Problems

Scenario: A high school student wants to practice solving algebraic equations.

Sample Prompt: "Generate three algebraic equations with variables on both sides for me to solve."

Customer Support

ChatGPT can help provide responses to common customer queries, providing instant support and freeing up space to focus on more brain-demanding issues. Here's how:

1. Personalized Customer Interactions

Scenario: You have just read an article saying that customers appreciate a personalized touch in their interactions with customer support. ChatGPT can help you craft personalized responses by analyzing customer data and understanding their needs.

Sample Prompt: "How can I address a customer who has just purchased our premium subscription?"

2. Handling Escalated Complaints

Scenario: A customer has escalated their complaint as they are dissatisfied with the customer support they have received so far. ChatGPT can help you draft empathetic and reassuring responses to ensure you address the customer's concerns.

Sample Prompt: "How should I respond to a customer who is unhappy with our service and demanding a refund?"

3. Multilingual Support

Scenario: You are in an international marketplace now. A Spanish customer has contacted you, and you are unfamiliar with the language. ChatGPT can act as a translator to communicate with customers in various languages.

Sample Prompt: "How do I greet a customer in Spanish who has reached out for support?"

Sample Prompts for you to Try Out

- "What are the key features of our latest product?"
- "Can you help me troubleshoot a connectivity issue with our device?"
- "How can I handle a customer who is having difficulty accessing their account?"
- "Can you provide me with a sample script to handle a customer complaint about a delayed shipment?"

Human Resources and Recruitment

Recruitment and HR professionals can rely on ChatGPT to assist with writing compelling job descriptions, screening candidates with predefined questions, and providing onboarding information for new hires. Here's how ChatGPT can help:

1. Writing Job Descriptions

Scenario: A human resources manager is tasked with creating a compelling job description for a new marketing manager position.

Sample Prompt: "I need help crafting a job description for a marketing manager role. The ideal candidate should have experience in digital marketing and a proven track record of successful campaign management. Can you help me develop a captivating and informative job description?"

2. Candidate Screening

Scenario: A recruitment specialist is going through a large pool of applicants for an entry-level customer support position and needs assistance screening potential candidates.

Sample Prompt: "I have hundreds of resumes for the customer support role, and I need to identify the most qualified candidates. Can you help me create a set of screening questions to assess their communication skills, problem-solving abilities, and customer-centric approach?"

3. Interview Questions

Scenario: An HR professional is preparing for an interview with a potential candidate for a sales position and needs help formulating relevant questions.

Sample Prompt: "I have an interview scheduled with a sales representative candidate. Can you assist me in crafting a list of behavioral and situational questions to assess their sales experience, negotiation skills, and ability to handle challenging situations?"

Other Sample Prompts for Human Resources

- "Generate a job description for a software engineer role focusing on front-end development skills."

- "Help me develop a set of interview questions to evaluate candidates for a project manager position."
- "Outline an onboarding checklist for new hires in our marketing department."
- "Create a performance evaluation template highlighting key performance indicators for sales representatives."

Financial Analysis and Reporting

ChatGPT can be very useful for financial analysts and accountants. It can help in data analysis, develop financial reports, and provide insights into market trends to make better financial decisions. Here's how:

1. Data Analysis Assistance

Scenario: A financial analyst wants to analyze a company's financial data to identify trends and key performance indicators (KPIs).

Sample Prompt: "I need help analyzing XYZ Company's financial data. Can you assist me in identifying the revenue growth and profit margin trends over the past three years?"

2. Generating Financial Reports

Scenario: An accountant must prepare a monthly financial report for the company's stakeholders.

Sample Prompt: "I have to create a comprehensive financial report summarizing our company's income statement, balance sheet, and cash flow statement for the past quarter. Can you help me draft the report?"

3. Market Analysis Insights

Scenario: A financial researcher wants to gain insights into market trends and competitor analysis.

Sample Prompt: "I'm researching the current market trends in the technology sector and need information on the top-performing tech companies and their market share. Can you provide me with some data and analysis?"

Other Sample Prompts for Financial Analysis

- "Please analyze the revenue and cost trends of ABC Corporation for the last five years and identify any patterns or fluctuations."
- "I'm researching the consumer goods industry. Can you generate a comparative analysis of the financial performance of three major companies in this sector?"
- "I'm considering investing in tech start-ups, but I need insights into their financial stability and growth prospects. Can you help me assess the financial health of three potential startup investments?"
- "I need to create a financial report for my department's budget presentation. Can you assist me in summarizing our expenses and revenue data for the past quarter?"

Healthcare and Research

Even in the medical field, ChatGPT has a role to play. It can aid healthcare professionals in diagnosing symptoms, researching medical literature, and suggesting treatment options based on scientific findings.

1. Diagnosis Assistance

Sample Prompt: "I'm a medical professional evaluating a patient with fever, cough, and fatigue symptoms. Can you help me narrow down possible diagnoses and suggest appropriate tests?"

2. Medical Literature Research

Sample Prompt: "I'm researching the effectiveness of a new drug for diabetes treatment. Can you provide me with recent studies and clinical trial results published in medical journals?"

3. Treatment Options for a Specific Condition

Sample Prompt: "I'm a physician seeking alternative treatment options for a patient with severe migraines who has not responded well to standard medications. Can you suggest some innovative therapies or approaches?"

4. Public Health Strategies

Sample Prompt: "I'm a public health officer tasked with designing an intervention to reduce obesity rates in our community. Can you provide evidence-based strategies and best practices used in similar successful programs?"

Other Sample Prompts for Healthcare & Research

- "I'm interested in learning about the current research on Alzheimer's disease. Can you suggest some reputable sources?"
- "I'm conducting research on genetic disorders. Can you help me find relevant case studies and genetic testing methods?"
- "Can you explain the mechanism of action for a specific medication used to treat depression?"
- "I need information on the long-term effects of concussions on athletes. Can you provide some insights?"

With ChatGPT as a versatile tool, professionals from all walks of life can use it to increase productivity at work. ChatGPT can help teams and individuals to reach new heights of success by streamlining tasks, suggesting new ideas, and providing useful information.

Microsoft and ChatGPT

Microsoft is taking big steps in adding artificial intelligence to its popular tools like Outlook, PowerPoint, Excel, and Word. Their goal is to simplify the way millions of users work every day.

Microsoft plans to introduce an AI "Co-pilot" to Microsoft 365 users. This is capable of editing, summarizing, creating, and comparing documents. With this feature, you can transcribe meeting notes while chatting on Skype, quickly get summarized email replies, request custom charts in Excel, and convert Word docs into PowerPoint presentations in a blink. These advancements promise to make workflows easier for Microsoft 365 users.

There is more! Microsoft is also introducing Business Chat to the digital world. It's like a super-smart assistant that understands and organizes all your data—emails, calendar events, documents, presentations, chats, and meetings—within Microsoft 365.

However, it's not just Microsoft in the AI race. Google, their rival, is also gearing up to integrate AI into their tools like Gmail, Sheets, and Docs.

The tech industry is buzzing with excitement as AI tools are changing how we work, shop, and live. And you know what? These developments will open doors of opportunities to those who can harness these tools.

Key Takeaway

In this chapter, we explored the practical and effective ways ChatGPT can boost productivity in the workplace across various professions and industries. We delved into how marketing, content creation, software development, design, project management, education, customer support, human resources, finance, and healthcare professionals can leverage ChatGPT to enhance their work processes and outcomes. Also, Microsoft's integration of ChatGPT into Word and Excel will bring AI-powered assistance directly to users' fingertips, simplifying tasks in all fields.

What Next?

Now that we have explored the impact of ChatGPT on individual productivity and creativity in various workplace scenarios, it's time to look further into its role in the business world. In the next chapter, we will explore how enterprises and professionals across various industries use ChatGPT to improve efficiency, decision-making, and customer engagement. From customer support to market research, ChatGPT can redefine how businesses operate, ensuring they stay ahead in the ever-evolving business world.

6. ChatGPT in Business

As a solopreneur, my days were always filled to the brim with endless tasks, deadlines, and a never-ending list of ideas to explore. It was tiring going through the same routine over and over again; I needed something that could make my work easier and boost my income. That's when I started using ChatGPT.

From the moment I integrated ChatGPT into my business, I felt an immediate shift in my workflow. The time-consuming process of writing compelling marketing copy became a breeze. With ChatGPT, I could create engaging content ideas and craft captivating email campaigns in less time. This allowed me to focus on other aspects of my business, like building client relationships and strategizing for growth.

But perhaps the most significant impact of ChatGPT was on my creativity. I was free from routine tasks; I had more mental space to think strategically about my business. ChatGPT also sparked innovative ideas that breathed new life into my products and services to capture my audience's attention and drive sales like never before.

As my business boomed, so did my income. My productivity led directly to increased revenue and a growing customer base. With ChatGPT by my side, I was able to achieve more in less time and chart a course to new heights. In this chapter, we will discuss the practical applications of ChatGPT in businesses, showing how it can significantly help you increase productivity and income.

Practical Ways to Use ChatGPT to Boost Productivity and Income in Your Business

Use ChatGPT as your Marketing Wizard

Gone are the days of endless buzz sessions and hours spent fine-tuning marketing materials. With ChatGPT, you can develop ideas, creative concepts, and persuasive messaging with just a few keystrokes. This tool can guide you through the marketing maze with unique strategies. Let's see how:

1. Market Trends and Insights

ChatGPT can scour the web for market trends and consumer insights. You can provide specific prompts like, "What are the emerging trends in the tech industry?" or, "What are the preferences of Gen Z consumers?" to get information that can help you develop sound marketing strategies and campaigns.

2. Competitor Analysis

Gaining a competitive edge is important for any business. With ChatGPT, you can ask for a thorough analysis of your competitors, like, "Compare our product features against Company X" or, "What marketing strategies does Company Y employ?" With ChatGPT's responses, you can tweak your marketing approach and stand out.

3. Customer Personal Development

Understanding your target audience is crucial in marketing. ChatGPT can assist in developing detailed customer personas. Simply ask for prompts like, "Create a customer persona for a fintech company target audience." ChatGPT will provide information to tailor your marketing messages accordingly.

4. Keyword Research

ChatGPT can perform keyword research for an effective SEO strategy. Use prompts such as: "Identify relevant keywords for luxury clothing category" or "What are the top search terms in the fashion industry?" ChatGPT's responses will help optimize your content and improve search engine rankings.

Other Sample Prompts for Marketing

- "Analyze consumer sentiment toward our brand on social media."
- "Create a customer persona for our luxury product line."
- "Provide insights on market trends for health and wellness products."

- "We are launching a new fitness product aimed at young professionals. Can you provide insights on potential customer segments and content ideas to target them effectively?"

ChatGPT as Your Finance Maestro

Finance teams deal with mountains of data daily. With ChatGPT, you can simplify financial analysis and reporting. From preparing financial statements to crunching complex numbers, ChatGPT can assist in crafting detailed reports and interpreting financial data with ease. This saves time and reduces the chance of errors.

1. Financial Reporting Made Easy

Imagine you have to create detailed financial reports regularly; that's stressful and tiring. With ChatGPT, you can simply provide the necessary data and ask it to create the report. Whether it's balance sheets, income statements, or cash flow analysis, ChatGPT can analyze the numbers and deliver the report in no time.

Sample Prompt: "Create a monthly balance sheet report for Q3 2023 based on the provided financial data."

2. Investment Research and Analysis

When researching potential investment opportunities, ChatGPT can be your research assistant. It can analyze market trends, study historical data, and provide information on specific companies or industries.

Sample Prompt: "Analyze the performance of XYZ Company's stock over the last five years and provide an overview of potential investment risks."

3. Financial Forecasting and Budgeting

ChatGPT can assist in financial forecasting and budgeting to boost your business's future financial performance. ChatGPT can analyze historical data and market trends to aid decision-making, whether sales projections or expense forecasts.

Sample Prompt: "Create a budget forecast for the next fiscal year, taking into account historical revenue and expense data."

4. Financial Presentations and Reports

Creating engaging financial presentations can be time-consuming. ChatGPT can help draft slides, summaries, and visuals to support your financial presentations.

Sample Prompt: "Create a PowerPoint presentation summarizing our financial performance for the board meeting."

Other Sample Prompts for Finance

- "Forecast our cash flow for the next quarter based on our historical data."
- "Analyze the financial performance of our top three competitors over the past year."
- "Recommend investment options for diversifying our portfolio."
- "Explain the impact of inflation on our purchasing power."

- "Assess the financial risks associated with launching a new product."

Innovative Product Development

ChatGPT can be your guide when it comes to innovation. It can ideate on new product features, explore customer needs and preferences, and predict market trends to manage product development efforts. You can use ChatGPT to stay ahead of the innovation curve and create groundbreaking solutions that resonate with your customers. Here is how:

1. Prototyping and Design

ChatGPT can help in the initial stages of design and prototyping. Prompt it with questions like, "What should our product's user interface look like?" or, "Suggest design elements for our prototype."

2. Ideation and Brainstorming

Use prompts like, "Generate new product ideas for our target market," and watch as ChatGPT generates different concepts you can try. Your team can work on these unique ideas and refine them into actionable plans.

3. User Feedback Analysis

Feedback from users is a goldmine of information for product development. With prompts like, "Analyze customer feedback on our latest product release," ChatGPT can summarize and categorize user responses, allowing you to address your customer's concerns and improve their product experience.

4. Content Creation

ChatGPT can help create engaging content for product descriptions, marketing materials, and user guides. Use prompts like, "Write a compelling product description for our cosmetic product," ChatGPT will craft convincing narratives that captivate potential customers.

Other Sample Prompts for Product Development

- "What are the latest trends in wearable technology?"
- "Suggest innovative features for a smart home device."
- "Describe a user-friendly interface for a productivity app."
- "Describe an eco-friendly packaging solution for our new product line."
- "Compare our product's pricing strategy with our main competitor and identify potential adjustments."

Use ChatGPT as your Customer Support Champion

ChatGPT can be your aid in providing exceptional customer support. It can understand customer queries, respond accurately, handle routine inquiries, and free up your support team to focus on more important tasks. This means happier customers and a more efficient support team.

1. Personalized Responses

ChatGPT can help you build strong customer relationships by crafting personalized and heartfelt responses. This leads to higher customer retention rates.

Sample Prompt: "Draft a personalized response to a customer who had a positive experience with our product."

2. Automated FAQs

ChatGPT can generate FAQs about your product. This reduces the burden on the support team and allows your customers to find quick answers to common queries on their own.

Sample Prompt: "Create a list of FAQs and their answers for our website's support page."

3. Language Translation

ChatGPT helps you overcome language barriers with its multilingual support system. This allows you to communicate with customers from diverse backgrounds efficiently.

Sample Prompt: "Translate the customer's query from Italian to English."

4. Crisis Management Responses

In times of crisis, ChatGPT can quickly develop empathetic responses, assuring customers that their concerns are acknowledged.

Sample Prompt: "Provide a response template for customers affected by the recent service disruption."

Other Sample Prompts for Customer Support

- "Generate an apology email for a delayed order delivery."

- "Draft a response for a customer asking about our refund policy."
- "Provide a step-by-step guide for setting up our software on a new device."
- "Create a response template for handling customer complaints about damaged products."

HR and Recruitment

ChatGPT eases the burden on HR by automating the screening process for job applicants. It can review resumes, identify qualified candidates, and conduct preliminary interviews. This ensures a fair and unbiased selection process in your organization. ChatGPT can help streamline the process by crafting documents like employee handbooks or answering frequently asked questions for new hires.

1. Crafting Engaging Job Descriptions

ChatGPT can develop a well-written and compelling job description that attracts top talent by feeding it details about the role, required skills, and company culture.

Sample Prompt: "Help us create a captivating job description for a Senior Software Engineer position."

2. Screening and Shortlisting Candidates

ChatGPT can analyze resumes and match candidates based on specified criteria. This saves time in the initial screening process and ensures that only the most suitable candidates move forward.

Sample Prompt: "Review these resumes and shortlist candidates for the Sales Representative role."

3. Interview Question Preparation

HR teams can use ChatGPT to create a list of interview questions for specific job roles.

Sample Prompt: "Provide a set of behavioral interview questions to assess a candidate's problem-solving skills."

4. Employee Onboarding

ChatGPT can assist in creating onboarding materials for new hires, including welcome emails and orientation documents.

Sample Prompt: "Draft a comprehensive onboarding package for our new software engineer, covering key company policies and department overviews."

Other Sample Prompts for HR and Recruitment

- "Develop a set of questions to assess a candidate's adaptability and teamwork skill."
- "Help me create a job posting for a Customer Support Specialist focusing on empathetic communication and problem-solving skills."
- "Assist us in pre-screening applicants for a Graphic Designer role by asking about their design experience and preferred tools."
- "I need to conduct a second-round interview for a Marketing Manager. Generate a list of strategic marketing questions to evaluate their leadership skills."

- "Help us craft a rejection email that provides constructive feedback to candidates who did well."

Legal Insights

Legal teams can benefit from using ChatGPT to analyze and summarize legal documents. It can provide information, from contract reviews to researching case laws. As a lawyer or paralegal, here is how to use ChatGPT to your advantage:

Contract Review and Summarization

ChatGPT can help in analyzing lengthy contracts and legal documents. By providing a prompt like, "Please analyze and summarize the key terms of the contract between Company X and Company Y," ChatGPT can develop a summary highlighting important clauses and potential areas of concern.

Sample Prompt: "Please review this contract and concisely summarize the key terms and conditions."

Legal Research and Case Analysis

With ChatGPT's vast knowledge base, you can use it for your legal research. Prompting it with questions like, "Find recent case laws related to intellectual property disputes," can yield relevant results.

Sample Prompt: "Can you research recent case laws related to product liability in the healthcare industry?"

Regulatory Compliance Assistance

ChatGPT can keep the legal team updated on changing regulations and compliance requirements. A prompt such as: "Provide a summary of the recent changes in data protection laws," enables the team to address compliance issues.

Analyzing Legal Arguments

With ChatGPT, your team can gain a deeper understanding of legal arguments. It can help identify potential weaknesses, evaluate counterarguments, and support your team in building persuasive cases.

Sample Prompt: "Analyze the strengths and weaknesses of this legal argument in the pending litigation."

Other Sample Prompts for Legal Insights

- "Analyze and summarize the key provisions of the employment contract for John Doe, including termination clauses."
- "Research recent case laws related to copyright infringement in the digital content industry."
- "Provide a legal opinion on the potential liability of Company ABC in the recent product liability case."
- "Review the lease agreement for potential issues related to property maintenance responsibilities."
- "Identify any compliance requirements for conducting business operations in Country X."

Business Strategy

ChatGPT can be very useful when it comes to strategic planning. It can help you explore different scenarios, conduct SWOT analyses, and help in developing business plans. ChatGPT's knowledge base makes it an excellent resource for data-driven decision-making. Let's see how you can use this tool:

1. Ideation and Brainstorming

ChatGPT can serve as your collaborator in developing ideas to fuel your business strategy. It can provide new perspectives, explore different market opportunities, and suggest potential features or improvements for existing products.

Sample Prompt: "Come up with ideas for a new product or service that aligns with our company's vision and market trends."

2. SWOT Analysis

ChatGPT can identify your business's strengths, weaknesses, opportunities, and threats. It can provide information on market trends, customer preferences, and potential risks. This can help you develop an all-inclusive business strategy to increase your revenue.

Sample Prompt: "Conduct a SWOT analysis for an online fashion retail business."

3. Scenario Planning

ChatGPT can simulate different scenarios, considering factors like market dynamics, consumer behavior, and economic trends. You can make data-driven decisions with confidence by exploring potential outcomes.

Sample Prompt: "Explore various scenarios for entering a new market or launching a product."

4. Competitive Positioning

ChatGPT can help express your brand's unique selling points, stating key determiners that resonate with your target audience. It can craft compelling messaging that sets your business apart to ensure a strong position in the market.

Sample Prompt: "Develop a unique value proposition that differentiates our brand from competitors."

5. Crafting Business Proposals

ChatGPT can be your co-pilot when drafting business proposals.

Sample Prompt: "Generate a compelling business proposal for our new product launch, highlighting its unique selling points and potential market impact."

Other Sample Prompts for Business Strategy

- "Perform a detailed analysis of our target audience's preferences and buying behaviors."

- "Create a plan for entering the Asian market, considering cultural differences and local competition."
- "Provide information on potential partnerships or acquisitions to expand our market reach and competitive advantage."
- "Devise a contingency plan to navigate potential supply chain disruptions in times of crisis."
- "Evaluate the potential impact of emerging technologies on our business model and suggest adaptation strategies."

How Businesses are Incorporating ChatGPT to Improve Business Operations

In recent years, businesses have seen the potential of ChatGPT in improving and streamlining various systems to increase productivity and income. It is becoming a must-have tool—for everything from customer service to data analysis. Let's explore how businesses are incorporating ChatGPT to achieve their goals:

1. Customer Support and Engagement

ChatGPT helps in handling routine queries, providing personalized recommendations, and troubleshooting common problems while maintaining a human-like conversational experience. Businesses can build stronger customer loyalty and enhance customer satisfaction with ChatGPT on their side.

2. Data Analysis and Decision-Making

Businesses use ChatGPT to analyze customer sentiment, extract information from customer feedback, and analyze market trends. With ChatGPT's assistance, your business can increase operational efficiency and identify new opportunities by making data-driven decisions.

3. Content Generation and Marketing

ChatGPT is making big waves in content creation and marketing efforts. It can craft engaging blog posts, social media content, email newsletters, and ad copy. ChatGPT is helping businesses maintain a consistent online presence, attract more leads, and drive higher conversions.

4. Process Automation and Efficiency

Integrating ChatGPT with existing systems can help your business automate repetitive tasks and simplify internal processes. From scheduling meetings and managing appointments to handling administrative tasks, ChatGPT can reduce manual workload and allow employees to concentrate on other things.

5. Training and Onboarding

ChatGPT can also be used in employee training and onboarding processes. It can mimic real-world scenarios and interactive learning experiences. This helps your recruit get used to their roles faster.

6. Innovation and Ideation

Businesses are tapping into ChatGPT's creative potential to drive innovation and creativity. With ChatGPT as a brainstorming partner, you can come up with new product concepts and solve complex problems while stimulating creativity and collaboration.

Callback to the Importance of Fact-Checking and Revising

As we wrap up this chapter, we must address an aspect: the importance of fact-checking and revising ChatGPT's responses. ChatGPT is undoubtedly mind-blowing; you may have tried the above prompts and are surprised at its great responses. But here is a little reminder: ChatGPT is not an all-knowing oracle.

As we discussed earlier, exercising caution and human judgment in interpreting its output is important. ChatGPT is trained on large amounts of data; hence, it can produce errors or provide inaccurate information. Therefore, fact-checking and verifying its responses is very important, especially when dealing with legal matters where precision and accuracy are undebatable.

When drafting legal documents or making important business decisions, you should never solely rely on ChatGPT's output. It's always wise to consult legal experts and subject matter specialists to validate the information generated by ChatGPT.

Similarly, in any context, fact-checking ChatGPT's responses enhances the quality of the content and ensures it aligns with your company's values and objectives. Human input and creativity play a key role in refining ChatGPT's suggestions and tailoring them to the unique needs of your business.

You need to always remember that ChatGPT, regardless of how amazing it is, is a tool meant to complement human abilities and not to replace them. It can boost your productivity and inspire creativity, but your expertise is key in evaluating, refining, and applying ChatGPT's ideas. Use ChatGPT as a collaborative partner, working hand in hand with your team to achieve the best possible outcomes.

Key Takeaway

In this chapter, we explored the practical and effective ways ChatGPT can increase productivity and income in your business. We delved into real-life examples and scenarios where you can use ChatGPT as an asset, assisting in market research, strategic planning, competitive intelligence, and more. Integrating ChatGPT into business workflows can ease processes, improve efficiency, and ultimately lead to better business performance.

What Next?

As we continue our journey exploring the power of ChatGPT, our next chapter takes us into personal development. Beyond its business and workplace applications, ChatGPT can play a life-changing role in your growth and self-improvement. In this upcoming chapter, we will look at how ChatGPT can support personal development goals, whether improving communication skills, setting and achieving personal milestones, managing stress, or simply finding inspiration and motivation.

7. ChatGPT in Personal Development

I was speaking to my very close friend about ChatGPT. My initial thought was to spread the good news of how it has been helping me in my career; I didn't know he had also started using the tool. I will share his experience to show you that ChatGPT is beyond the four walls of your office. Its benefits can extend to your personal life.

Isaac is a very curious person. He is always looking for ways to level up his life. But he faced the usual challenges of juggling work, personal goals, and a never-ending to-do list. Little did he know that a change was about to enter his life—ChatGPT!

He was skeptical at first but decided to give it a try. As a digital marketer at heart, he often faces writer's block. But with ChatGPT by his side, he found a wellspring of inspiration. It never failed to impress and became his companion, always ready to work with him.

ChatGPT made interactions look like a conversation with a supportive friend. He would use this tool during late-night study sessions, buzz sessions for work projects, and moments of creative thinking.

But that's not all! ChatGPT has been an excellent life coach to him. He has used it in learning new habits and routines. With its motivational pep talks, he was able to form healthier habits.

From his life, I could say that ChatGPT has gone beyond just a tool; it's a companion, mentor, and confidant. The best part? ChatGPT has helped him develop lifelong learning for him to evolve and grow continually.

In this chapter, we will look into the possibilities of self-development with ChatGPT. You will learn about the advantages of using this tool in your life for personal and professional growth.

Practical Ways ChatGPT Can Improve Your Personal and Professional Life

Let's look at the ways ChatGPT can supercharge your daily routines and maximize your potential:

Personal Productivity Partner

ChatGPT is like having a digital assistant at your fingertips. It can help you stay organized by creating to-do lists and managing your schedule. It can also help in goal setting and tracking your progress, keeping you motivated and on top of your game. ChatGPT can provide suggestions, helping you make better decisions on your project, schedule, and others. Here's how it works:

1. Overcoming Procrastination

Scenario: Procrastination is a constant roadblock in your pursuits, and you need strategies to overcome this productivity killer.

Sample Prompt: "How can I beat procrastination and stay motivated to work on my hobby regularly? I need effective techniques to stay on track."

2. Balancing Screen Time

Scenario: You find yourself spending excessive time on social media and digital distractions. This can hinder your growth and prevent you from exploring new ideas.

Sample Prompt: "Help me reduce my screen time and create a healthier balance between online activities and pursuing my new hobby."

3. Time Management

Scenario: You need personalized time management tips and strategies to stay on track throughout the day.

Sample Prompt: "ChatGPT, how can I better manage my time to be more productive at work?"

Skill Development Support

Looking to learn a new skill or study a topic of interest? ChatGPT is your go-to knowledge companion. It can curate personalized learning resources, recommend online courses, and explain complex concepts. Just fire away with your questions; it will serve relevant information and resources like a seasoned expert.

1. Advancing Professional Skills

Scenario: Like my friend Isaac, you are career-driven, aiming to improve your professional skills. You want to take online courses, but with so many options, you are confused about which ones will benefit your career most.

Sample Prompt: "I'm looking to boost my professional skills through online courses. Can you suggest some courses that align with a marketing and project management career?"

2. Mastering a Specific Skill

Scenario: You've been eyeing that interesting skill, be it playing the guitar, learning to code, or cooking like a chef. It's time to unlock it with ChatGPT by your side.

Sample Prompt: "I've always wanted to learn how to play the guitar. Can you suggest a step-by-step learning plan and some helpful online tutorials?"

3. Personalized Learning Path

Scenario: You want to go into a particular field, but you're looking for a customized learning path. ChatGPT's got your back.

Sample Prompt: "I'm interested In psychology. Can you help with a list of books, podcasts, and courses to help me explore this field?"

Creative Muse

Have a creative block? ChatGPT can help you with imaginative ideas and writing prompts. ChatGPT can be your creative muse, whether you're an artist, writer, or someone who just loves exploring their creative side. It can provide you with ideas and help you overcome creative blocks.

1. The Writer's Block Dilemma

Scenario: You're a passionate writer, but lately, the writer's block has left you feeling uninspired. Your mind draws blanks, and you struggle to start that next chapter or write a captivating story.

Sample Prompt: "Help me brainstorm an interesting plot twist for my historical romance novel."

2. The Artist's Creative Stagnation

Scenario: You long to create captivating art pieces as an artist, but lately, you've hit a wall of stagnation. Your inspiration seems blank, and you're yearning to explore new artistic techniques.

Sample Prompt: "I'm looking to experiment with new art styles. Can you guide me through some contemporary art movements for inspiration?"

3. Exploring Creative Hobbies

Scenario: You want to explore new creative hobbies but don't know where to start.

Sample Prompt: "Recommend a beginner-friendly craft or DIY project to enhance my home decor."

Mental Health Buddy

Taking care of your mental well-being is important, and ChatGPT can lend a helping hand. With ChatGPT, you can engage in reflective conversations, practice mindfulness exercises, or receive supportive messages to maintain a positive outlook on life.

1. Managing Stress and Improving Sleep

Scenario: Stress and lack of sleep affect your overall well-being. You need strategies to manage stress and improve your sleep quality for a healthier lifestyle.

Sample Prompt: "I've been feeling stressed lately, and it's affecting my sleep. Can you recommend some relaxation techniques and bedtime routines to help me manage stress and sleep better?"

2. Boosting Self-Esteem

Scenario: You're struggling with low self-esteem and self-doubt, impacting your confidence and self-worth.

Sample Prompt: "I could use a confidence boost. Can you provide positive affirmations or self-love exercises to help me improve my self-esteem?"

3. Managing Emotions

Scenario: You find it challenging to handle intense emotions like anger, sadness, or frustration in a healthy way.

Sample Prompt: "I need some advice on managing my emotions better. How can I practice emotional regulation techniques to respond more calmly to situations?"

Language and Communication Improvement

Want to level up your communication game? ChatGPT can be your language tutor. It can help in improving your writing skills, grammar, and vocabulary. Practice conversing in different languages or fine-tune your public speaking abilities with ChatGPT.

1. Public Speaking Nerves

Scenario: Public speaking fills you with anxiety, and you want to feel more confident during presentations.

Sample Prompt: "I have a big presentation coming up, and I'm nervous about speaking in front of a crowd. Can you advise me on overcoming nervousness and delivering a compelling speech?"

2. Learning a New Language

Scenario: You've always wanted to learn a new language but don't know where to start or how to practice conversational skills.

Sample Prompt: "I want to learn Spanish, but I don't have anyone to practice with. Can you help me with my pronunciation and some basic conversational phrases?"

3. Improving Grammar and Vocabulary

Scenario: Your grammar and vocabulary could sound more polished and professional.

Sample Prompt: "I want to enhance my writing style by improving my grammar and vocabulary. Can you give me tips on how to expand my word choices and avoid common grammatical errors?"

4. Effective Communication in Conflict Resolution

Scenario: Communicating during conflicts can be challenging. ChatGPT can guide you on active listening and how to develop effective communication skills to resolve conflicts amicably.

Sample Prompt: "I had an argument with a friend. How can I approach them to discuss the issue and mend our relationship?"

Job Search and Career Advancement

Are you seeking career growth? ChatGPT can guide you through resume writing and interview preparation and provide industry-specific advice. It can help you identify potential career paths and suggest opportunities aligned with your skills and aspirations.

1. Tailored Resumes and Cover Letter

Scenario: You're struggling to create a resume that catches the eye of potential employers.

Sample Prompt: "I need assistance crafting a compelling resume and cover letter. Can you give me some tips on how to show-case my experience and skills better?"

2. Interview Preparation

Scenario: Nerves get the best of you during interviews, and you want to confidently ace your next one.

Sample Prompt: "I have an important job interview coming up. Can you help me practice common interview questions and provide feedback on my answers?"

3. Negotiating Job Offers

Scenario: You've received a job offer but are unsure about nego-tiating for better terms.

Sample Prompt: "I have a job offer on the table. Can you help me strategize my negotiation approach to secure a better compen-sation package?"

Financial Planning Advisor

Get your finances on track with ChatGPT's financial planning knowledge. It can help you create budgets, set financial goals, and provide investment tips to secure your future.

1. Investment and Retirement Planning

Scenario: You want to secure your financial future and grow wealth through investments, but you're uncertain where to start and which investment options suit your risk appetite and goals.

Sample Prompt: "I want to start investing to secure my future, but I'm a bit overwhelmed by all the options. Can you help me understand the basics of investing and suggest suitable investment strategies to help secure my future?"

2. Managing Debt and Improving Credit Score

Scenario: Debt can be tiring, and you're looking for ways to manage it and improve your credit score for better financial health.

Sample Prompt: "I have some credit card debt and worry about my credit score. How can I plan to pay off my debts faster and boost my credit score? Are there any debt consolidation options I should consider?"

3. Budgeting and Saving

Scenario: You want to create a budget that allows you to save more effectively but don't know where to start.

Sample Prompt: "I want to create a budget to save more money each month. Can you help me understand how to allocate my income wisely and identify areas where I can cut expenses? Any tips on how to stay disciplined and meet my saving goals?"

4. Financial Goal Setting

Scenario: You have various financial goals but need assistance setting clear and achievable targets.

Sample Prompt: "I have multiple financial goals, like buying a home, starting a business, and saving for my child's education. How can I prioritize these goals and create a realistic roadmap?"

Health and Fitness

Health is Wealth. ChatGPT can help you craft personalized fitness routines, offer healthy recipes, and provide wellness advice to live a balanced lifestyle. Simply share your fitness goals, lifestyle, and preferences, and ChatGPT can provide tailored workout routines, nutrition tips, and motivational messages to keep you on the go.

1. Finding the Right Fitness Regimen

Scenario: You're eager to begin a health and fitness routine, but you feel overwhelmed with so many routines. ChatGPT to the rescue.

Sample Prompt: "I want to start a fitness routine but don't know where to begin. Can you recommend some beginner-friendly exercises?"

2. Staying Motivated

Scenario: You've been working hard on your fitness journey, but lately, you've been struggling to stay motivated.

Sample Prompt: "I feel like I'm losing interest in my fitness routine. How can I add variety to keep it engaging and exciting?"

3. Navigating Nutrition and Healthy Eating

Scenario: You understand the importance of nutrition in your health journey, but you're confused about making healthy choices.

Sample Prompt: "I often find myself snacking on unhealthy foods. What are some healthier alternatives that can satisfy my cravings?"

4. Overcoming Time and Resource Constraints

Scenario: You're determined to prioritize your health and fitness, but your busy schedule and limited resources are holding you back.

Sample Prompt: "I have a tight schedule with work and family commitments. How can I add short, effective workouts into my day?" or, "I can't afford a gym membership. What are some budget-friendly fitness options that I can do at home or in my neighborhood?"

Virtual Travel Companion

Can't hop on a plane right now? ChatGPT can whisk you away on virtual adventures. ChatGPT can provide you with vivid descriptions and interesting trivia to quench your adventure thirst.

1. Wanderlust While Staying Home

Scenario: You're longing to travel, but current circumstances restrict your ability to do so. You yearn to experience new cultures, marvel at historical sites, and explore breathtaking landscapes.

Sample Prompt: "Take me on a virtual adventure. Describe the beautiful beaches of Bali and share some interesting facts about Balinese culture."

2. Finding the Perfect Virtual Tour

Scenario: You want to embark on a virtual tour that caters to your specific interests, with different options online.

Sample Prompt: "I'm passionate about ancient history and architecture. Can you recommend a virtual tour that takes me through the historical wonders of Rome and its iconic landmarks?"

3. Getting Lost in Cultural Immersion

Scenario: You crave the joy of exploring the culture and traditions of a distant land, but you are far away.

Sample Prompt: "Immerse me in the rich culture of Japan. Tell me about traditional tea ceremonies, origami art, and the beauty of cherry blossom festivals."

4. A Taste of Global Cuisine

Scenario: You miss the thrill of trying exotic dishes from around the world, but you're stuck at home with limited dining options.

Sample Prompt: "I want to tantalize my taste buds with a virtual food adventure. Describe the flavors and aromas of authentic Thai street food, and recommend a delicious recipe I can try at home."

Trying New Hobbies

Scenario: You've decided to go into photography but are not sure which camera suits your needs, what photography style to pursue, or how to get started. This leaves you feeling stuck and unable to take the first step.

Sample Prompt: "I'm excited to start a new hobby in photography. Can you help me find the right camera and suggest a photography style that aligns with my interests [state your interest]?"

Scenario: You've been stuck in your daily routine, craving something exciting and meaningful to engage your mind and soul.

Sample Prompt: "I'm looking to start a new hobby that can add some excitement and fulfillment to my life. I enjoy being outdoors and love exploring creative activities. Can you suggest some hobbies that might suit my interests? I'd love to hear your ideas and get started on this new adventure."

Scenario: You find some extra free time on weekends and want to explore a new hobby that brings joy and satisfaction.

Sample Prompt: "I'm looking to start a new hobby I can enjoy on weekends. I'd love something creative and relaxing, but I don't know what suits me best. Can you suggest some hobbies that might be a good fit for me?"

Take Caution!

After trying these prompts, you must have seen testimony to the powers of ChatGPT. However, there is a need for fact-checking and consulting with professionals, especially concerning overall health.

When it comes to personal health and medical concerns, relying solely on ChatGPT is not advised. ChatGPT is an AI language model, but it is not a substitute for personalized medical advice from qualified healthcare professionals. Health issues vary from person to person. What works for you may not be suitable for another. Healthcare professionals consider your medical history, lifestyle, and individual needs to provide treatment.

If you have health-related concerns while using ChatGPT, consider the following guidelines:

- **Fact-Checking:** Always fact-check the information you receive from ChatGPT by referring to credible sources or consulting reputable websites, journals, or articles. This way, you can verify the accuracy of the information you receive.

- **Seek Professional Guidance:** Consult a qualified healthcare professional or physician if you have health concerns or need medical advice. A doctor, nurse, or other medical expert can provide advice based on your health history and needs. Do not rely solely on ChatGPT advice for decision-making.

- **Be Cautious with Self-Diagnosis:** Avoid using ChatGPT or any other online resource to self-diagnose medical conditions. Self-diagnosis can lead to misunderstandings and unnecessary anxiety. Instead, consult a healthcare expert for an accurate diagnosis.

- **Privacy and Security:** Be cautious about sharing sensitive personal health information with ChatGPT or any AI tool. Protect your privacy and only discuss health concerns with your healthcare provider.

Remember, your health is of utmost importance, and seeking guidance from qualified professionals ensures you receive the best care and advice. ChatGPT can be useful in various aspects of life, but exercise caution and put your well-being first when dealing with health issues.

Key Takeaway

In this chapter, we looked at the practical ways ChatGPT can significantly improve one's personal life. ChatGPT can be your digital friend in navigating various aspects of your life, from boosting productivity and finding fulfilling hobbies to providing emotional support. However, there is a need to exercise caution, fact-check information, and consult professionals, especially when dealing with health issues. ChatGPT should never replace expert advice and guidance from qualified professionals.

What Next?

Having experienced the potential of ChatGPT to change our personal lives for the better, it's time to go on to the next exciting chapter, which will explain even more ways that ChatGPT can affect our lives positively beyond the confines of a regular workday. You will see its impact in helping you earn passive income, enriching your leisure time, and positively impacting society. Let's seize this opportunity and shape a fulfilling and purpose-driven life with ChatGPT.

8. ChatGPT Beyond the 9 to 5

You might ask yourself, "What else can ChatGPT do outside the workspace?" I am here to tell you that ChatGPT can do more than you can imagine. The power of ChatGPT goes beyond the regular 9–5 jobs you have. Its use cuts across all spheres of life.

A brand designer and writer shared on Twitter how he used ChatGPT to turn $100 into a business, making as much money as possible with just prompts. Sounds like a pipe dream, right? How did ChatGPT become the beast turning $100 into a thriving business venture?

Jackson Greathouse Fall, a brand designer and writer, challenged ChatGPT with a task. He typed, "You have $100, and your goal is to turn that into as much money as possible in the shortest time possible without doing anything illegal. I'll be your 'human counterpart' and follow every instruction."

The chatbot, in seconds, replied with a dazzling idea. "Launch a business called Green Gadget Guru, offering products and tips to help people live a more sustainable lifestyle." ChatGPT gave him four steps to follow. In the first step, ChatGPT asked him to buy a domain and hosting for $15. Step two was to buy a niche affiliate site focused on eco-friendly products. That left $62.84 from the $100 budget. Step three was to create social media content and captivating articles; the last step was to optimize for search engines. In the end, he was able to secure $500 in investment.

In one day, Green Gadget Guru raised $1,378.84 in funds, and the business is now valued at $25,000. He explored the idea of manufacturing new products and ventured into selling existing ones for commissions. With ChatGPT, Jackson sees through the challenges of entrepreneurship with confidence.

That's just the tip of what ChatGPT can do. In this last chapter, we will look into ChatGPT and how it can be a partner when it comes to creating passive income. You will learn the advantages of using ChatGPT to set yourself up for success and unlock the doors to financial freedom.

Maybe you are looking to start a side hustle or create a full-blown passive income stream; ChatGPT can guide you through the process. Provide ChatGPT with a brief description of your interests, skills, or the industry you're interested in, and boom! You will get a list of potential ideas to explore.

Now, let's talk planning. Once you have your ideas, ChatGPT can help you organize your thoughts. You can engage in interactive conversations to map out the steps in setting up your passive income venture. ChatGPT can provide you with tips and help you identify potential pitfalls to avoid in your new business idea (whether creating an online course, launching a dropshipping store, or starting a blog).

Once it's time to execute those brilliant ideas, ChatGPT can serve as your virtual business partner, guiding you through the setup process. It can assist with website creation and content writing and also help you come up with social media posts to promote your business.

Earning money while you're sleeping, lounging on the beach, or binging your favorite shows sounds like a dream come true, right? But hold on, let's face the reality here—setting up passive income isn't all smooth sailing. It's a journey full of challenges and hurdles you must conquer. Let's look at these challenges to keep you ahead in the game.

- **Knowledge and Expertise:** Unless you have a magic genie to do all the work for you, you'll need the right knowledge and expertise to start a successful passive income stream. Continuous learning is key to whatever you venture into. It may be understanding the stock market, mastering affiliate marketing, or knowing the ins and outs of rental property management; learning never stops.
- **Consistency and Dedication:** Building passive income requires consistency and dedication. You can't set it and forget it—you need to keep nurturing and growing your income streams. This might require updating your

website, staying up to date with market trends, or creating content for your business.

- **Time and Effort:** Despite the term "passive," don't be fooled—starting a passive income stream takes time and effort. It's a labor-intensive process, especially in the beginning. You need to research, plan, create content, and market, which can be a lot. Balancing this side hustle with your regular job and other commitments can also be draining. Take your time and put in the effort.

- **Patience:** Patience is a virtue, and it's certainly true when it comes to passive income. Building a passive income stream doesn't happen overnight. It can take months, if not years, for your efforts to bear fruit. Impatience can lead to frustration; you could abandon the venture prematurely. Be patient.

- **Funding Frenzy:** Money is the lifeblood of any startup. Securing enough funding to kickstart your dream can be a battle. Investors might be skeptical, and banks might be hesitant. And let's be real: not everyone has piles of cash to kickstart their passive income dream. But don't worry; perseverance pays off, and other funding options like crowdfunding and angel investors can come to the rescue.

- **Competitive Circus:** You're not alone under the big top in the startup circus. Breaking through the noise and standing out in a crowded market requires a lot. You can do this by setting your product or service apart, understanding your target audience, and delivering value like no other.

Don't let these challenges scare you away. Every successful entrepreneur faces hurdles on their way to financial freedom. It's all about learning, adapting, and staying persistent. With the right mindset, you can turn these challenges into stepping stones to achieve your goals.

How ChatGPT Can Help You Earn Passive Income

Here we are, the money part of this book.

Build an App, Website, or Service

With ChatGPT, you can build your own tech product without writing a single line of code. Yes, you heard that right—no coding required.

Ihor Stefurak from Ukraine used ChatGPT to build a Chrome extension. He had zero programming knowledge. But within 24 hours of launching his extension, he raked in $1000. That's some cool cash rolling in.

Let's talk about code generation. ChatGPT can help you make a sleek, eye-catching HTML page, integrate Stripe for seamless checkout, and handle any hiccups along the way. You only need to ask ChatGPT to debug the code, and it'll do it in a snap.

However, you will need to subscribe to ChatGPT Plus for access to premium services. While you don't need to be a seasoned programmer, a basic understanding of coding will help you grasp what's going on under the hood.

Here are sample prompts to try:

- "Help me create an awesome HTML landing page for my new startup."
- "I want to integrate Stripe for payments. Can you guide me through the process?"
- "Having a little trouble with my code here, ChatGPT. Can you find the bug and fix it for me?"

Get Business Ideas from ChatGPT

Do you want to start your side hustle business and earn passive income? Let's look at some prompts to generate business ideas.

Type this prompt into ChatGPT: "I want to start a side hustle. I'm a huge fan of animals and love spending time outdoors. Can you help me with pet-related business ideas that align with my passions?"

Or how about this: "I have a knack for crafting DIY projects. I want to channel my creativity into a side hustle I can do from home. Any brilliant ideas to get me started?"

And here's another one: "I'm a tech-savvy person, and I'm keen on using your expertise. Can you help me explore online business ideas involving innovative technology?"

Looking to indulge your taste buds in a side hustle? Try this: "I'm a foodie at heart, and I dream of turning my passion for cooking into a profitable venture. Any delicious food-related business ideas that you can cook up for me?"

For wellness and fitness enthusiasts, try this prompt: "I'm all about leading a healthy lifestyle and motivating others to do the same. Can you help me with some wellness-focused side hustle ideas that positively impact people's lives?"

And for travelers out there, this one's for you: "Wanderlust has taken over my soul, and I want to turn my love for travel into a lucrative side hustle. Any exciting travel-related business ideas to fuel my adventurous spirit?"

Go ahead and give it a try.

Email Affiliate Marketing

Email affiliate marketing is another means for you to earn passive income. With ChatGPT, you can write emails that entice users to click on affiliate links and make purchases or sign up for services.

Getting started is a breeze. First, pick an affiliate program that suits your interests and target audience. Whether it's Amazon, Shopify, ConvertKit, or any other program, there's something out there for you.

Next, build an email list focused on your marketing campaign. Use lead magnets and email signups to gather a pool of interested subscribers. The more targeted your list, the better your chances of success.

Now comes the exciting part. Fire up ChatGPT and put it to work.

Here are some sample prompts you can use to help solve any doubts or questions you have along the way:

- "Can you help me find the best affiliate program for my niche [provide your niche]?"
- "I need some ideas for lead magnets to build my email list. Any suggestions?"
- "How do I make my email campaigns more engaging and persuasive?"
- "How often should I email my subscribers to keep them engaged?"
- "I'm seeing some clicks but not many conversions. Any tips to improve my conversion rates?"

Create Videos with ChatGPT

ChatGPT can be your buddy in helping you craft video ideas in any specific category you desire. Maybe gaming, travel, DIY, or even something as niche as underwater basket weaving, ChatGPT has got you.

Once you have your video idea, ask ChatGPT to create a script for a YouTube video specific to your style and personality.

Head to Pictory.ai or invideo.io to breathe life into your script. With your video ready to roll, hit that publish button on YouTube. Sit back, relax, and let the money roll in as your content attracts viewers and ad revenue.

And here's a bonus tip: Consider making reaction videos, especially in Shorts format (clips under 60 seconds). People love to watch genuine reactions, and with ChatGPT, you can add your unique spin to the mix and rake in those views.

Sample Prompts:

- "I'm passionate about fitness. Can you suggest some unique video ideas for my fitness channel?"
- "I want to start a cooking channel. What are some trending recipe ideas I can create videos on?"
- "I'm a tech enthusiast. What are some tech-related video ideas that will appeal to my audience?"
- "I want to create entertaining skits for my comedy channel. Can you give me some hilarious sketch ideas?"
- "I'm interested in history and documentaries. Can you suggest video ideas that will educate and engage my viewers?"

E-book Publishing

Writing and coming up with new ideas has never been easier, thanks to ChatGPT. People are now going into topics from niche and relevant subjects to motivational lectures, all the way to epic sci-fi novels that will take you to the stars and beyond.

With ChatGPT's creativity, you can start with a simple outline and then watch as each paragraph flows.

Before you decide to publish a book entirely using only ChatGPT or any other artificial intelligence, take note: AI-generate content cannot be copyrighted based on a ruling from a federal judge. However, you are allowed to copyright protect any part that is human generated. Be sure to disclose any AI-generated content if you are publishing on platforms such as Amazon following the guidelines for both text and images.

Here is a little bonus for you. If you want to take your e-book game to the next level, check out Book Bolt. It's the fairy godmother for authors. It allows you to create, publish, and market your e-books like a pro on Amazon. That's what I call a winning combo.

Let's get into action and see how ChatGPT can help you on your way to e-book stardom. Try these prompts:

- "I'm eager to write a children's e-book that sparks imagination and wonder. Any ideas for an enchanting adventure in a mystical forest?"
- "I want to pen down a motivational e-book that will inspire people to chase their dreams fearlessly. Can you help me kickstart the first chapter with an electrifying pep talk?"
- "I'm a sci-fi fanatic dreaming of creating an intergalactic saga. How about we craft an epic space battle scene that leaves readers at the edge of their seats?"

Become a Data Analyst

ChatGPT can be your data-analyzing wizard and help you earn some cash. You can upload various file types like XLS, CSV, XML, JSON, and SQLite.

Let's say you have a massive dataset lying around that you want to analyze; just upload that file to ChatGPT and use the ChatGPT Code Interpreter.

Here are some sample prompts you can try:

- "I've got this CSV file with sales data from the last quarter. Can you help me visualize the top-selling products?"
- "I'm struggling to understand the correlation between marketing expenses and revenue in this XLS file. Show me a line chart to analyze the trends!"
- "I've got this JSON file with customer feedback. Can you create a pie chart representing the positive, negative, and neutral sentiments?"
- "I need to analyze the inventory levels from this SQLite database. Show me a bar chart to highlight the most stocked items."
- "I'm dealing with some XML data containing weather statistics. Help me out with a scatter plot to understand temperature patterns."

With these prompts, ChatGPT will come up with graphs, charts, and diagrams to help you understand your data's trends. You don't need to be a data whiz; ChatGPT can guide you through it all.

If you are wondering how to use Code Interpreter, OpenAI has a guide to help you. Once you are all set up, you will be walking through the data universe like a pro.

Freelance and Create Content

Want to make money as a freelance content writer? You can use ChatGPT as your translation partner to break down language barriers and provide sound translations for your clients across the globe.

ChatGPT can also be your digital marketing dynamo in writing marketing materials and persuasive copy that keeps your clients and customers glued to you. Say goodbye to typos and hello to great content with ChatGPT by your side as a proofreading prodigy. You can become a guardian of grammar and style by using ChatGPT to polish your written works.

You can use ChatGPT to decode complex technical jargon into easily digestible content. Clients will love your ability to explain difficult concepts with simplicity.

If you are wondering how to get started, here are some sample prompts to guide you on your content writing journey:

- "I need help writing a compelling blog post about the latest trends in fashion. Can you give me some creative ideas and key points to include?"
- "I'm working on a website for a travel agency, and I need some captivating content for their destination pages. Can you assist me in describing exotic locations in a way that sparks Wanderlust in readers?"
- "I want to start offering translation services. Can you help me translate a short paragraph from English to Spanish, ensuring accuracy and cultural nuance?"

- "My e-commerce store needs attention-grabbing product descriptions. Can you come up with some witty and persuasive copy for my latest line of sustainable fashion products?"
- "I have a technical whitepaper that needs some polishing. Can you help me refine the language and make it more understandable for a non-technical audience?"

Importance of Fact-Checking

As we explore the wonders of this tool, we must remember that ChatGPT's responses are generated based on patterns in the data it has been trained on. Although it's constantly learning and evolving, it can still make mistakes or provide inaccurate information. Hence, it's important not to blindly rely on it as your sole source of information.

See ChatGPT as your guide, not the ultimate oracle. It can provide creative ideas and solutions but is not a replacement for human intelligence, expertise, and critical thinking. ChatGPT is a knowledgeable friend who may occasionally get things wrong.

When using ChatGPT, always cross-reference its responses with reliable sources. Fact-check the information it provides to ensure accuracy. Seek advice from human experts in the field and consult trustworthy sources, books, and articles.

Treat ChatGPT as a source of inspiration or a starting point for your ideas. Let it ignite your curiosity and imagination, but don't let it be the sole determinant of your decisions or actions.

Always remember that the beauty of human intelligence lies in its ability to analyze, reason, and use information from various sources. You can make decisions and interpret the world in ways that AI can't replicate. Therefore, use ChatGPT wisely, trust your instincts, and seek knowledge from different perspectives to broaden your horizons.

Key Takeaway

In this exciting journey through ChatGPT, we have learned that it is a powerful tool that can help you in various ways. We have tried creative, social media management, code optimization, travel planning, and more prompts to help you have a better grasp of how ChatGPT works. We also emphasized the importance of fact-checking its responses and not relying on it alone for critical information. Understanding its limitations and treating it as a source of inspiration and a starting point should be your guiding principle.

Look at ways you can use it to enhance your personal and professional life, whether as a creative writer, social media manager, programmer, curious learner, or virtual assistant. You have the knowledge and power to engineer prompts tailored to your unique needs and goals. Let ChatGPT be your partner in exploring new ideas and reaching heights you never thought possible. Now, you have evolved from being a curious novice to a confident user who understands how to use AI to their advantage.

As we wrap up this chapter, remember to use the U.S.E. Method (Understand, Source, Evaluate) as your guiding light. Use ChatGPT's responses wisely and responsibly to ensure accuracy and credibility. With ChatGPT on your side, the possibilities for achieving your goals are endless. It is the future; embrace it with optimism, caution, and enthusiasm.

You Are Irreplaceable

"I want word of mouth to be our biggest voice."

— Jasmine Guy

AI is a wonderful tool, but it can't be used for everything – and I'm glad for that. As much as it's transformed my business, I would never want it to replace the work I love to do, and it will never be a substitute for a real person's voice.

When I was thinking about how I could get what I've learned about using AI in business to a wider audience, my first thought was, "Could AI help me here?" And the answer is no.

The way people find the information they're looking for is by reading reviews of different books on the market, and ChatGPT, thankfully, won't write a book review for me. Why am I thankful? Because I would feel like I was cheating. I want to know that my book has helped real-life people, and I want new readers to be able to trust the reviews they've read. When I asked ChatGPT (out of interest more than anything else) if it could write a review for this book, it told me that it would need to know more about how it was received by audiences… so there's no getting around it: In order for this information to help more people, I'm going to need your assistance.

By leaving a review of this book on Amazon, you'll let other

people who are looking to harness the power of AI know exactly where they can find the guidance they're looking for.

With just a few minutes of your time, you can help this book reach the hands of the people who are looking for it – and they'll know they can trust it because it's come from a real-life reader. AI is an incredible asset, but it will never replace human intelligence. The trick is for us to use it as a tool to enhance what we can do on our own.

Thank you for your support. I'm so happy to have you onboard.

Conclusion

It's been a long ride through the eight chapters of prompt engineering with ChatGPT. We have immersed ourselves in the potential of ChatGPT and what it can do. The key takeaway from this book is crystal clear: ChatGPT can be your ultimate partner if you use it responsibly and wisely.

Throughout this book, we have looked at how ChatGPT can boost your creativity, income, and productivity in both your career and your life. You have learned about prompt engineering and how to create personalized interactions with ChatGPT to optimize its benefits for your specific needs.

And let's not forget the potential for passive income. With ChatGPT, you can set yourself up for financial freedom to create opportunities beyond the traditional 9 to 5 grind.

However, ChatGPT, in all its power, is not a replacement for human intelligence. Instead, it's your loyal assistant to help you achieve more without losing your personal touch. It won't take over your job or business but will push you toward new heights.

With the knowledge gathered from this book, you are better equipped to seize ideas, outshine competitors, and stay ahead in your game.

As we conclude, remember that change is inevitable, and those who embrace it survive and thrive in this fast-paced world. Know that the sky is the limit with ChatGPT as your companion.

I encourage you to implement what you have learned. Embrace ChatGPT, engineer prompts, and use it to transform your career. Your success story awaits; we can't wait to hear about it. And don't forget to share your stories with others, inspiring them to embark on their journey with AI.

Your feedback and reviews are so important. Please take a moment to share your thoughts on this book to encourage others.

With ChatGPT and prompt engineering, you have the tools to thrive and flourish in this digital world. Go out there, grab the opportunities, and make your mark with the power of AI by your side. The future awaits, and you are ready to conquer it.

Reference

10 Jobs AI Might Soon Replace (And Those It Won't). (n.d.). https://sensoriumarc.com/articles/jobs-ai-might-replace-and-those-it-wont

Abelis, V., & Abelis, V. (2023). 10 Productive Ways to Use Chatgpt at Work (Your Boss Won't Mind) | DeskTime Blog. DeskTime Insights. https://desktime.com/blog/how-to-use-chatgpt-at-work

ACL Anthology - ACL Anthology. (n.d.). https://aclanthology.org/

AcroYogi. (2023, April 19). AI Training Datasets: The Books1+Books2 That Big AI Eats for Breakfast - Musings of Freedom. Gregoreite: Harbinger of the AI Tsunami. https://gregoreite.com/drilling-down-details-on-the-ai-training-datasets/

Admin. (2023, April 22). How Does ChatGPT Handle Ambiguous or Vague Queries from Users? ChatGPT Online. https://chatgptonline.us/how-does-chatgpt-handle-ambiguous-or-vague-queries-from-users/

Alston, E. (2023). ChatGPT vs. GPT-3 and GPT-4: What's the Difference? zapier.com. https://zapier.com/blog/chatgpt-vs-gpt/

AnimusHerb. (n.d.). I Just Spend the Entire Day Using ChatGPT to Solve Business Problems. I Can't Believe How Helpful It Is: r/aiconvolibrary. https://www.reddit.com/r/aiconvolibrary/comments/10lq8ap/comment/j70c2wh/?utm_source=share&utm_medium=web2x&context=3&rdt=55926

AppMySite. (2023). ChatGPT and App Development: Here's All You Need to Know. AppMySite. https://www.appmysite.com/blog/all-you-need-to-know-about-chatgpt-and-app-development/

Artificial intelligence (AI) | Definition, Examples, Types, Applications, Companies, & Facts. (2023, September 5). Encyclopedia Britannica. https://www.britannica.com/technology/artificial-intelligence/Alan-Turing-and-the-beginning-of-AI

ArXiv.Org e-Print archive. (n.d.). https://arxiv.org/

Association for Healthcare Philanthropy. (n.d.). How to Use ChatGPT to Boost Productivity and Improve Performance. www.linkedin.com. https://www.linkedin.com/pulse/how-use-chatgpt-boost-productivity/

Author, G. (2023). 7 Most Common Challenges Faced by Startups. Creately Blog. https://creately.com/blog/culture/challenges-faced-by-startups/

Ayelol. (2023). 15 Ways to Use ChatGPT for Business: Harnessing the Power of ChatGPT to Scale Your Business. Amigo: No-code Data Integrations to Google Sheets. https://blog.tryamigo.com/15-ways-to-use-chatgpt-for-business/

Baskar, N. (2023, January 20). A Look at the Rise of AI and How It's Changing Our Lives. Skill-Lync. https://skill-lync.com/blogs/a-look-at-the-rise-of-ai-and-how-its-changing-our-lives

Biswal, A. (2023). AI Applications: Top 18 Artificial Intelligence Applications in 2023. Simplilearn.com. https://www.simplilearn.com/tutorials/artificial-intelligence-tutorial/artificial-intelligence-applications

Blaha, L. M., Abrams, M., Bibyk, S., Bonial, C., Hartzler, B. M., Hsu, C. D., Khemlani, S., King, J., St Amant, R., Trafton, J. G., & Wong, R. (2022). Understanding Is a Process. Frontiers in Systems Neuroscience, 16. https://doi.org/10.3389/fnsys.2022.800280

Brod, G. (2021). Toward an Understanding of When Prior Knowledge Helps or Hinders Learning. Npj Science of Learning, 6(1). https://doi.org/10.1038/s41539-021-00103-w

Careerera. (2021, June 22). What Are the Advantages and Disadvantages of CHATGPT? Careerera.com. https://www.careerera.com/blog/what-are-the-advantages-and-disadvantages-of-chatgpt

Challenges and Risks of Starting a Business | Red Tape Reduction. (n.d.). https://www.westerncape.gov.za/red-tape-reduction/our-guides-and-resources/starting-your-own-small-business/challenges-and-risks-starting-business

ChatGPT Lifts Business Professionals' Productivity and Improves Work Quality. (n.d.). Nielsen Norman Group. https://www.nngroup.com/articles/chatgpt-productivity/

Cloudbooklet, & Cloudbooklet. (2023). Google Search Engine and OpenAI's ChatGPT: Differences and Uses - Cloudbooklet. Cloudbooklet. https://www.cloudbooklet.com/google-search-engine-and-openais-chatgpt-differences-and-uses/

Colwill, E. (2023). ChatGPT Invades the Workplace. www.kornferry.com. https://www.kornferry.com/insights/this-week-in-leadership/chatgpt-invades-the-workplace

Connect Invest, (2022, April 26) Passive Income Barriers. Connect Invest.

https://www.connectinvest.com/resources/blogs/learn-how-to-overcome-barriers-to-passive-income/

Copeland, B. (2023, September 5). Artificial intelligence (AI) | Definition, Examples, Types, Applications, Companies, & Facts. Encyclopedia Britannica. https://www.britannica.com/technology/artificial-intelligence

Correspondent, R. W. T. (2023, March 27). Half of Students Are Using ChatGPT to Cheat, and It Could Rise to 90%. Mail Online. https://www.dailymail.co.uk/sciencetech/article-11899475/Half-students-using-ChatGPT-cheat-rise-90.html

Coursera. (2023). 4 Types of AI: Getting to Know Artificial Intelligence. Coursera. https://www.coursera.org/articles/types-of-ai

Cousins, B. (2023, March 31). Uncovering the Different Types of ChatGPT Bias. Forbes. https://www.forbes.com/sites/forbestechcouncil/2023/03/31/uncovering-the-different-types-of-chatgpt-bias/?sh=52c14b0b571b

DALL·E 2. (n.d.). https://openai.com/dall-e-2

Delua, J. (2021, March 13). Supervised vs. Unsupervised Learning: What's the Difference? – IBM Blog. IBM Blog. https://www.ibm.com/blog/supervised-vs-unsupervised-learning/

DEV Community. (2001, September 7). DEV Community. https://dev.to/

Diaz, M. (2023, August 15). How to Use ChatGPT. ZDNET. https://www.zdnet.com/article/how-to-use-chatgpt/

Dilmegani, C. (2023). How to Use ChatGPT for Business in 2023: Top 40 Applications. AIMultiple. https://research.aimultiple.com/chatgpt-for-business/

Dils. (2023). How to Learn Any New Skill With ChatGPT (10 Prompts). WGMI Media. https://wgmimedia.com/how-to-learn-a-new-skill-with-chatgpt/

Dils. (2023). How To Write An eBook With ChatGPT (Best Prompts). WGMI Media. https://wgmimedia.com/ebook-chatgpt-prompts/

DorsDrinker. (n.d.). I Like Letting ChatGPT Rate My Prompts before Executing Them. If GPT Think My Prompt Isnt Good Enough It Tells Me Why and Gives an Example of a Better Prompt: r/ChatGPT. https://www.reddit.com/r/ChatGPT/comments/120fx2v/i_like_letting_chatgpt_rate_my_prompts_before/?utm_source=share&utm_medium=web2x&context=3

Duggal, N. (2023). What Is Artificial Intelligence: Types, History, and Future. Simplilearn.com. https://www.simplilearn.com/tutorials/artificial-intelligence-tutorial/what-is-artificial-intelligence

Eadicicco, L. (2023, January 14). You'll Be Seeing Chatgpt's Influence Everywhere This Year. CNET. https://www.cnet.com/tech/services-and-software/chatgpt-is-going-to-be-everywhere-in-2023/

Edwards-Schachter, M. (2018). The Nature and Variety of Innovation. International Journal of Innovation Studies, 2(2), 65–79. https://doi.org/10.1016/j.ijis.2018.08.004

Eightify. (2023). 38 Tips to Boost Productivity with ChatGPT AI Language Model. Eightify YouTube Summaries. https://eightify.app/summary/artificial-intelligence-and-programming/38-tips-to-boost-productivity-with-chatgpt-ai-language-model

Elodie. (2023). Who Is behind the Giant Open AI? Waalaxy. https://blog.waalaxy.com/en/open-ia-chatgpt/

Experts, E. D. (2023). How to Use Chat GPT: A Simple Guide for Beginners. Master Data Skills + AI. https://blog.enterprisedna.co/how-to-use-chat-gpt/

Frankenfield, J. (2022). Weak AI (Artificial Intelligence): Examples and Limitations. Investopedia. https://www.investopedia.com/terms/w/weak-ai.asp

Frankenfield, J. (2023). Artificial Intelligence: What It Is and How It Is Used. Investopedia. https://www.investopedia.com/terms/a/artificial-intelligence-ai.asp

Gewirtz, D. (2023). How Does ChatGPT Actually Work? ZDNET. https://www.zdnet.com/article/how-does-chatgpt-work/

Gewirtz, D. (2023, August 11). How to Write Better ChatGPT Prompts for the Best Generative AI Results. ZDNET. https://www.zdnet.com/article/how-to-write-better-chatgpt-prompts/

Gindham, A. (2023). How to Write Better ChatGPT Prompts & Become a Prompt Writer. The Writesonic Blog – Making Content Your Superpower. https://writesonic.com/blog/how-to-write-chatgpt-prompts/

Glover, E. (2022). Strong AI vs. Weak AI: What's the Difference? Built In. https://builtin.com/artificial-intelligence/strong-ai-weak-ai

Griffith, E. (2023, February 15). ChatGPT vs. Google Search: In Head-to-Head Battle, Which One Is Smarter? PCMAG. https://www.pcmag.com/news/chatgpt-vs-google-search-in-head-to-head-battle-which-one-is-smarter

Hazelcast. (2020, July 4). What is Machine Learning Inference? | Hazelcast. https://hazelcast.com/glossary/machine-learning-inference/

Heath, A. (2023, February 27). Snapchat Releases 'My AI' Chatbot Powered by

ChatGPT. The Verge. https://www.theverge.com/2023/2/27/23614959/ snapchat-my-ai-chatbot-chatgpt-openai-plus-subscription

Heaven, W. D. (2023, February 8). ChatGPT Is Everywhere. Here's Where It Came From. MIT Technology Review. https://www.technologyreview. com/2023/02/08/1068068/

Hughes, A. (n.d.). CHATGPT: Everything You Need to Know About OpenAI's GPT-4 Tool. www.sciencefocus.com. https://www.sciencefocus.com/ future-technology/gpt-3

Ibrahim, H. (2023). How to Use ChatGPT on Android and iOS. MUO. https:// www.makeuseof.com/how-to-use-chatgpt-on-android-and-ios/

Ina. (2023). The History of Chatbots – From Eliza to ChatGPT. AI-chatbot Software for Complex Requirements. https://onlim.com/en/the-history-of-chatbots/

Johnson, A. (2022, December 13). Here's What to Know About OpenAI's CHATGPT – What It's Disrupting and How to Use It. Forbes. https://www. forbes.com/sites/ariannajohnson/2022/12/07/heres-what-to-know-about-openais-chatgpt-what-its-disrupting-and-how-to-use-it/?sh= 6b30a5452643

Joshbersin, & Joshbersin. (2023). Why Is the World Afraid of AI? The Fears Are Unfounded, and Here's Why. JOSH BERSIN. https://joshbersin.com/2023/ 04/why-is-the-world-afraid-of-ai-the-fears-are-unfounded-and-heres-why/

Justdoit_Leo. (n.d.). How ChatGPT Changed My Daily Routine as an Engineer. Share Your Specific Examples!: r/ChatGPT. https://www.reddit. com/r/ChatGPT/comments/13mmuxu/how_chatgpt_changed_my_dai ly_routine_as_an/

K, T. (2023). 💬 One Powerful ChatGPT Prompt Generator to Rule Them All 👑. Get Rich Now – Learn Money Making Methods. https://getrichnow. com/chatgpt-prompt-generator/

Kelly, S. M. (2023, March 16). Microsoft Is Bringing ChatGPT Technology to Word, Excel and Outlook. CNN. https://edition.cnn.com/2023/03/16/ tech/openai-gpt-microsoft-365/index.html

Kemper, J. (2023, August 19). ChatGPT Guide: Use These Prompt Strategies to Maximize Your Results. THE DECODER. https://the-decoder.com/chat gpt-guide-prompt-strategies/

Korn Ferry. (2023, March 27). ChatGPT in the workplace: Korn Ferry survey shows majority of professionals would use the tool, though less than half trust its accuracy. https://www.kornferry.com/about-us/press/chatgpt-in-the-workplace

Landwehr, J. (2023, May 13). People Are Using ChatGPT in Place of Therapy – What Do Mental Health Experts Think? Health. https://www.health.com/chatgpt-therapy-mental-health-experts-weigh-in-7488513

Leighton, N. (2023, February 22). 6 Ways Business Leaders Should Integrate ChatGPT. Forbes. https://www.forbes.com/sites/forbescoachescouncil/2023/02/22/6-ways-business-leaders-should-integrate-chatgpt/?sh=229a1f1a6c61

Leswing, K. (2023, February 18). Microsoft's Bing A.I. Is Producing Creepy Conversations with Users. CNBC. https://www.cnbc.com/2023/02/16/microsofts-bing-ai-is-leading-to-creepy-experiences-for-users.html

Lomas, N. (2023, April 29). ChatGPT Resumes Service in Italy after Adding Privacy Disclosures and Controls. TechCrunch. https://techcrunch.com/2023/04/28/chatgpt-resumes-in-italy/

Mack, L. E. (2023). Can ChatGPT Design Safe and Effective Workout Plans for You? MUO. https://www.makeuseof.com/can-chatgpt-design-safe-effective-workout-plans/

Master ChatGPT Prompts: Ultimate Cheat Sheet & Guide – EcoAGI. (2023, August 20). https://ecoagi.ai/articles/chatgpt-prompt-cheat-sheet

McCallum, B. S. (2023, April 1). ChatGPT Banned in Italy over Privacy Concerns. BBC News. https://www.bbc.com/news/technology-65139406

McCoy, L. (2023) Microsoft Azure Explained: What It Is and Why It Matters. CCB Technology. https://ccbtechnology.com/what-microsoft-azure-is-and-why-it-matters/

McCormick, K. (2023, July 6). 6 Ways to Use ChatGPT for Small Business Marketing (+6 Ways NOT to Use It). WordStream. https://www.wordstream.com/blog/ws/2023/03/06/how-to-use-chatgpt-for-small-business-marketing

Microsoft Azure Tutorial - Javatpoint. (n.d.). www.javatpoint.com. https://www.javatpoint.com/microsoft-azure.

Miszczak, P. (2023). Chat GPT Affiliate Marketing in 2023 [Step by Step Guide]. businessolution.org. https://businessolution.org/chat-gpt-affiliate-marketing/

Mok, A., & Zinkula, J. (2023, March 21). A Guy Is Using ChatGPT to Turn $100 into a Business Making as Much Money as Possible. Here Are the First 4 Steps the AI Chatbot Gave Him. Entrepreneur. https://www.entrepreneur.

com/business-news/how-to-start-a-business-with-100-using-chatgpt-ai-tools/448066

Mok, A., & Zinkula, J. (2023, September 4). ChatGPT May Be Coming for Our Jobs. Here Are the 10 Roles That AI Is Most Likely to Replace. Business Insider. https://www.businessinsider.com/chatgpt-jobs-at-risk-replace ment-artificial-intelligence-ai-labor-trends-2023-02

Mortensen, J., Mortensen, J., & Mortensen, J. (2023). Why Is Technology Evolving So Fast? Tech Evaluate. https://techevaluate.com/why-is-technol ogy-evolving-so-fast/

Mrbullwinkle. (2023, July 19). What Is Azure OpenAI Service? – Azure AI services. Microsoft Learn. https://learn.microsoft.com/en-us/azure/ai-services/openai/overview

Neo, B. (2021, December 14). Top 20 Must-Watch Artificial Intelligence Movies – Towards Data Science. Medium. https://towardsdatascience.com/top-20-movies-about-machine-learning-ai-and-data-science-8382d408c8c3

Oluwaniyi, R. (2023). 7 Reasons Why Artificial Intelligence Can't Replace Humans at Work. MUO. https://www.makeuseof.com/reasons-artificial-intelligence-cant-replace-humans/

Ortiz, S. (2023). What Is ChatGPT and Why Does It Matter? Here's What You Need to Know. ZDNET. https://www.zdnet.com/article/what-is-chatgpt-and-why-does-it-matter-heres-everything-you-need-to-know/

Panel, E. (2021, June 14). 14 Ways AI Could Become a Detriment to Society. Forbes. https://www.forbes.com/sites/forbestechcouncil/2021/06/14/14-ways-ai-could-become-a-detriment-to-society/?sh=5902899227f

Pocock, K. (2023). What Is CHATGPT? Why You Need to Care about GPT 4. PC Guide. https://www.pcguide.com/apps/what-is-chat-gpt/

Pymnts. (2023, March 24). Shopify, Coca Cola Harness the Power of ChatGPT. PYMNTS.com. https://www.pymnts.com/news/retail/2023/shopify-coca-cola-harness-power-chatgpt/

Raschka, S. (2023, February 9). Understanding and Coding the Self-Attention Mechanism of Large Language Models from Scratch. Sebastian Raschka, PhD. https://sebastianraschka.com/blog/2023/self-attention-from-scratch.html

Romans, C. (2023). How to Create a Healthy Meal Plan Using ChatGPT. MUO. https://www.makeuseof.com/create-healthy-meal-plan-using-chatgpt/

Sant, H. (2023). ChatGPT-4 vs ChatGPT-3.5 Default vs. ChatGPT-3.5 Legacy: Differences Tested. Geekflare. https://geekflare.com/chat-gpt-versions-comparison/

Sha, A., & Sha, A. (2023). How to Make Money with ChatGPT (10 Easy Ways). Beebom. https://beebom.com/use-chatgpt-make-money/

Sheen, A. P. B. T. (2023, March 23). What is DALL-E? Definition from Techopedia. Techopedia. https://www.techopedia.com/definition/dall-e

Slater, Derek. (2023). How to Use ChatGPT to Find a New Hobby – Griproom. GripRoom. https://www.griproom.com/fun/how-to-use-chatgpt-to-find-a-new-hobby.

Smith, D. (2023, March 23). 'Of Course It's Disturbing': Will AI Change Hollywood Forever? The Guardian. https://www.theguardian.com/film/2023/mar/23/ai-change-hollywood-film-industry-concern

Somoye, F. L. (2023). Who Created ChatGPT – And Who Owns OpenAI? PC Guide. https://www.pcguide.com/apps/who-created-chat-gpt/

Substantial_Rush. (n.d.). What Are Some Ways ChatGPT and Other AI Is Helping Your Business?: r/Entrepreneur. https://www.reddit.com/r/Entrepreneur/comments/11drj3h/what_are_some_ways_chatgpt_and_other_ai_is/

Team, X. (2021, November 19). Top 10 Benefits of Artificial Intelligence (AI) | 10XDS. 10XDS – Exponential Digital Solutions. https://10xds.com/blog/benefits-of-artificial-intelligence-ai/

Terrasi, V. (2023). How to Write ChatGPT Prompts to Get the Best Results. Search Engine Journal. https://www.searchenginejournal.com/how-to-write-chatgpt-prompts/479324/

The Implications of ChatGPT for Legal Services and Society – Harvard Law School Center on the Legal Profession. (2023, March 24). Harvard Law School Center on the Legal Profession. https://clp.law.harvard.edu/knowledge-hub/magazine/issues/generative-ai-in-the-legal-profession/the-implications-of-chatgpt-for-legal-services-and-society/

The Politics of AI: ChatGPT and Political Bias | Brookings. (2023, June 28). Brookings. https://www.brookings.edu/articles/the-politics-of-ai-chatgpt-and-political-bias/

Thomas, M. (2022). The Future of AI: How Artificial Intelligence Will Change the World. Built In. https://builtin.com/artificial-intelligence/artificial-intelligence-future

Top Applications of Artificial Intelligence (AI) in 2023. (2023, August 14). InterviewBit. https://www.interviewbit.com/blog/applications-of-artificial-intelligence/

TOP 25 WORD OF MOUTH QUOTES (of 87). A-Z Quotes. Accessed October 4, 2023. https://www.azquotes.com/quotes/topics/word-of-mouth.html.

Vanian, J. (2023, March 17). Microsoft Adds OpenAI Technology to Word and Excel. CNBC. https://www.cnbc.com/2023/03/16/microsoft-to-improve-office-365-with-chatgpt-like-generative-ai-tech-.html

Wadhwani, S. (2023, August 21). AI-Generated Content Cannot be Copyrighted - Spiceworks. Spiceworks. https://www.spiceworks.com/news/ai-generated-content-cannot-be-copyrighted/

Wankhede, C. (2023). Does ChatGPT Have a Character Limit? Here's How to Bypass It. Android Authority. https://www.androidauthority.com/chatgpt-character-limit-3292997/

What Are the Advantages of Artificial Intelligence? | HCLTech. (n.d.). https://www.hcltech.com/technology-qa/what-are-the-advantages-of-artificial-intelligence

What Is Strong AI? | IBM. (n.d.). https://www.ibm.com/topics/strong-ai

Writer, R. C. (2023). Everything You Need to Know About ChatGPT Bias. Rock Content. https://rockcontent.com/blog/chatgpt-bias/

Wu, G. (2022). 15 Creative Ways to Use ChatGPT by OpenAI. MUO. https://www.makeuseof.com/creative-ways-to-use-chatgpt-openai/

Zandan, N. (2023). 8 Ways ChatGPT Can Help to Improve Sales Skills and Knowledge. Quantified AI. https://www.quantified.ai/blog/8-ways-chatgpt-can-help-to-improve-sales-skills-and-knowledge/

ChatGPT for Business 101

AI-Driven Strategies to Cut Costs, Skyrocket Productivity and Boost Your Bottom Line

Introduction

As the sun began to set behind the horizon, casting a warm glow over the tranquil scenery, I couldn't help but marvel at how far my business had come. It felt like just yesterday when I was struggling to keep up with the demands of running a growing furniture business. Back then, the idea of using AI to streamline my operations seemed like a distant dream. The rise of social media and online advertising sounds foreign, one that I struggled to understand as an old-fashioned craftsman.

When I first encountered ChatGPT, I was hesitant, skeptical of its capabilities, and unsure of how it could fit into my traditional, hands-on approach to business. Yet, with each prompt and response, I witnessed the power of AI unfold before my eyes. It was as if a window had been opened to a world of endless possibilities where creativity knew no bounds. My first book on Prompt Engineering and ChatGPT chronicled my initial skepticism and eventual adoption of AI technology, which changed how I approached marketing and content creation for my business today.

Since then, I have used ChatGPT to craft engaging social media posts, write compelling email campaigns, and even create product descriptions. Its ability to generate content and ideas that resonated with my audience helped me expand my reach far beyond my local town, attracting customers from across the country.

ChatGPT has changed everything. The time saved through automation has helped me focus more on designing and crafting new pieces, pushing the boundaries of my creativity further than ever before. Looking back, I realized that embracing AI was the best decision I have ever made for my business.

Steering a business in today's digital world feels like running a never-ending marathon, doesn't it? With fierce competition at every turn and customers expecting the moon, it seems like you're constantly being pulled in a million directions. Cutting operational costs while boosting productivity and innovation isn't just a goal—it's your daily challenge. But what if there's a powerful ally that can not only help you meet these challenges but turn them into your biggest opportunities for growth?

Imagine being able to handle customer inquiries, personalize marketing campaigns, and boost operational efficiency—all with the help of AI. This is the promise of ChatGPT for business. Small businesses and industry giants like Slack, Shopify, Coca-Cola, Snap Inc., etc., are exploring the power of AI to enhance customer satisfaction and stay ahead in this digital age.

According to Strata, 46% of American companies have saved between $25,000 and $70,000 by using ChatGPT (Statista, 2023). Take Nutella, for example; they launched an advertising campaign where they used AI to create 7 million unique Nutella jar labels—each jar with a one-of-a-kind design. This AI-driven campaign tapped into customers' desire for uniqueness and personalization with every single jar of Nutella sold.

Despite the undeniable benefits, you may still perceive AI as a distant, complex frontier reserved only for the tech elite. If you've ever found yourself thinking, "AI sounds like a hassle," or "Tech isn't my forte; how am I supposed to use this?" or if you have ever thought that AI is too complex or that it wasn't for you, think again. AI and ChatGPT are more within your grasp than ever before, ready to blend into your business operations, no matter your business size or tech-savvy.

But here's the kicker: while you have undoubtedly heard of ChatGPT and its 180 million user base and 1.7 billion monthly site views as of December 2023, you may still be struggling with how to leverage this technology to its fullest potential in your business. That's where *ChatGPT for Business 101* comes in.

This book is an essential guide to everything about ChatGPT in the business world, as it provides practical guidance and strategies to help scale your growing business. You will learn how to integrate cost-effective chatbots into your business operation to provide personalized assistance, answer customer queries, and streamline support processes for a seamless customer experience. You will also discover techniques for boosting conversion rates in e-commerce through targeted messaging and recommendations while using AI to analyze customer behavior and tailor marketing strategies to drive sales and increase revenue.

With *ChatGPT for Business 101*, you will gain a deep understanding of AI and ChatGPT applications, learn tips for implementation, and gain insights into optimizing content creation, from crafting engaging social media posts to generating converting email campaigns that captivate your audience and enhance brand visibility. Whether you are a seasoned entrepreneur or just starting out, this book will help you stay ahead of the curve and grow in the business world.

And what result should you expect? A business that runs smoother, engages customers more effectively, and outshines the competition while you feel confident and equipped to tackle any obstacle that comes your way in your business. So, if you are tired of struggling with inefficiency and lackluster results and ready to take your business to the next level, then let's embark on this exciting learning journey together.

1. The Dawn of Artificial Intelligence in Business

In the not-so-distant past, the notion of artificial intelligence (AI) seemed like something out of a science fiction novel—an interesting concept that belonged to the realm of imagination, not reality. Yet, today, AI has become an integral part of our everyday lives, changing the way we work, communicate, and interact with the world around us.

Nowhere is this transformation more evident than in the world of business. Over the past decade, AI has rapidly evolved from a novelty to a necessity, reshaping industries, redefining business models, and restructuring the way companies operate.

According to IBM, businesses that have adopted AI technologies are experiencing up to a 40% improvement in efficiency and a notable increase in customer satisfaction rates. For instance, Netflix uses AI algorithms to analyze user behavior and offer personalized content recommendations. This strategy has led to a 30% increase in user retention and a significant 40%

increase in viewing hours. As a result, customers are more engaged, spend longer periods on the platform, and are more likely to recommend Netflix to others. These are not just incremental improvements; they are capable of elevating a business in today's hyper-competitive marketplace.

AI tools like ChatGPT are helping businesses communicate with their customers and streamline their operations. As we move on in this chapter, we will explore the impact of AI and ChatGPT on the business world and why understanding and integrating these technologies is no longer optional but essential for business success and competitiveness. We will look into real-world examples of how businesses are leveraging AI to gain a competitive edge, drive growth, and enhance customer experiences. We will also discuss the practical steps that businesses can take to adopt AI and ChatGPT to unlock new opportunities and achieve sustainable growth in the digital age, just like I did.

The Role of AI in Business

Artificial intelligence (AI) refers to the ability of a computer or computer-controlled robot to perform tasks that typically require human intelligence. This includes tasks such as reasoning, problem-solving, understanding language, and learning from experience. AI aims to replicate human-like cognitive functions in machines, which can involve developing algorithms and systems that can process information, draw conclusions, and make decisions based on that information. One key aspect of AI is its ability to learn from past experiences. This is known as machine learning, a subset of AI that focuses on developing algorithms that improve automatically through experience.

Artificial intelligence, once the "stuff" of science fiction, has become a reality in the business world. From customer service chatbots to predictive analytics, AI is at the beck and call of today's businesses. According to a report by PwC, AI is expected to contribute up to $15.7 trillion to the global economy by 2030, making it one of the most significant drivers of economic growth in the coming decade.

One of the key reasons for the rapid adoption of AI in business is its ability to automate mundane and repetitive tasks, allowing your employees to focus on other activities. The use of AI in businesses is beyond what you can imagine or think of. However, let's look at how AI and ChatGPT are used in business today.

Content Generation

One of the key ways AI is used in content generation is through natural language processing (NLP) models like ChatGPT. These models are trained on vast amounts of text data and are capable of generating human-like text based on the prompt you input into it. This enables businesses to create blog posts, articles, product descriptions, and other types of content quickly and efficiently.

For example, a marketing team could use ChatGPT to generate social media posts or email newsletters, saving time and resources compared to writing them manually. Similarly, a content creator could use AI to generate ideas or outlines for articles, helping them overcome writer's block and stay productive. Another use case for AI in content generation is content optimization. AI-powered tools can analyze existing content and provide recommendations for improving readability, SEO, and engagement. Likewise, ChatGPT can suggest relevant keywords, meta tags, and content structures to improve SEO rankings. Tools like MarketMuse, Jasper AI, SurferSEO, Frase, Scalenut, etc., use AI to analyze top-performing content and suggest ways to optimize your content for better results.

Marketing

Using AI and ChatGPT in marketing is a move forward in how businesses engage with their audience, personalize their messaging, and optimize their campaigns. One way to leverage these technologies is through content creation. AI can generate high-quality, relevant marketing copy, helping marketers maintain a consistent presence across different channels.

AI-powered chatbots can enhance customer interactions by providing instant responses to queries with personalized recommendations and even facilitating transactions. This improves customer satisfaction and can lead to increased sales and loyalty. Moving on, it can analyze customer data quickly and accurately and identify patterns and trends that can inform marketing strategies. For example, a clothing retailer can use AI to analyze customer data and see trends in fashion preferences. Based on this analysis, the retailer can create personalized recommendations for each customer, increasing the likelihood of a purchase.

Sales

In sales, you can use AI algorithms to analyze customer data, generate tailored product descriptions and promotional messages, and use past interactions to provide personalized product recommendations. AI can also use leads based on customers' behavior and interactions with your website or emails to prioritize high-potential leads. It can assist you in engaging with leads through automated messaging, providing information and assistance in real time.

Also, AI is efficient in using algorithms to analyze historical sales data and market trends to forecast future sales. Generating reports and insights based on this data can help the sales team in your company make informed decisions. AI tools like Levity, Incendium, and many others can help analyze customer preferences and behavior to personalize email marketing campaigns while you use ChatGPT to generate email content, subject lines, and call-to-action messages that resonate with customers.

Customer Service

Businesses can streamline interactions, resolve issues more quickly, and provide a more tailored experience for their customers by integrating these technologies into customer service operations. One way AI and ChatGPT are being integrated into customer service is through chatbots. These AI-powered assistants can handle routine inquiries, such as FAQs, product information, and basic troubleshooting. Chatbots provide 24/7 support, ensuring that customers always have access to assistance when they need it.

Another use case for AI and ChatGPT in customer service is in sentiment analysis. Through customer interactions, including emails, chat transcripts, and social media posts, AI algorithms can detect customer sentiment and identify potential issues before they escalate. This allows businesses to proactively address customer concerns and improve overall satisfaction.

IT Operations

AI is a trailblazing tool that can help you manage your tasks. For example, AI-powered chatbots provide instant support to employees, troubleshooting technical issues and answering queries in real time. This reduces the burden on IT support teams and improves overall efficiency.

Also, AI can be used to automate routine tasks, such as system monitoring and maintenance. AI algorithms detect anomalies and predict potential issues before they occur, allowing IT teams to address them even before they happen. As a business owner, you don't need to always send reminder emails to your workers about an upcoming meeting, as it can assist in project management, providing updates and reminders to your team members. With AI, you have time for other things, either personal or business-related.

Human Resources

Human resources (HR) departments are increasingly turning to AI and ChatGPT to enhance their effectiveness. One key application of AI in HR is in recruitment and talent acquisition. With detailed prompts, ChatGPT and other AI-powered tools can scrutinize resumes, screen candidates, and even conduct initial interviews. This saves HR professionals time and helps them identify the best candidates more efficiently.

AI in HR offers benefits in employee engagement and retention. AI-powered systems can use employee feedback, performance data, and other relevant metrics to identify patterns that can help HR teams better understand and address employee needs and concerns. This leads to higher employee satisfaction and lower turnover rates.

Cybersecurity

One of the many ways AI is used in cybersecurity is through the development of AI-powered threat detection systems. These systems work on large amounts of data to check for anomalies that may indicate a potential cyberattack. Organizations can use this to detect and respond to threats in real time, minimizing the impact of attacks.

You can also use AI in the development of AI-powered authentication systems. These systems use machine learning algorithms to examine user behavior and verify identities, making it more difficult for hackers to gain unauthorized access to systems and data.

Legal Department

In legal departments, AI-powered contract analysis tools are useful in quickly reviewing and extracting key information from contracts, saving time and reducing the risk of human error. Similarly, ChatGPT can assist lawyers in drafting legal documents, conducting legal research, and even providing legal advice to clients. Also, AIs can analyze legal data, such as case outcomes or judges' rulings, to assist lawyers in making more informed decisions.

Accounting and Finance

In accounting and finance, AI-powered tools can automate repetitive tasks, such as data entry and reconciliation. ChatGPT can be used to generate financial reports and provide insights that aid in decision-making. For example, AI algorithms can analyze financial data and make predictions about the performance of a product or the stock market. ChatGPT can also generate natural language summaries of financial reports, making it easier for stakeholders to understand complex financial information, detect fraudulent activities, and improve compliance with regulatory requirements.

The Evolution of AI

The evolution of artificial intelligence (AI) spans several decades and has been marked by significant advancements and breakthroughs. In the early 1950s, a groundbreaking idea took root in the minds of visionary scientists and mathematicians—a concept that would forever change the course of human history. This concept was artificial intelligence (AI), the notion that machines could be injected with intelligence akin to that of humans to help them reason, learn, and make decisions autonomously. Let's look through the beginning and growth of AI.

The Birth of AI (1950–1956)

The birth of AI can be traced back to 1950 when Alan Turing proposed the famous Turing Test, which aimed to determine a machine's ability to exhibit intelligent behavior indistinguishable from that of a human. This period also saw the creation of the first neural network-based learning machine by Marvin Minsky and Dean Edmonds, laying the groundwork for future AI research.

AI Maturation (1957–1979)

The late 1950s and 1960s witnessed significant advancements in AI, with the development of programs capable of solving algebra word problems and playing chess at a rudimentary level. In 1966, the first AI laboratory was established at Stanford University, which serves as the formalization of AI as a distinct field of study.

AI Boom (1980–1987)

The 1980s saw a surge of interest and investment in AI. This sudden surge was fueled by advancements in computer technology and the emergence of expert systems capable of mimic-king human expertise in specific domains. During this period, there was the development of expert systems for medical diagnosis, financial forecasting, and other applications, showcasing AI's potential in different industries.

AI Winter (1987–1993)

The AI boom of the 1980s was short-lived, as unrealistic expectations and overhyped promises led to a period of anticlimax known as the AI winter. Funding for AI research dried up, and interest in the field waned as progress failed to meet expectations.

AI Agents (1993–2011)

The early 1990s marked a resurgence of interest in AI as there were increased advancements in machine learning and the development of intelligent agents capable of autonomous decision-making. This period saw the emergence of AI applications in areas such as data mining, natural language processing, and robotics, paving the way for AI's integration into mainstream business operations.

AI General Intelligence

In recent years, the concept of artificial general intelligence (AGI), or AI with human-level intelligence across a wide range of domains, has gained prominence. While AGI remains a distant goal, advancements in deep learning, neural networks, and other AI technologies have brought us closer to achieving this ambitious vision.

The evolution of AI from its rudimentary stage to its current state has significantly influenced business operations. In 2022, OpenAI released ChatGPT, a groundbreaking AI-powered conversational agent that is now the fastest-growing consumer internet app of all time. ChatGPT's ability to engage in natural, human-like conversations has transformed customer service, marketing, sales, and other business functions, helping organizations deliver personalized experiences at scale and revolutionizing the way they interact with customers and stakeholders. As businesses continue to embrace AI technologies like ChatGPT, the future promises even greater opportunities for innovation and growth in the business world.

ChatGPT Chatbot vs. ChatGPT API

ChatGPT offers two distinct ways to interact with its powerful language processing capabilities. Understanding the difference between the ChatGPT chatbot and the ChatGPT API is important for choosing the right approach for your needs.

The Conversationalist: ChatGPT Chatbot

ChatGPT chatbot is like a friendly, ever-learning companion you can chat with. It is a readily available interface that is accessible directly through OpenAI's website. This user-friendly platform allows anyone to engage in conversation with the AI and ask questions across diverse topics.

The beauty of the ChatGPT chatbot lies in its simplicity. It doesn't require any technical expertise—you simply start typing, and the conversation unfolds. This makes it ideal for casual exploration. If you're curious about what ChatGPT can do, the chatbot is a fantastic starting point. You can experiment with different prompts and questions, getting a feel for its fluency and range of responses. Or idea generation as a brain-storming partner, generating new ideas for stories, poems, or marketing slogans. Or simple question-and-answer for basic questions that don't require in-depth analysis.

The Powerhouse: ChatGPT API

While the chatbot offers a straightforward interaction, the real magic lies beneath the surface—the ChatGPT API. This API functions as the engine powering the chatbot, granting developers access to the core functionalities of ChatGPT.

Think of it like this: The chatbot is a prebuilt website you can visit and interact with, but you can't modify its design or features. The API, on the other hand, provides the building blocks (the code and functionalities) that developers can leverage to create entirely new applications.

With ChatGPT API, you can build chatbots tailored to specific purposes, like a customer service bot trained to answer product inquiries or a virtual assistant optimized for scheduling tasks. Developers have greater control over how ChatGPT is used. They can define specific parameters for the AI's responses, ensuring they align perfectly with the application's goals.

The API allows ChatGPT to be seamlessly integrated into existing applications. This could be used to enhance customer support systems, personalize marketing campaigns, or even develop educational tools powered by AI-driven explanations.

Real-Life Stories

Beyond this, let's look at some real-life examples of how multinational companies have integrated AI into their operations and taken advantage of what it offers to be ahead in this competitive digital age.

Alibaba

Alibaba Group is a multinational conglomerate specializing in e-commerce, retail, the internet, and technology. They faced the challenge of managing a large inventory and optimizing product recommendations to enhance user experience and drive sales.

However, with AI algorithms, including natural language processing (NLP) and machine learning, they were able to analyze customer behavior, preferences, and browsing history. This data was used to personalize product recommendations and tailor marketing strategies to individual users. Alibaba uses AI in its City Brain Project, Cloud Computing Division, and inventory management systems to optimize supply chain logistics, reduce costs, and improve overall operational efficiency.

Amazon

Amazon, a global leader in e-commerce and cloud computing, uses AI in many parts of its business. One of Amazon's stores, called Amazon Go, uses AI to track the items customers pick up. Customers don't need to check out; they just grab what they want and leave. Cameras in the store watch what customers take, and they are automatically charged for those items through the Amazon Go app on their phones. This makes shopping quicker and easier for customers.

Also, Amazon uses AI-driven inventory management tools to predict demand, leading to a 25% reduction in inventory carrying costs and a significant decrease in stockouts. This has resulted in higher customer satisfaction levels. The improved efficiency has also led to a 20% increase in fulfillment rates, allowing Amazon to deliver orders faster than ever.

Tencent

Tencent, a leading Chinese social media company, uses artificial intelligence (AI) in various aspects of its operations. With over 1 billion users on its app WeChat, Tencent has expanded into gaming, digital assistants, mobile payments, cloud storage, live streaming, sports, education, movies, and self-driving cars. The company reflects its commitment to integrating AI into its services by collecting data from its users to improve its products and services.

Tencent also uses AI-powered fraud detection and prevention systems that use user behavior, transaction patterns, and network activity to look out for suspicious activities in real time. These systems utilize machine learning algorithms to adapt and evolve based on emerging threats and evolving attack techniques.

This helps Tencent mitigate fraud risks and protect user data from unauthorized access and malicious activities while also reducing financial losses associated with fraudulent transactions and improving user trust and confidence in Tencent's platforms and services.

Addressing Common Misconceptions and Fears

Artificial intelligence (AI) has become a force today, yet there are still common misconceptions and fears surrounding its adoption. Let's debunk some of these myths:

Myth 1: GenAI Won't Affect My Business

Many businesses mistakenly believe that AI, particularly generative AI (GenAI), won't affect their operations. However, the reality is that AI is already reshaping industries across the board. Major software providers like Microsoft, Google, and Salesforce are integrating generative AI features into their software offerings. From customer service automation to data analysis and content generation, AI technologies like ChatGPT are becoming integral to business processes. This presents businesses with a unique opportunity to use AI technologies for increased efficiency, improved customer experiences, and enhanced decision-making processes.

Myth 2: It's So Massive, We Have to Go Slow

Some businesses fear that implementing AI requires massive overhauls and extensive investments, leading them to proceed cautiously or avoid adoption altogether. However, AI implementation doesn't have to be an all-or-nothing endeavor. Companies can start small, focusing on specific use cases or departments, and gradually scale their AI initiatives as they gain confidence and see positive results. Also, leveraging AIaaS (AI as a Service) solutions allows businesses to access AI capabilities without the need for significant upfront investments or infrastructure changes.

Myth 3: Generative AI Is Too New and Risky

While generative AI, which includes technologies like ChatGPT, is relatively new, it has already demonstrated its potential across various industries. Businesses may hesitate to embrace generative AI due to concerns about reliability, security, and ethical implications. However, advancements in AI research, coupled with rigorous testing and validation processes, have enhanced the reliability and safety of generative AI models. Moreover, by adhering to ethical guidelines and implementing robust security measures, you can mitigate potential risks and use generative AI to increase your business's overall performance.

Myth 4: Generative AI Will Replace Employees

Generative AI can indeed automate certain tasks and streamline processes, but it's unlikely to replace human employees entirely. Instead, AI serves as a complement to human work, augmenting capabilities to enhance productivity and efficiency. Using AI will help businesses automate repetitive tasks while employees can focus on higher-value work that requires human creativity and critical thinking.

Myth 5: We'll Need to Hire a Lot of New Talent for Generative AI

Although implementing AI may require some expertise in AI technologies, businesses don't necessarily need to hire a large number of new employees. Many AI tools and platforms are designed to be user-friendly and accessible. This allows existing employees to learn and use them without extensive technical knowledge. Also, businesses can take advantage of external resources, such as AI consultants or training programs, to support their AI initiatives without significant hiring costs.

Myth 6: We Don't Need Generative AI for Our Digital Transformation

In today's rapidly evolving business world, digital transformation is essential for staying competitive and meeting customer demands. AI plays a crucial role in digital transformation by allowing businesses to innovate, personalize customer experiences, and create new revenue streams. It can be used to automate tasks, optimize processes, and drive business growth and success. Businesses that embrace AI are better positioned to stay competitive and adapt to the evolving digital landscape.

Setting the Stage for AI Integration

Integrating AI into your business can be both exciting and daunting, but with the right approach, it becomes an achievable and rewarding endeavor. To ensure a successful integration, it's important to follow a systematic approach. Here are ten steps to help your business start their AI journey:

Step 1: Find Out What AI Is All About

Begin by gaining a basic understanding of AI and its potential applications in your industry. Do your research and educate yourself and your team on the fundamentals of AI technologies and how they can benefit your business.

Step 2: Determine the Business Problem You Can Solve with AI

Identify specific challenges or opportunities within your business that AI can address. To do this, you need to understand the types of services your business provides. A problem, such as long wait times for customer support inquiries, can guide AI initiatives toward implementing a chatbot system to provide immediate assistance and reduce response times.

Step 3: Determine the Internal Capability

Assess your organization's existing capabilities and resources related to AI, including technical expertise, data infrastructure, and budget. Identify any gaps that need to be addressed to successfully implement AI solutions.

Step 4: Assess the Potential Value for AI Implementation

Evaluate the potential benefits and ROI of integrating AI into your business. Consider factors such as cost savings, efficiency gains, revenue growth, and competitive advantage to determine the value proposition of AI implementation.

Step 5: Hire the Right Personnel

Invest in hiring or training employees with the necessary skills and expertise to drive your AI initiatives forward. Look for individuals with experience in data science, machine learning, software development, and domain-specific knowledge relevant to your industry.

Step 6: Appreciate Small Beginnings

Start small and focus on quick wins to build momentum and demonstrate the value of AI to stakeholders. Begin with pilot projects or proofs-of-concept that address specific use cases and deliver tangible results.

Step 7: Carry Out the Integration of Data

Ensure that your data infrastructure is robust and capable of supporting AI applications. Cleanse and organize your data to make it accessible and usable for AI algorithms, and establish protocols for data governance and security.

Step 8: Include AI in Your Daily Tasks

Incorporate AI tools and solutions into your daily workflows and processes to familiarize employees with AI technologies and encourage adoption. Provide training and support to help employees use AI effectively in their roles.

Step 9: Integrate AI with Balance

Strike a balance between using AI to automate tasks and augmenting human capabilities, and ensure it complements rather than replaces human expertise. Be mindful of ethical considerations, privacy concerns, and potential biases in AI algorithms, and prioritize transparency and accountability in your AI initiatives.

Step 10: Reconsider Storage in Your AI Plan

Review your data storage infrastructure and consider how it can support the growing volume and complexity of data generated by AI applications. Explore options for scalable and flexible storage solutions that can accommodate the demands of AI-driven analytics and insights.

Wrap-Up

AI offers many benefits to businesses, and it is important to start by identifying specific challenges or opportunities that AI can address. Think about the areas of your business where AI could make a significant impact and how it could help you streamline processes, make more informed decisions, and unlock new possibilities for innovation. Envisioning the potential applications of AI in your business can better prepare you for the detailed strategies that will be discussed in later chapters. In the next chapter, we will look into the practical aspects of AI integration, starting with automation. Automation serves as the first practical step for many businesses in their AI integration process. We will explore how automation can be used to streamline workflows, reduce manual labor, and enhance overall productivity.

2. Automation

Today's business world is so fast-paced that the need for efficiency and productivity has never been greater. Companies are constantly seeking new ways to simplify their operations and gain a competitive edge. This is where automation comes in.

According to McKinsey, companies that have integrated automation reported saving an average of 40% in operational costs and increasing productivity by up to 25%. In 2022, Amazon's robotic handling system, Robin, sorted 1 billion packages, accounting for one-eighth of all orders delivered worldwide. Robots handle tasks like picking and packing, allowing human workers to take charge of quality control and the shipping process. This explains the significant impact of automation in the business world.

Automation is more than just a buzzword—it's a basic shift in how businesses operate. It allows you to achieve unprecedented levels of efficiency and productivity. Automation is efficient in easing workflows, reducing costs, and improving the overall quality of your products and services.

In this chapter, we will look into the key principles of automation, examining its role in enhancing operational efficiency and driving business growth. We will also explore how GenAI, with its advanced natural language processing capabilities, can be used to automate routine tasks so you can create time and resources for other important things.

Benefits of Automation

Automation refers to the use of technology to perform tasks with minimal human intervention. It involves the use of software, robots, and other technologies to automate processes and operations. The use of automation reduces the need for manual labor and increases efficiency.

Automation can range from simple tasks like email notifications and data entry to more complex processes like customer service interactions and manufacturing operations. Automating these tasks increases efficiency and reduces errors.

In recent years, advancements in artificial intelligence and machine learning have expanded the possibilities for automation. These technologies allow systems to learn from data, make decisions, and perform tasks that previously required human intelligence. As a result, businesses can automate even more complex processes and achieve higher levels of productivity. Let's look at the additional benefits of automation.

1. **Increased Productivity:** Automation can significantly increase productivity by allowing machines to perform repetitive tasks more quickly and accurately than humans. This allows your employees to work on other tasks that add value to your business, resulting in higher overall productivity levels.

2. **Stronger Security:** Automation enhances security measures by reducing the risk of human error, consistently applying access controls, monitoring unusual activity, and promptly responding to potential threats. Automated security protocols help safeguard sensitive data and protect against cyberattacks.

3. **Streamlined Compliance:** Compliance with regulations and standards is critical for businesses in many industries. Automation can help streamline compliance processes by ensuring that relevant rules and regulations are consistently applied and monitored, reducing the risk of noncompliance penalties.

4. **Greater Operational Efficiency:** Automation can lead to greater operational efficiency by reducing the time and resources required to complete tasks. This can result in cost savings and improved service delivery.

5. **Better Collaboration:** Automation facilitates better collaboration by providing employees with access to real-time data and insights. This can help teams work more effectively together to improve decision-making and outcomes within the company.

6. **Enhanced Service Delivery:** It helps businesses deliver faster, more efficient services to customers. Tasks that once required manual intervention can now be automated, with quicker response times and improved customer satisfaction.

7. **Significant Cost Savings:** One of the most significant benefits of automation is its ability to cut operational costs. Automating manual processes in businesses can save time and resources, minimize labor costs, and boost profitability.

8. **Reduced Errors:** Automation helps minimize the risk of errors that can occur during manual data entry or processing. With automation, your businesses can achieve greater accuracy and consistency in their operations. This leads to the production of higher-quality goods and services.

9. **Reliable Insights:** With automation, businesses can gather and analyze data more efficiently with valuable insights into customer behavior, market trends, and business performance. This can help businesses make better-informed decisions, improve overall performance, and stay ahead of the competition.

10. **Standardized Processes:** Automation helps standardize processes across an organization, ensuring consistency and efficiency. This can be particularly beneficial for businesses operating in multiple locations or dealing with large volumes of data. With automation, businesses can establish clear workflows and standard operating procedures to reduce variability and improve overall efficiency.

11. **Gained Transparency:** Organizations can track and monitor activities in real time, gaining insights into performance, resource allocation, and potential bottlenecks with automation. This increased transparency allows businesses to make informed decisions, note down areas for improvement, and optimize their operations for maximum efficiency.

12. **Heightened Morale:** Automation can enhance employee morale by eliminating repetitive tasks; this allows them to focus on more challenging work, resulting in greater job satisfaction and engagement. Also, automation reduces the likelihood of human error, boosting employees' confidence in their work.

How ChatGPT Integration Can Help with Automating Tasks

Artificial intelligence (AI) and natural language processing (NLP) have made it possible to create chatbots, which are computer programs that can have conversations with people and do certain tasks automatically.

One way to use ChatGPT is as a chatbot for customer support. It can answer frequently asked questions and handle many inquiries at once, which can save time and reduce the need for human support. Another application involves automating the creation of documents such as contracts or reports. This process relies on prompts and user-provided information. Using ChatGPT can minimize errors and facilitate the updating of templates to maintain document consistency. However, it may require additional training for optimal performance.

ChatGPT can also be used for language translation tasks. This AI tool is capable of translating large volumes of text in a short time, potentially reducing the dependence on human translators. Nonetheless, it may struggle to capture the nuanced meaning or cultural context of the original text.

Sentiment analysis is another valuable application of ChatGPT. It's adept at sorting extensive text datasets like customer feedback, with insights into customer sentiment and preferences. It can generate content tasks such as blog posts, social media posts, news articles, or product descriptions. It simplifies the content creation process and delivers content on time and consistently.

It can also function as a virtual assistant, helping with different administrative tasks like scheduling appointments to enhance efficiency and accessibility, as it is available round-the-clock. However, additional security measures may be needed to safeguard user data.

Hence, before automating with ChatGPT, you need to understand that certain tasks can and cannot be automated. Now, let's look at the step-by-step guide on how your business can identify tasks that are suitable for automation.

Step 1: Assess Your Current State

The first step is to evaluate your current business processes and look for areas where automation could be beneficial. Consider tasks that are repetitive, time-consuming, or prone to human error. Look for patterns in your workflows and pinpoint tasks that could be enhanced with automation.

Step 2: Define Your Automation Criteria

Next, establish clear criteria for determining which tasks are suitable for automation with AI. Consider factors such as the complexity of the task, frequency and volume of the task, the potential for automation using natural language processing, and the expected benefits in terms of efficiency, cost savings, or improved quality. Define what success looks like for each automated task.

Step 3: Prioritize Your Automation Opportunities

Once you have identified potential tasks for automation and defined your criteria, prioritize them based on their potential impact and feasibility. Assess the resources required for automation, the expected return on investment, and any dependencies or constraints that may affect implementation. You should focus on automating tasks that offer the greatest benefits with the least amount of effort.

Step 4: Choose Your Automation Tools

It's time to select the appropriate tools for implementation. ChatGPT's large language model is a tool that can be integrated into various automation platforms or used as a standalone solution. Factors such as ease of integration, scalability, and compatibility with your existing systems should influence your decision. Several automation platforms offer ChatGPT integration. Your business can opt to develop custom automation solutions using ChatGPT APIs for better flexibility and control over the automation process. This allows you to tailor solutions to your specific needs and requirements.

Step 5: Implement and Monitor Your Automation Solutions

To do this, set up ChatGPT within your chosen automation platform or integrate it into your existing systems. Depending on the complexity of the tasks being automated, this may involve configuring workflows, defining triggers, and setting up rules for ChatGPT interactions. If you are using ChatGPT in a customer service chatbot, you might use a platform like Dialogflow or Rasa to define the conversation flow, set triggers for specific responses, and establish rules for handling different types of inquiries. This involves designing the conversation logic, defining the actions ChatGPT should take based on user inputs, and ensuring that the chatbot responds appropriately to various scenarios.

Once implemented, you will need to monitor the performance of your automation solutions and make adjustments as needed. Track key metrics such as task completion times, error rates, and overall efficiency to evaluate the effectiveness of ChatGPT in automating tasks. You should also review regularly and optimize your automation workflows to ensure they remain aligned with your business goals and objectives.

Chatbots for Business Automation

ChatGPT, with its advanced natural language processing capabilities, is a valuable tool for automating various aspects of business operations beyond what you can imagine. Here are key areas where ChatGPT can be used for automation:

Customer Support and Service

Automating customer support processes is easy with chatbots. It does this by handling routine inquiries, providing 24/7 assistance, and resolving common issues. You can integrate ChatGPT into your website or messaging platforms to offer instant responses to customer queries, thereby improving response times.

To implement this, you would need to set up the ChatGPT system on your website or messaging platforms using an API or SDK provided by the platform hosting ChatGPT. Once integrated, ChatGPT can analyze incoming messages from customers in real time and generate instant responses based on the content of the messages and any predefined rules or knowledge bases you have set up. These responses will help address common customer queries, provide information about products or services, or offer assistance with specific tasks.

Content Creation

Many businesses use ChatGPT to generate content for marketing campaigns, industry trends, FAQs, blog posts, social media posts, product descriptions, and more. To do this, you need to provide ChatGPT with prompts or input data to generate content that aligns with their brand voice and messaging. A marketing agency can use ChatGPT to generate social media captions for their clients by inputting relevant information such as the client's industry, target audience, and key messages, while ChatGPT generates engaging captions tailored to each client's needs.

Employee Training and Onboarding

Employee onboarding software tools, such as BambooHR, Rippling, Talmundo, Happyfox, Capacity, etc., can assist your HR team in delivering a seamless onboarding experience for new hires. Businesses can create interactive training modules for new employees using AI. The training material can be developed by crafting detailed scripts that cover various aspects of the onboarding process and employee training. These scripts may include common questions, step-by-step guides, simulations of real-world scenarios, etc.

AI can then be integrated into the training platform, allowing employees to interact with it just like they would with a human trainer. Employees can ask questions, seek clarification, and receive guidance tailored to their needs and progress. It can also provide instant feedback on the completion of tasks, quiz responses, or simulations to help employees learn from their mistakes and improve their skills.

Automated Scheduling

Scheduling appointments, interviews, meetings, and events can be time-consuming; you could divert such time into doing other things or simply taking a break. Although ChatGPT does not have the capability to schedule appointments directly, you would need to integrate the Zapier ChatGPT plugin with a scheduling tool or platform like Motion, TARS, ArtiBot.ai, etc., that can handle appointment bookings.

For instance, you can use the ChatGPT-powered chatbot to understand appointment preferences such as date, time, or type of appointment, and then you can use this information to schedule the appointment through the integrated scheduling system. The chatbot could also provide you with confirmation details once the appointment is successfully booked. This automation reduces the need for manual scheduling.

Summary and Outline Writing

After a hectic meeting and long day, ChatGPT can help automate the creation of summaries and outlines for documents, reports, or presentations. You can use ChatGPT to automatically summarize lengthy documents or draft outlines based on key points or themes. For instance, your marketing team can use ChatGPT to summarize customer feedback from surveys or create outlines for upcoming blog posts or marketing campaigns.

Responsive Chatbots

ChatGPT can be used to create responsive chatbots that are capable of interacting with customers and providing information or assistance. To create responsive chatbots, you need to collect relevant data such as FAQs, product information, and troubleshooting guides to teach ChatGPT how to generate appropriate responses. Once trained, ChatGPT can then be integrated into a chatbot platform or messaging app to provide support for common customer service issues. ChatGPT's natural language processing capabilities allow it to understand and respond to customer queries in a human-like manner, improving the overall customer experience.

Market Research

ChatGPT is effective in streamlining market research efforts by automating tasks such as data collection, analysis, and report generation. Your business can use AI to scour online forums, social media platforms, and customer feedback channels to gather insights on consumer preferences, trends, and sentiment. This is done by crafting personalized review request messages you can send to your customers and analyzing them using ChatGPT natural language processing (NLP) algorithms to understand the sentiment, extract key topics, and identify common trends. This analysis helps businesses gauge customer satisfaction, pinpoint areas for improvement, and make informed decisions based on customer feedback.

For instance, a cosmetics company that wants to understand consumer preferences for skincare products can use ChatGPT to craft customers' review requests so as to collect and analyze these reviews. ChatGPT then identifies recurring keywords and themes, such as "anti-aging," "moisturizing," and "natural ingredients," indicating high consumer demand for these features. Based on this analysis, the company develops a new line of skincare products tailored to meet these preferences, resulting in increased sales and customer satisfaction.

Data Analysis and Reporting

Data analysis and reporting tasks become less stressful with ChatGPT. It extracts actionable information from large datasets quickly and efficiently. ChatGPT can process financial data, sales figures, or customer surveys to generate reports, charts, and graphs summarizing key findings and trends.

A retail chain can analyze sales data to identify top-performing products and optimize inventory management using ChatGPT. It analyzes sales figures from different store locations, identifies trends, and generates a comprehensive report highlighting best-selling products, sales trends, and customer demographics. This helps the company adjust its inventory levels and improve store layouts to maximize sales.

Social Media Management

ChatGPT can help in managing social media presence by automating tasks such as content creation, scheduling posts, and responding to customer inquiries. For instance, businesses can use ChatGPT to generate engaging social media posts, write product descriptions, or draft responses to customer comments and messages. It can also schedule posts with tools like UpGrow, Flick, Content Studio, etc., at optimal times, monitor engagement metrics, and respond to customer queries in real time. This automation helps you maintain a consistent and active presence on social media platforms and drive engagement to build customer relationships.

Prompts for Business Automation

Here are practical examples of prompts you can feed ChatGPT to help you generate reports, manage emails, and schedule meetings. Be sure to give ChatGPT relevant information about your business, including any specific requirements, preferences, or constraints that need to be considered when automating the task.

Generating Reports

- Create a comprehensive customer segmentation report based on demographic data, purchase history, and behavioral patterns, identifying key customer segments and their preferences.
- Produce a market research report on emerging trends and opportunities in the healthcare industry, focusing on advancements in medical technology, regulatory changes, and consumer demand.
- Generate a financial performance report for the current fiscal year, analyzing key metrics such as revenue growth, profit margins, and operating expenses and providing insights into financial health and stability.
- Provide an inventory management report detailing current stock levels, inventory turnover rates, and stockout occurrences, and offer recommendations for optimizing inventory levels and reducing carrying costs.
- Produce a marketing campaign performance report, evaluating the effectiveness of recent marketing initiatives, such as email campaigns, PPC advertising, and social media promotions, and measuring ROI and conversion rates.
- Create a website traffic analysis report, summarizing website traffic patterns, user behavior, and conversion metrics and identifying opportunities for improving website performance and user experience.
- Provide a supply chain efficiency report, analyzing supply chain processes, lead times, and inventory

turnover ratios and recommending strategies for reducing costs and improving operational efficiency.

- Produce a customer churn analysis report, analyzing churn rates, reasons for customer attrition, and customer retention strategies and providing recommendations for reducing churn and improving customer loyalty.
- Provide a risk management report, identifying potential risks and vulnerabilities, assessing their potential impact on business operations, and outlining risk mitigation strategies and contingency plans.

Managing Emails

- Create a follow-up email for a sales lead, expressing appreciation for their interest in your products or services and offering additional information or assistance to facilitate the sales process.
- Write a response to a customer complaint or negative feedback, acknowledging their concerns, apologizing for any inconvenience, and outlining steps taken to address the issue and ensure customer satisfaction.
- Draft an email announcement for an upcoming product launch or promotion, highlighting key features, benefits, and promotional offers and encouraging recipients to take advantage of the opportunity.
- Create a thank-you email for a recent purchase, expressing gratitude for the customer's business, providing order details, and inviting feedback or suggestions for improvement.

- Write a response to a partnership inquiry or collaboration proposal, expressing interest in the opportunity, outlining potential benefits and synergies, and proposing the next steps for further discussion.
- Draft an email newsletter for subscribers featuring company updates, product announcements, industry insights, and relevant content to engage and inform recipients and encourage continued interaction with your brand.
- Write a response to a job application or inquiry, thanking the applicant for their interest, providing information on the hiring process, and requesting any additional materials or information needed for consideration.
- Draft an email announcement for a company policy update or procedural change, clearly communicating the changes, the reasons behind them, and any actions employees need to take to comply with the new policies.
- Write a reminder email for an upcoming deadline or important meeting, providing details on the event, any required preparations, and a friendly reminder to ensure attendance or completion of tasks.
- Create an email outreach campaign for prospecting or lead generation, introducing your company or services, highlighting key benefits or features, and inviting recipients to learn more or schedule a consultation.

Schedule Planning

With the Zapier ChatGPT plugin, you can integrate ChatGPT with over 5,000 compatible apps. This means you can direct ChatGPT to perform tasks in other apps, like scheduling meetings in Google Calendar or updating spreadsheets in Notion. Let's look at some ChatGPT prompts that can help you schedule planning:

- Can you help me prioritize my tasks this week/month? I need to do the following: (Provide your to-do list).
- Create a project plan for implementing a remote work policy detailing communication strategies, technology requirements, and employee training.
- Develop strategies to ensure successful project delivery and minimize the risk associated with (type of project).
- Develop a timeline template for (type of project) that can be easily adjusted to accommodate changing requirements.
- I need tips on effective team collaboration and communication during marketing campaigns to ensure all team members are on the same page.
- Create a project plan for (type of project) that will help me stay organized at work.
- Develop strategies for tracking progress on (type of project) to ensure deadlines are met and expectations are exceeded.
- Devise a strategy for communicating project progress and updates to stakeholders and team members on (type of project) to maintain transparency.

Wrap-Up

In business automation, it's important to look ahead and far beyond operational efficiency and consider the impact it can have on customer support and overall customer experience. Customer support is easier with chatbots, as they offer opportunities to provide instant, personalized assistance to customers around the clock—from answering common questions to resolving issues and processing transactions—while reducing wait times and improving response times. The next chapter will be an eye-opener into the wonders of chatbots and explore how they can ease customer support operations and elevate customer experience to new heights.

3. Customer Support

Businesses are constantly looking for ways to improve their customer support services and deliver exceptional experiences to their customers. One notable solution that has emerged in recent years is the use of chatbots. These AI-driven bots have significantly changed customer support services with unparalleled 24/7 assistance and enhanced customer satisfaction.

Did you know that businesses implementing chatbots have seen a significant improvement in customer satisfaction? According to Uberall, 80% of customers who interact with an AI chatbot say they have a positive experience, explaining the growing importance of AI-driven chatbots in delivering top-notch customer support.

With chatbots, customers can get instant answers to their queries, any time of day or night, without having to wait in long queues or walk through complex phone menus. It promises a seamless and efficient customer support experience that meets the needs of today's on-demand consumers.

However, in this chapter, we will discuss the huge impact that chatbots can have on customer support in your business. We will guide you through integrating AI into your customer service framework, exploring the benefits, challenges, and best practices for implementing chatbots effectively.

The Transformation with Chatbots

For almost every website you visit, you get a "Hi, this is Adriana. How can I help you today?" and it's interesting to know that you get an instant response like you are chatting in real life with customer support personnel about your concern. It wasn't like this many years ago, as you had to wait for human response, which can take more time and require more customer service personnel working shifts—extra costs for the company. Who would have thought that customer service could be auto-mated? But here we have it, changing our business world.

One of the main jobs of chatbots is to handle common ques-tions that customers often ask. They do this by finding the right answers from the information available to them. This is super handy because it means that customers can get help in no time without having to wait for a human to respond. Rather than your workers providing similar answers to the same questions from customers all the time, they can handle more complicated issues that need human attention in the organization.

Another interesting thing about these chatbots is that they can make it seem like you are talking to a real person. They are trained to understand different types of questions and respond in a friendly and helpful way. So, even though you are chatting with a machine, it feels like you are chatting with a human.

Now, let's look at the numerous advantages of integrating chatbots into your business.

Fast, 24/7 Customer Service

Chatbots offer lightning-fast responses to customer inquiries. These chatbots can instantly assist round-the-clock, ensuring that customers receive help whenever they need it, regardless of time zones or business hours. This quick response time enhances customer satisfaction by addressing issues promptly, reducing wait times, and preventing frustration.

More Personalized Experiences

AI-powered support systems can deliver personalized experiences to each customer. It analyzes customer data and interaction history and then tailors responses to suit individual preferences and needs. This personalization creates a more engaging and meaningful customer experience, increasing customer loyalty and driving repeat business. Also, AI support systems can remember past interactions with customers, allowing for continuity and consistency in service, which further enhances customer experience and relationships.

Deliver Multilingual Support

With AI-powered support systems, your business can communicate with customers in multiple languages. This capability breaks down language barriers and ensures that your business can effectively serve customers from diverse language backgrounds. Whether it's answering questions in Chinese, German, Italian, English, Arab, and many more—just name it—or providing product information or resolving issues, AI can do so in the customer's preferred language. This enhances the accessibility of support services and expands the reach of businesses to a global audience.

Ensure More Consistent Support

One of the key advantages of AI-powered support is its ability to provide consistent assistance to customers. Unlike human agents, who may vary in their responses due to factors like mood, fatigue, or knowledge level, AI-powered systems deliver consistent and standardized support every time. This ensures that all customers receive the same level of service quality, regardless of when they reach out for assistance. Consistency in support leads to increased customer satisfaction, as businesses can rely on AI to consistently meet customers' needs and expectations.

Convenient Self-Service Options

With chatbots, you can respond quickly and accurately to common inquiries by providing relevant information and assisting your customers with basic tasks, all without the need for human intervention. This means that customers can get help whenever they need it without having to wait for a human agent to be available. This allows customers to find solutions on their terms, whether it's checking account balances, tracking orders, or troubleshooting issues, improving their overall experience with the brand.

Proactive Customer Service

AI-powered support systems allow businesses to provide proactive customer service by anticipating and addressing customer needs before they even arise. Through predictive analytics and machine learning algorithms, these systems can use customer data and behavior patterns to check for potential issues or opportunities for engagement. For instance, if a customer frequently buys a specific product, the system might proactively offer information about related products or provide tips on how to use the product effectively. This proactive approach helps businesses anticipate and resolve customer problems more effectively and build trust and loyalty in customers.

Delivering Omnichannel Support

Chatbots break the barrier that customers face with having to use different channels of communication to voice their complaints or reach out to your business. AI-powered chatbots provide seamless support across multiple channels, such as chat, email, phone, and social media. This allows customers to reach out for help through their preferred communication channel, making it more convenient for them to get assistance.

Also, AI-powered systems can maintain context across channels, ensuring a consistent and personalized experience for customers regardless of how they choose to interact with the business. This omnichannel approach improves customer satisfaction and builds loyalty by providing a cohesive and streamlined support experience.

Improving Service with Every Interaction

AI-powered support systems are capable of learning and improving over time through machine learning algorithms. However, you need to feed the AI system with a large amount of customer data. This includes past interactions like chats, emails, and even voice recordings. The AI can learn to identify patterns in customer inquiries, categorize issues, and match them with the most appropriate responses by analyzing the data using machine learning algorithms.

With a feedback loop, customers can rate the helpfulness of the AI's response, allowing the system to learn from its mistakes and improve over time. Also, human experts should be involved in reviewing AI responses and refining the data used for training to ensure that it stays accurate and addresses evolving customer needs.

Continuously improving its capabilities can enhance the overall quality of service and deliver more personalized and effective support to customers. This helps your business optimize support processes and drive operational efficiency.

Collect Customer Feedback

AI can efficiently collect and analyze customer feedback, which provides your business with insights into customer preferences, satisfaction levels, and pain points. AI uses a mix of direct and indirect methods to collect customer feedback. On the direct side, it might ask to rate their helpfulness with a thumbs up/down or a star system. You can also add short surveys to the AI algorithm after an interaction to gauge customers' experiences.

On the flipside, AI can analyze language in chats or emails to help understand customers' sentiments—happy, frustrated, or somewhere in between. This allows businesses to identify trends, prioritize areas for improvement, and make informed decisions to enhance the overall customer experience.

Reduce Customer Requests

It can help reduce the volume of customer requests by providing self-service options and automating routine tasks. AI chatbots offer instant answers to common inquiries, guide customers through simple processes, such as account updates or order tracking, and deflect a significant number of requests that would otherwise require human intervention. Incorporating AI chatbots into your business operation increases efficiency and reduces operational costs.

Integrating AI Agents for 24/7 Support

Integrating ChatGPT chatbots into existing customer support channels can be a strategic move to improve customer service and your business as a whole. Here's a step-by-step guide to help you through the process:

Step 1: Choose Your Data Type

First, determine the type of data you want your chatbot to access and respond to. This could include FAQs, product information, troubleshooting guides, or any other relevant data that customers might inquire about.

Step 2: Using Website URLs

One way to integrate ChatGPT chatbots into your customer support channels is by providing access to specific website URLs. This allows the chatbot to crawl through your website's content and extract relevant information to answer customer queries. Ensure that the URLs provided contain up-to-date and accurate information.

Step 3: Using Single Links

Alternatively, you can provide single links to specific resources or documents that contain the information your chatbot needs to respond to customer inquiries. This method is useful for accessing resources such as PDF manuals, knowledge base articles, or support documentation.

Step 4: Using Sitemap Data

The next step is to use sitemap data to train your chatbot. Sitemaps provide a structured overview of your website's content, making it easier for the chatbot to navigate and access relevant information. Integrating sitemap data into your chatbot's training process helps ensure easy access to a comprehensive repository of information to assist customers effectively.

Step 5: Training the Chatbot

Once you have determined the data type and access method for your chatbot, it's time to train it. Use machine learning techniques to train your chatbot on the specific data sources and information relevant to your business. This may involve providing examples of questions and corresponding answers, refining responses based on feedback, and continuously updating and improving the chatbot's knowledge base.

Step 6: Adding Bot Details

To do this, start by defining the purpose and scope of your ChatGPT chatbot. Determine the specific tasks and inquiries it will handle, such as answering FAQs, providing product information, or assisting with troubleshooting. Then, customize the bot's name, avatar, and tone to align with your brand identity and customer preferences.

Step 7: Editing and Adding More Knowledge

Continuously update and refine your chatbot by editing existing responses and adding new knowledge based on user feedback and evolving customer needs. You should also regularly review chat transcripts and analytics to identify areas for improvement.

Step 8: Retraining the Chatbot

The next step is to periodically review and retrain your ChatGPT chatbot to keep it up-to-date with the latest information and customer inquiries. Analyze your customer interactions and feedback to check for ways you can improve or new topics to add. Then, use this feedback to refine the bot's responses, adjust its training data, and enhance its conversational abilities.

Step 9: Testing Your Chatbot

Before deploying your ChatGPT chatbot to live customer support channels, thoroughly test its functionality and performance. Conduct various test scenarios to ensure that the bot accurately understands user queries and provides relevant responses. You can test for different use cases, language variations, and edge cases to discover any potential issues or limitations in the future. Make necessary adjustments and iterations based on test results to optimize the bot's performance.

Step 10: Further Learning

Continuous learning is essential for maximizing the effectiveness of your ChatGPT chatbot. Monitor its interactions with customers in real time and gather feedback from users to spot areas for improvement. Focus on analyzing chat transcripts, user ratings, and customer satisfaction metrics to measure the bot's performance and identify opportunities for further learning and refinement.

Look for patterns where the chatbot stumbles. Are there frequent misunderstandings of user queries? Are conversations going off track? Are specific keywords tripping the bot up? Are there repeated questions? Is a negative tone emerging as the conversation progresses? Does the conversation feel natural or clunky? Are there opportunities for the chatbot to offer more information or make proactive suggestions to enhance the user experience? Analyzing the flow of conversation helps identify areas where the chatbot can be more helpful and engaging. Use this feedback to enhance the bot's knowledge base, refine its conversational abilities, and improve overall customer satisfaction.

Although ChatGPT chatbots have a lot of benefits when integrated into your business operation, you might, however, have to face certain challenges in their integration process. Knowing these challenges ahead can help you stay prepared and ahead of your game. Below are potential challenges you should expect and ways to overcome them:

Natural Language Understanding

One of the primary challenges businesses may face is ensuring that the chatbot can accurately understand and interpret user queries, especially when they are phrased in natural language. The chatbot may struggle with understanding different phrasings, slang, or misspelled words, which can result in inaccurate or irrelevant responses.

To overcome this challenge, you can invest in training the chatbot with a diverse range of training data and examples to improve its natural language understanding. Also, using prebuilt models and frameworks for natural language processing can help enhance the chatbot's ability to comprehend user inputs accurately.

Domain Knowledge and Training Data

Integrating AI chatbots into customer support systems may pose a problem due to the need for extensive training data. Sourcing for sufficient domain knowledge and training data to provide relevant and accurate responses to user queries, particularly in specialized or niche industries, can be time-consuming and resource-intensive.

You can address this by regularly curating and updating the chatbot's training data to reflect the latest trends and developments in their industry. Integrate your chatbot with external knowledge bases and resources to supplement its domain knowledge and leverage transfer learning techniques to generalize its knowledge from one domain to another, improving its overall effectiveness.

User Experience and Personalization

Ensuring a seamless user experience and personalized interactions can be challenging when integrating ChatGPT chatbots. Customers expect chatbots to understand their queries accurately and provide relevant responses tailored to their needs. However, without proper customization and personalization, the chatbot may struggle to meet these expectations.

To solve this hurdle, businesses can customize the chatbot's responses based on user data and behavior. Implementing user profiling and context awareness can help the chatbot deliver more personalized interactions. Also, providing options for users to escalate to human agents when needed can enhance the user experience.

Integration with Existing Systems

You may struggle with integrating ChatGPT chatbots with existing systems and platforms in your business's infrastructure. Your businesses may encounter compatibility issues, data silos, and technical complexities when trying to connect the chatbot with CRM systems, databases, and other backend systems.

Businesses can overcome this challenge by selecting chatbot platforms that offer seamless integration with existing systems through APIs and connectors called webhooks. Prioritize compatibility and data consistency between systems to ensure smooth operation. Consider working closely with IT and development teams to help address any technical issues that arise during integration.

Enhancing Customer Satisfaction with AI

Customer service plays a pivotal role in determining business success. To improve customer satisfaction using ChatGPT chatbots, businesses can employ several strategies that include the following:

Provide 24/7 Support

Use ChatGPT chatbots to provide round-the-clock support to your customers, ensuring that they can receive assistance anytime, even during holidays or nonbusiness hours. For instance, as a travel agency, you can integrate chatbots into your business's website to help customers book flights and hotels. The chatbot operates 24/7, allowing customers to make reservations or inquire about travel plans at any time. This availability enhances customer satisfaction by providing timely responses to queries and issues.

Instant Issue Resolution

With the speed and efficiency of chatbots, your business can attend to customers' inquiries and provide quick resolutions to their issues. Integrating chatbots can assist customers with product inquiries and order tracking. Visitors can receive immediate responses to their questions, such as product availability or delivery status, improving their overall shopping experience.

Cost-Effective Solution

Opt for ChatGPT chatbots as a cost-effective alternative to hiring, training, and managing human customer support agents. Your small business can use a chatbot on its website to handle customer inquiries and support requests. This can help save on staffing costs while still providing efficient and responsive customer service.

Integration with Live Chat

Combining live chat with chatbots allows businesses to offer a hybrid support solution. Customers can interact with a live agent when needed while still benefiting from the efficiency of chatbots. Customers have the option to make simple inquiries with chatbots or escalate issues to a live agent for more complex issues to ensure personalized assistance.

Personalized Recommendations

With the intelligence of ChatGPT chatbots, you can study customer preferences and provide personalized product recommendations or assistance. For example, an online fashion store can use a chatbot to interact with customers and gather information about their preferences and past purchases. The chatbot will use the data to suggest relevant products and offer personalized shopping assistance for customers.

Transcript Analysis

Data and transcripts from chatbot conversations are useful in helping businesses gain valuable insights into customer preferences, behaviors, and pain points. A clothing business can implement chatbots to analyze transcripts to identify common customer issues and improve its services and delivery.

Prompts for Customer Service

Here are a few ChatGPT prompts for customer service. These prompts combine direct instructions with hypothetical situations to guide customer service personnel on how to address various issues customers may encounter using ChatGPT:

- As a customer service representative at (your company name), imagine dealing with an irate customer. Respond by acknowledging their frustration and expressing empathy. Assure them that you are there to help resolve their issue and provide a positive experience.
- Generate a script to engage with a potential customer who is curious about your products/services. Introduce yourself warmly, express gratitude for your interest, and offer helpful information about your offerings without being pushy.
- As a customer service agent for (company name), you will be addressing an issue with our (software product) that causes it to crash upon opening. Many customers are unable to use the product, and some are seeking

refunds. Draft a response to empathize with their frustrations and politely request their patience as our team works on a fix.

- A customer is curious about our product and wants to know how it stands out from similar products in the market. Respond as a knowledgeable customer service agent and provide the customer with relevant information about our product (product name), highlighting its unique features and benefits (provide ChatGPT with its key features and benefits).
- We offer fixed packages with fixed pricing, but a customer wants to customize their package to suit their needs. Respond as a customer-centric service provider and offer to accommodate their request within reason, as we occasionally allow for personalization on special requests.
- Craft an email to express appreciation for a customer's business or purchase and reiterate the company's commitment to providing excellent service.
- Draft a response to acknowledge customers' wait times, offer an estimated wait, and suggest alternative solutions like browsing self-help resources while they wait.
- Our website is experiencing technical glitches, causing issues with order placement, viewing recent orders, and tracking order status. Provide three variations of empathetic scripts to handle customer queries regarding the issue with patience and understanding.
- A customer seeks assistance in understanding the technical process behind our software (name of

software). Summarize a knowledge base article to provide step-by-step instructions you can use to guide customers through the process (provide ChatGPT with the article).

- Craft a response when a customer inquires about a product you cannot access information about due to department specialization (e.g., tech support for a clothing store).
- Develop a polite and clear script to direct customers to our self-help knowledge base and chatbot to resolve generic queries and issues efficiently.

Wrap-Up

In conclusion, the advancements in AI-powered customer support have changed the way businesses interact with their customers and improved the customer experience. The e-commerce sector, in particular, has benefited greatly from these advancements, resulting in more personalized and seamless shopping experiences for consumers. In the next chapter, we will look into how AI and ChatGPT are transforming the e-commerce sector, creating tailored shopping experiences that cater to individual preferences and needs. From personalized product recommendations to intelligent virtual assistants, the potential applications of AI in e-commerce are vast and promising. Stay glued as we explore the future of online shopping powered by AI.

4. E-Commerce

The digital world is vastly advancing, and companies/organizations are ready to utilize this technology to their advantage to make customer experience the highlight among their competitors. E-commerce is one of the major areas that has undergone tremendous technological advancement. The creation of language processing technology has enabled organizations and companies to offer incredibly individualized and effective customer service.

ChatGPT is one technological advancement that is topping the list. According to Twinkle, businesses implementing AI have seen an average increase of 35% in customer conversion rates. It has a human language working ability and is built on crafting and comprehending meaningful and relevant texts. This makes it an excellent tool for building human-like relationships with clients in e-commerce. This and more are promises of AI in e-commerce.

In this chapter, we will explore the various ways AI, particularly ChatGPT, is being used in the e-commerce sector. We will look at case studies, industry trends, and practical applications to unveil the power of AI in creating seamless shopping experiences online.

Personalized Shopping Experience with ChatGPT

Personalization in e-commerce deals with tailoring individuals' online shopping experiences to their preferences. This can be done through targeted marketing messages, customized website interfaces, and recommending personalized products based on the client's browsing history. The motive is to improve user satisfaction and drive conversions by rendering useful content to each shopper.

Natural language processing (NLP) is important in achieving personalization in e-commerce. By clarifying customers' language and desires, e-commerce companies can deliver a more personalized experience that meets customers' expectations. Also, customer feedback, comments, or reviews by NLP can help e-commerce companies make better recommendations to customers.

This can be done by overviewing the client's purchasing history and suggesting goods and services that agree with the customer's preferences. This is a win-win for both customers and businesses, as companies are able to deliver an authentic experience to each customer, which will, in turn, build trust and loyalty while customers get excess value for their money.

Future Applications of AI in E-Commerce

In the coming years, the use of AI in e-commerce will go beyond creating optimized content for your business website. You should be prepared to embrace the soon-to-be transformation that will happen with AI in a few years' time. However, here's a glimpse into some exciting potential applications of AI that will reshape the online shopping experience:

- **Pricing Optimization:** AI will be more effective in analyzing market trends, competitor pricing, demand forecasting, and customer behavior to optimize pricing strategies. This will help e-commerce businesses maximize revenue, increase competitiveness, and capitalize on market opportunities.
- **Hyper-Personalization:** AI will go beyond simple product recommendations. In the future, it can act as a virtual stylist, suggesting outfits based on customers' preferences, body types, and even weather conditions by analyzing customers' past purchases, browsing history, and social media activity to create an individualized shopping experience.
- **Voice Search Revolution:** With AI advancements, voice search will become a dominant force in e-commerce. Customers will be able to seamlessly search for products and complete purchases using just their voice. This will be transformative for mobile shopping and hands-free interactions, especially for busy customers.
- **AI-Powered Logistics and Delivery:** AI can streamline logistics by optimizing delivery routes, predicting

potential delays, and enabling autonomous delivery vehicles. This will lead to faster deliveries, reduced costs, and a more transparent delivery experience for customers.

- **Visual Search and Personalized Recommendations:** AI will be able to power advanced image recognition, allowing customers to search for products using images or even by taking a picture of an item they like. This will further personalize product recommendations and bridge the gap between physical and online shopping experiences.
- **Augmented Reality (AR) and Virtual Try-On:** AI will integrate with AR and virtual try-on technology to allow customers to visualize products in their environment, try on virtual clothing or accessories, and make more informed purchase decisions.

As technology keeps evolving, we are expecting to see more interesting applications of AI in the e-commerce industry.

How to Integrate ChatGPT for E-commerce Website

Integrating ChatGPT with e-commerce platforms can significantly improve your customer shopping experience by providing personalized product recommendations and offers. Here are the steps to incorporating ChatGPT into your e-commerce business:

Select a Chatbot Platform

Begin by choosing a platform or service that provides a chatbot or conversational AI powered by GPT. Examples of such platforms include Giosg, Chatfuel, Flow XO, etc. These platforms offer tools and APIs for building and deploying your chatbot.

Plan Conversation Flow

Design the flow of conversation for your chatbot. Consider the various features and functionalities you want your chatbot to offer. This could include providing product information, assisting with order tracking, personalized recommendations, answering FAQs, and more.

Develop Chatbot Responses

The next step is to develop possible questions, answers, and responses to help train your chatbot for better performance. Ensure that the responses are structured and tailored to your target audience. Depending on the type of platform you choose, it will provide guidelines on how to prepare and format the data for training your chatbot.

Integrate with Your Webshop

After training your chatbot, the next step is to integrate it with your webshop. This involves embedding the chatbot interface or incorporating JavaScript codes into your website so that customers can easily access this feature while browsing products on your website.

1. **Test and Refine**: Before launching your chatbot, thoroughly test it to ensure that it functions correctly and provides the right responses when prompted. Gather feedback from test users, and use this feedback to refine and improve your chatbot's performance.

2. **Launch and Monitor**: Once you are satisfied with your chatbot's performance, launch it on your webshop. Monitor its performance closely and make adjustments as necessary to enhance its effectiveness.

3. **Continuously Improve**: Regularly review and analyze your chatbot's interactions with customers. Use this data to identify areas for improvement and make updates to your chatbot to enhance its capabilities and improve the overall shopping experience for your customers.

Inventory Management Optimization

AI is useful in inventory management in a good number of ways. Integrating AI into your inventory management system helps to monitor stock levels in real time, send notifications when inventory levels are low, and suggest when to place new orders with suppliers.

With AI, it becomes easier to sort and process useful historical data, current inventory levels, and market trends to forecast demand and optimize inventory levels. This proactive approach helps reduce stockouts, minimize excess inventory, and improve overall inventory turnover rates. Also, it streamlines inventory management tasks by automating routine processes such as order processing, inventory tracking, and supplier communication. This automation saves time and reduces the risk of human error. Some of the best AI-powered inventory management software solutions include Fishbowl, SkuVault, Zoho Inventory, etc.

Now, let's look at more ways artificial intelligence optimizes your inventory:

1. **Scheduling Production Runs:** AI has the ability to analyze sales data and customer demand to figure out the product that will be in high demand and use the findings to plan production affairs in a way that limits waste and maximizes efficiency. It can provide concrete information about market trends and patterns, pricing systems, and product quality, directing the course of the decision process in the company.

2. **Monitoring Inventory Levels:** Your business can adopt AI with a manufacturer's inventory management system to track stock levels in real time. Notifications will be sent at low inventory levels, showing recommendations for when to place orders for new products from suppliers. Users can monitor cost and performance easily.

3. **Coordinating with Suppliers:** Distribution of delivery processes can be done with AI from suppliers to

producers and vice versa. Items can be selected, and the selection of the right route, including transportation costs, can be optimized. Automated information will be sent to confirm delivery time and quantity while providing accurate updates on inventory levels and production time. In optimizing inventory management with AI, it is important to use accurate and comprehensive tags and descriptions; these tags should be properly categorized. It helps quicken data analysis and facilitation.

Leveraging Customer Data for Smart Decisions

ChatGPT's role in analyzing customer data for smart decisions is multifaceted and impactful. Its natural language processing (NLP) and deep learning capabilities allow it to process vast amounts of unstructured customer data, such as reviews, feedback, and interactions, to extract valuable insights.

ChatGPT's human-like manner of understanding is what makes it stand out among other AI technologies in the market. Customers do not have to repeatedly submit their problems for the system to understand. It provides loads of benefits in customer service as it uses natural and familiar words to interact with its users— including sarcasm and humor. Customers derive more satisfaction when they "feel" like they are interacting with a person who is interested in solving their problem rather than a robot.

Also, AI tools can analyze customer behavior patterns to predict future trends and anticipate customer needs. To do this, you need to gather customer data. This isn't just about purchases but also browsing habits, time spent on your site, and even social media interactions. By collecting this data and cleaning it up, you can feed it into AI models.

These AI models are like smart machines that learn from the data. Some recommend products based on past purchases (think "Customers who bought this, also bought ..."), while others identify groups of customers with similar behavior for targeted marketing campaigns. There are even models that predict future actions, like when a customer might buy something or what they are interested in.

Once the AI is trained, it's time to put it to work. You integrate it with different parts of your business, like your website, app, or email marketing. This allows the AI to personalize the customer experience in real time. You also constantly monitor how the AI performs, seeing if customers click on recommendations or if they are happy with the experience. This new data is fed back into the AI, keeping it up-to-date and improving its ability to predict customer needs.

Prompts for E-commerce

Below are some interesting ChatGPT prompts you can try out on your own:

- **Prompt for creating engaging product titles**: Create seven attractive and persuasive product titles for mini electronic hand fans.

- **Prompt for building e-commerce landing pages**:
Create a compelling landing page for our new
product line of sustainable fashion accessories.
Focus on key selling points such as eco-friendly
materials, unique designs, and social impact. The
landing page must be persuasive and include clear
calls-to-action.

- **Prompt for e-commerce social media content ideas**:
Brainstorm creative social media content ideas for our
e-commerce fashion brand, targeting young adults,
incorporating trending fashion topics, styling tips, and
user-generated content.

- **Prompt for e-commerce email campaign ideas**:
Create an email campaign that targets personalized
recommendations and new product promotions for a
virtual kitchen utensil store.

- **Prompt for e-commerce product launch strategies**:
Create a product launch plan that focuses on targeting
influencers, adopting marketing mediums, and
monitoring the performance of launch campaigns for a
new model of smartphone device.

- **Prompt for e-commerce FAQ**: Create a list of FAQs
and provide accurate answers for an upcoming social
media application launch.

- **Prompt for e-commerce online shopping payment
method**: Come up with five payment method ideas that
are accessible and easy to navigate for digital book
purchases in an online bookshop.

- **Prompt for e-commerce advertisement**: Design three
major templates that contain quality, appealing, and

compelling video, image, and written content for an interior decoration brand.

- **Prompt for e-commerce homepage content**: Create informative and exciting homepage content on a blog that deals with international travel experiences. Include pictures and theme designs.
- **Prompt for e-commerce sales boost**: Write an intriguing product description for a company that sells creamy yogurt with quality traits and health benefits, persuading a potential customer to make a purchase.
- **Prompt for e-commerce value showcase and cost-effectiveness:** Write a compelling product description for a premium light bulb, highlighting its top-tier features. Mention that the product includes free delivery and is available at a discounted price without disclosing the original price.
- **Prompt for e-commerce title optimization for search engines**: Generate sample titles for an agricultural product company specializing in organic fertilizers, ensuring optimization for ranking on various search engines. The titles should include relevant keywords related to organic farming, soil health, and sustainable agriculture practices.
- **Prompt for e-commerce Meta descriptions to deploy scarcity and urgency**: Create meta description content for fashion houses that focus on only corporate wear, indicating the urgency for limited stock available for purchase.
- **Prompt to identify e-commerce market opportunities**: Analyze the latest market trends and

consumer demand to recognize potential opportunities for growth in the e-commerce market.

- **Prompt for e-commerce sales funnel**: Highlight a constructive e-commerce sales funnel for optimization and create awareness for sales and maximum conversions.
- **Prompt for e-commerce customer segmentation ideas:** Suggest seven factors to segment customers to target marketing and effectively improve customer satisfaction.
- **Prompt for e-commerce user-generated content ideas:** Motivate customers to create and share reviews and media posts featuring the company's product.
- **Prompt for e-commerce blogging ideas:** Propose engaging and educative content ideas for a blog to attract traffic and educate potential customers.
- **Prompt for seasonal campaign planning:** Develop a seasonal marketing campaign for our outdoor apparel collection. Include ideas for social media content, email newsletters, and promotional offers.
- **Prompt for e-commerce customer survey questions**: Get customer feedback through targeted surveys that identify dissatisfaction and reveal opportunities for improvement.

Wrap-Up

There is a whole lot more in this book as we continue to explore different business sectors where AI and ChatGPT are game-changers. Having seen the booming effects of AI on e-commerce, it's evident that AI is reshaping not just online shopping but also customer engagement. The next chapter will look into content creation and marketing, explaining how AI enriches customer interactions with personalized content in your business.

5. Content Creation

If you have ever found yourself stuck trying to come up with engaging content for your social media page or struggling to brainstorm ideas for your next newsletter, you are not alone. Coming up with fresh and creative content ideas can be a challenge, especially when you are pressed for time or feeling uninspired. But with AI tools, you get a simple solution to this common problem: you can generate new and innovative ideas for your content using your audience's interests and preferences.

A recent study by eMarketer revealed that 58% of marketers using generative AI for content creation saw a big boost in performance. JPMorgan Chase used Persado's Gen AI to create ad copy and achieved a remarkable 450% increase in click-through rates (CTR) for their marketing campaigns. This shows just how impactful AI is in content creation and enhancing campaign performance in the marketing world.

Content creation plays a versatile and multifaceted role across various aspects of business operations. It is not limited to a single function but rather serves multiple purposes and can be applied in different contexts to achieve various goals. Creating engaging content and effective marketing strategies are important for businesses to connect with their audiences.

As we go into the nitty-gritty details of this chapter, we will uncover how ChatGPT is changing content creation and marketing, allowing businesses to create more engaging and impactful content that resonates with their audience on a deeper level. We will also explore the potential of ChatGPT in content writing with practical strategies and actionable tips to help you navigate the digital marketing field.

Revolution in Content Creation with ChatGPT

The business world thrives on efficient communication, and content plays a central role in achieving that. The approach to content creation is undergoing a metamorphosis with ChatGPT, offering a multitude of benefits that can significantly impact a business's reach and engagement. However, let's look at the numerous benefits ChatGPT provides businesses with:

Enhancing Efficiency

ChatGPT is like a tireless assistant who can handle multiple tasks. It helps tackle repetitive work like generating first drafts, social media captions, and even basic blog posts. This allows time for your writers and marketing teams to focus on strategy, in-depth research, and audience analysis. ChatGPT also helps brainstorm topics, suggest outlines, and even generate different creative angles to keep content fresh and engaging. This means that you can produce more content at a faster rate to maintain a consistent content pipeline and capitalize on marketing opportunities.

Automated Research and Data Analysis

With ChatGPT, you no longer have to spend hours sifting through mountains of information. ChatGPT can summarize key points, analyze data, identify trends, and even generate reports using specific prompts. This helps businesses create data-driven content that resonates with their target audience. It can also research and compile this information, ensuring the content is factually accurate and reflects current market trends to help your business tailor its content for maximum impact.

Streamlining Content Production Processes

ChatGPT acts as a catalyst, streamlining workflows and breaking down content creation into manageable steps. If you are experiencing writer's block, ChatGPT can spark inspiration, helping you overcome creative roadblocks. If you need to adapt content for different platforms or audiences, ChatGPT can rewrite existing content in new formats or tones, saving you time and resources. This streamlined approach promotes consistency and quality control across all content channels, ensuring a cohesive brand message is delivered to various audiences.

Tailored Content for Specific Audiences

ChatGPT analyzes user data and preferences, allowing businesses to personalize content for different demographics or customer segments. It can help craft marketing materials that speak directly to a specific audience's needs and interests. ChatGPT can achieve this level of personalization by suggesting language, examples, and even content formats that resonate with your target audience. This approach leads to higher engagement and better conversion rates.

Optimizing Content for Search Engine Visibility

Keywords are the gateway to search engine visibility. ChatGPT understands search engine algorithms and can suggest optimal content structures to improve discoverability. This might include crafting clear and concise headlines, organizing the content with headings and subheadings, and suggesting internal linking to connect related content on your website. These seemingly small tweaks recommended by ChatGPT can have a significant impact on search engine ranking and organic website traffic.

Prompts for Enhancing Content Creation

Here's a series of thirty ChatGPT prompt examples tailored for generating different types of content:

- **Blog Post Introduction**: Write an engaging introduction for a blog post about the benefits of using AI in content creation.
- **Product Description**: Craft a compelling product description for our latest smartwatch model, focusing on its key features, such as heart rate monitoring, GPS tracking, and waterproof design, and highlighting the benefits of convenience, health tracking, and style.
- **Social Media Post**: Craft a catchy social media post promoting a new line of skincare products, highlighting their natural ingredients and eco-friendly packaging.
- **Email Newsletter:** Draft a friendly and informative email newsletter announcing a special sale event to loyal customers.
- **How-To Guide**: Write a step-by-step guide on how to create a budget for beginners.
- **Listicle**: Create a listicle featuring the top ten travel destinations for adventure seekers.
- **Product Review**: Write a detailed review of *The Alchemist* by Paulo Coelho, highlighting its plot, characters, and themes. Include your reflections on the book's impact and relevance to society.
- **FAQ Page**: Create an FAQ page for a software company, addressing common questions about their products.
- **Recipe**: Share a delicious and easy-to-make recipe for homemade chocolate chip cookies.
- **Company Announcement**: Draft a company announcement introducing a new CEO and outlining their vision for the future.

- **Press Release**: Write a press release announcing a partnership between two tech companies.
- **Job Description**: Craft a compelling job description for a marketing manager position at a startup.
- **About Us Page**: Create an engaging "About Us" page for a fashion brand, highlighting its history and values.
- **Ebook Introduction**: Write an intriguing introduction for an ebook about the future of remote work.
- **White Paper**: Write a white paper on the role of AI in improving patient outcomes in oncology treatment.
- **Travel Guide:** Craft a detailed travel guide for a weekend getaway to Paris, France, highlighting the best attractions, restaurants, and activities for a memorable experience.
- **Event Invitation**: Craft an elegant event invitation for a charity gala, including event details and RSVP instructions.
- **Customer Testimonial**: Write a customer testimonial for a fitness app, highlighting its effectiveness and user-friendliness.
- **Website Homepage Copy**: Develop compelling copy for the homepage of a sustainable fashion brand, showcasing its commitment to eco-friendly practices.
- **Advertisement Copy**: Write a catchy advertisement for a new energy drink, highlighting its refreshing taste and energy-boosting properties.
- **Podcast Episode Description**: Create a captivating episode description for a podcast episode featuring an interview with a renowned author.

- **Video Script**: Write a script for a promotional video showcasing the features of a new smartphone.
- **Survey Questions**: Develop survey questions to gather feedback from customers about their shopping experience.
- **Infographic Outline**: Design an infographic outline explaining the impact of regular exercise on mental and physical health, including benefits such as improved mood, increased energy levels, better sleep, and a reduced risk of chronic diseases.
- **Presentation Slides**: Design an outline for engaging presentation slides on a pitch deck to secure funding for a healthcare startup focused on developing AI-powered diagnostic tools for early cancer detection.
- **Course Syllabus**: Develop a course syllabus for a beginner's photography course, outlining topics and learning objectives.
- **Email Template**: Create a customizable email template for sending out monthly newsletters.
- **Product Comparison Chart**: Design a product comparison chart comparing the features and prices of different smartphones.

Prompts for Marketing Content Creation

Here are some ChatGPT prompts you should look to try in your free time on marketing content creation:

- **Writing Blog Headlines**: Write a compelling headline for a blog post about (insert topic).

- **Creating Meta Descriptions for Blogs**: Write a meta description for our (insert blog title, keyword, or topic) blog that will maximize click-through rates.
- **Compiling Ideas for How-To Guides**: Compile a list of ideas for a series of informative how-to guides or tutorials on (insert topic).
- **Generating Newsletter Subject Line Options**: Create engaging subject line options for an upcoming newsletter that will highlight (insert topic or theme).
- **Compiling Ideas for Gated Content**: Compile a list of ten ideas for gated content, such as downloadable templates or an ebook for a company in (insert industry).
- **Providing a List of SEO-Optimized Keywords**: Provide a list of fifteen keywords for blog posts to optimize our website's SEO performance (insert additional information for context).
- **Turning Your Content Strategy into a Pitch to Stakeholders**: Summarize our proposed content strategy so we can pitch its benefits to stakeholders and upper management. (Ensure to provide ChatGPT with a detailed description of your content strategy, which may include your objectives, target audience, content themes, and any other relevant details.)
- **Email Marketing**: Creating email greetings: Craft a personalized email greeting for a campaign promoting our new line of sustainable activewear to environmentally conscious fitness enthusiasts.

- **Drafting CTAs**: Draft options for a persuasive CTA on our landing page to promote our upcoming webinar on (topic).
- **Increasing Click-Through Rates**: Suggest innovative ways to increase click-through rates for our weekly newsletter.
- **Creating Customer Feedback Surveys**: Create a copy for a customer feedback survey email to be sent after a customer service interaction.
- **Proposing A/B Testing Headlines**: Propose two different email headlines that we can use for A/B testing in our next promotional campaign for our line of organic skincare products targeting Gen-Zs and millennials.
- **Composing Re-engagement Emails**: Compose a re-engagement email intended for customers who haven't made a purchase in the last six months.
- **Generating Campaign Ideas**: Generate ideas for a summer-themed email marketing campaign to promote our seasonal products.
- **Providing Email Templates**: Provide a framework or template that we can use for all of our marketing campaign emails.
- **Creating Taglines**: Create a memorable tagline or slogan for our brand, focusing on our commitment to sustainability.
- **Creating Copy for Instagram Stories**: Craft a series of Instagram Stories featuring tips and tricks on how to use a skincare product.

- **Writing Brand Guidelines:** Write a set of guidelines to ensure brand consistency across all marketing materials, focusing on our brand voice and tone.
- **Create an Informative Video Script That Demonstrates How Your Product** (let's say, a smart home security system) **Solves a Common Problem** (prevents break-ins and provides peace of mind for homeowners).

Integrating AI into Overall Marketing Strategy

Integrating AI into content marketing can significantly enhance your overall marketing strategy. Here's how you can strategically leverage AI:

Define Your Goals and Target Audience

- **Start with a Clear Understanding of Your Marketing Objectives:** What do you want to achieve? Increase brand awareness? Drive sales? Generate leads? Knowing your objectives will guide your AI selection.
- **Identify Your Target Audience:** Analyze your target audience's demographics, interests, and online behavior. Who are you trying to reach with your marketing efforts? Understanding their demographics, interests, and online behavior is crucial for successful AI implementation. This will help inform you on how you can leverage AI for personalized marketing efforts.

Identify Areas Where AI Can Add Value

- **Content Creation:** Explore AI tools for brainstorming ideas, generating content outlines, or even writing initial drafts.
- **Personalization:** Use AI to tailor your marketing messages, email campaigns, recommendations, social media ads, and offers based on user data and behavior.
- **Customer Journey Optimization:** AI-powered chatbots can answer customer inquiries 24/7, improving the customer experience at various touchpoints. It can analyze customer interactions and help suggest improvements to your marketing funnel for a smoother customer experience.
- **Marketing Analytics and Optimization:** AI can analyze vast amounts of marketing data to identify trends, optimize campaign performance, and predict customer behavior. This allows for data-driven marketing decisions and improved ROI.

Choose the Right AI Tools

- **Research and Compare:** With a plethora of AI marketing tools available, research and compare their features and functionalities. Look for tools that address your specific needs and integrate seamlessly with your existing marketing stack.
- **Start Small and Scale Up:** Don't try to overhaul your entire marketing strategy overnight. Begin by integrating AI into a single aspect of your marketing,

like content creation or email personalization. As you gain experience, you can expand your use of AI tools.

Prioritize Data Management

- **Clean and Organized Data:** AI relies on high-quality data to function effectively. Ensure your customer data is clean, organized, and up-to-date.
- **Data Security and Privacy:** Comply with data privacy regulations like the General Data Protection Regulation (GDPR) or the California Consumer Privacy Act (CCPA). Be transparent with customers about how you collect and use their data for AI-powered marketing initiatives.

Monitor and Measure Results

- **Track Performance Metrics:** Closely monitor the performance of your AI-powered marketing campaigns. Track key metrics like conversion rates, click-through rates, and customer engagement to assess the impact of AI on your marketing strategy.
- **Refine and Adapt:** Based on your results, continuously refine your AI integration strategy. Be prepared to adapt your approach as AI technologies evolve and customer behavior changes.

Wrap-Up

In summary, the integration of AI into content marketing offers numerous benefits, from improving content planning and SEO optimization to providing valuable information about marketing campaigns. However, the data-driven capabilities of AI extend far beyond content creation and marketing. AI plays a crucial role in strategic business decision-making by processing big chunks of data, which can be beneficial in understanding current and recasting future trends.

In the next chapter, we will look deeper into AI's role in data analysis and collection, exploring how businesses can leverage AI to gain competitive advantage. We will discuss various AI-powered techniques and tools for data analysis, including predictive analytics, sentiment analysis, and customer segmentation.

6. Data-Driven Decisions

The ability to make informed decisions on time and accurately can mean the difference between success and failure. Businesses deal with data every day, ranging from customer feedback to operational metrics, which can be overwhelming to analyze and interpret manually. This is where artificial intelligence (AI) comes in to help your business collect, process, and use data for better decision-making.

A study by Deloitte found that implementing artificial intelligence within a mining business allowed for improved data processes, making them eighteen times faster than what was previously done in the field. This remarkable leap explains the potential of AI in diverse industries by using data that was previously inaccessible or time-consuming to obtain to make accurate business decisions.

This chapter will explore the use of AI in facilitating the collection and analysis of data. We will look into real-world examples and case studies to explain how to use AI to make informed, data-driven decisions that drive success and create growth opportunities.

What Is Data Analysis?

Data analysis is the process of examining, cleaning, transforming, and interpreting data to extract useful information, inform conclusions, and support decision-making. It involves various techniques and methods to reveal patterns, trends, relationships, and insights from datasets. This helps you gain a deeper understanding of business operations, customers, and market dynamics.

In essence, data analysis is like mining for gold within a big mine of information. Just as miners sift through rocks and debris to find precious nuggets of gold, data analysts sift through vast amounts of data to discover information that will boost business growth.

One of the key aspects of data analysis is the use of statistical techniques and algorithms to identify patterns and relationships within the data. For example, in retail, data analysts may use sales data to check for correlations between certain products, customer demographics, and purchasing behaviors. Analyzing these patterns helps retailers optimize their product offerings, pricing strategies, and marketing campaigns to better meet customer needs and preferences.

Data analysis often uses visualization tools and techniques to present findings clearly and understandably. Visualizations, such as charts, graphs, and dashboards, help you better understand complex data patterns for decision-making. A hospital may use interactive dashboards to visualize patient data so that healthcare professionals can observe trends in patient health and make informed treatment decisions.

Real-life examples of data analysis cut across various industries. For instance, in finance, banks use data analysis to detect fraudulent transactions and assess credit risk. In manufacturing, companies use predictive maintenance techniques to analyze equipment sensor data and prevent costly downtime. In e-commerce, retailers use data analysis to personalize product recommendations and improve the shopping experience for customers.

Why Is Data Analysis Important?

Data analysis is important for businesses to make informed decisions and gain a competitive edge. Let's explore these aspects with examples:

Informed Decision-Making

Data analysis helps you make decisions based on evidence rather than intuition or guesswork. Access to accurate and relevant information is important for making informed decisions in business. AI tools like ChatGPT can process large amounts of data accurately to provide insights that humans might miss. This can help your business understand market trends, customer preferences, and potential risks, allowing them to make strategic decisions that lead to growth and success. For instance, Hulu uses data analysis to recommend movies and TV shows to its users. This works by analyzing viewing patterns and preferences and, hence, suggesting content that aligns with individual tastes for higher user satisfaction and retention.

Improved Understanding

Data analysis allows businesses to gain deeper knowledge of various aspects of their operations, customers, and market trends. Analyzing data from various sources with AI can help identify trends that provide useful insights. This deep understanding allows you to maximize opportunities and adapt strategies accordingly. For instance, Amazon uses data analysis tools to optimize its supply chain management on inventory levels, shipping times, and customer demand to ensure timely deliveries.

Competitive Advantage

Analyzing data provides you with a competitive edge in information that others may overlook. Information can be a source of differentiation in the marketplace. Companies that use data analytics can tailor their products or services more precisely to meet customer needs, setting themselves apart from competitors. For example, Walmart uses data analysis to optimize its pricing strategy. They can adjust prices in real time to remain competitive and maximize profits by analyzing sales data and market trends.

Risk Management

Data analysis plays a significant role in identifying and miti-
gating risks for businesses. Businesses can identify potential
risks early on to allow them to take proactive measures to
minimize or eliminate these risks. In the insurance industry,
data analysis is used to assess risk factors such as age, health,
and driving record to determine insurance premiums. This can
help insurance companies accurately assess the level of risk
associated with each policyholder and adjust premiums
according to the data results.

Efficient Resource Allocation

Effective resource allocation is essential for optimizing operational efficiency and maximizing ROI. Data analysis helps businesses identify areas where resources can be allocated more
efficiently. For instance, retailers analyze sales data to identify
high-demand products and allocate inventory as required.
Using predictive analytics models can help retailers forecast
demand trends and adjust inventory levels to meet customer
demands, thereby minimizing stockouts and excess inventory.

Continuous Improvement

Analyzing data facilitates continuous improvement by
providing insights into performance metrics and areas for
enhancement. Analyzing key performance indicators (KPIs) and
feedback data can help discover areas of weakness and implement strategies for improvement. Manufacturing companies

analyze production data to identify bottlenecks and optimize manufacturing processes. Using statistical process control techniques, such as Six Sigma, can identify sources of variation and implement corrective actions to improve product quality and reduce defects.

New Business Opportunities

Data-driven decisions help businesses spot and capitalize on new business opportunities. Data analyzed from various sources, such as market research, customer feedback, and competitor analysis, can help recognize untapped markets and niche segments. Analyzing website traffic data may reveal a growing interest in a particular product category, prompting businesses to expand their offerings in that area. Data-driven decisions also help businesses make strategic investments and partnerships that align with market trends and customer preferences.

Data Analysis Process

The data analysis process typically consists of several key stages, each of which is important for deriving meaningful insights from data. Here's an overview of the process:

- **Data Collection:** Data collection is the process of gathering relevant data from various sources, such as databases, surveys, spreadsheets, APIs, sensors, text documents, or external datasets. This step involves identifying the data needed for analysis, obtaining permission to access the data, and ensuring that the data is accurate and comprehensive.

- **Data Cleaning:** Data cleaning, also known as data preprocessing, is the process of identifying and correcting errors, inconsistencies, or missing values in the dataset. This step involves tasks such as removing duplicates, filling in missing values, correcting typos or formatting errors, and standardizing data formats. This is to ensure that the dataset is accurate, reliable, and suitable for analysis.

- **Exploratory Data Analysis (EDA):** EDA involves visually and statistically exploring the dataset to gain information and spot patterns or relationships between variables. This includes generating summary statistics, creating data visualizations (such as histograms, scatter plots, or heatmaps), and performing statistical tests or calculations. EDA helps analysts understand the structure of the data, detect outliers or anomalies, and generate hypotheses for further analysis.

- **Data Transformation:** Once the data is cleaned, it may need to be transformed into a format suitable for analysis. This could involve aggregating data, creating new variables, or applying mathematical transformations to normalize the data distribution. For example, converting text data into numerical values or normalizing data to a standard scale.

- **Model Building:** After the data is transformed, statistical or machine learning models are used to analyze the data and extract insights. This could involve regression analysis, clustering, classification, or other modeling techniques, depending on the nature of the data and the analysis goals.

- **Interpretation and Visualization:** Once the model is built and analyzed, the final step is to interpret the results and visualize them in a way that is easy to understand. This may involve creating charts, graphs, or other visualizations to represent the data and highlight key findings. The goal is to communicate the results gained from the data analysis process in a clear and meaningful way so that informed decisions can be made based on the findings.

- **Deployment:** Finally, the results derived from the analysis need to be deployed into actionable strategies or solutions. This may involve implementing recommendations, updating business processes, or integrating analytical tools into decision-making workflows. Continuous monitoring and refinement are crucial to ensuring the ongoing effectiveness of the data analysis process.

Utilizing ChatGPT in Data Analysis

Data analysis is a complex process that often requires expertise in programming and statistical methods. With ChatGPT's Advanced Data Analysis feature, data analysis becomes more accessible and efficient, even for users without extensive programming knowledge. This feature, available exclusively to premium (paid) accounts, uses the capabilities of GPT-4 to streamline the data analysis process and enhance the accuracy of results.

ChatGPT's Advanced Data Analysis feature is a tool integrated into the GPT-4 model to facilitate data analysis tasks by allowing users to upload data directly to ChatGPT for analysis. This feature is particularly useful for users seeking to explore data, write and test code, and solve data-related problems with the help of AI tools. Users can significantly increase the efficiency and accuracy of their data analysis workflows by running code directly on ChatGPT.

Key Features and Benefits

- **Direct Data Upload:** You can upload your data directly to ChatGPT, eliminating the need for external software or platforms. This integration streamlines the data analysis process and reduces friction in accessing and analyzing datasets.
- **Code Execution:** With ChatGPT's Advanced Data Analysis feature, users can write and execute code within the ChatGPT interface. This functionality allows you to perform a wide range of data manipulation, transformation, and analysis tasks without leaving the platform.
- **Increased Use Cases:** The Advanced Data Analysis feature expands the use cases for the model across various domains and industries by enabling code execution directly within ChatGPT. Whether you are analyzing financial data, conducting market research, or performing scientific experiments, ChatGPT's AI capabilities can assist in the analysis process.

- **Enhanced Accuracy:** The integration of data analysis capabilities into ChatGPT ensures a higher level of accuracy in the output produced by the model. Using GPT-4's advanced language understanding and reasoning abilities helps you trust the results generated by ChatGPT for your data analysis tasks.

How It Works

To use ChatGPT's Advanced Data Analysis feature, you simply need to upload your dataset and write the necessary code within the ChatGPT interface. ChatGPT then processes the code and executes it on the uploaded data, providing users with insights, visualizations, and analysis results. This workflow enables you to run through your data easily, refine their analysis, and make informed decisions based on the data.

Advantages of AI-Driven Analysis

AI-driven data analysis offers several advantages that can significantly improve the efficiency and effectiveness of data processing and interpretation.

- **Speed:** AI algorithms can process large volumes of data in a fraction of the time it would take a human analyst. This helps businesses make faster decisions and respond to changes. This speed is valuable in industries where real-time information is important, such as finance, healthcare, and e-commerce.

- **Scalability:** Since AI-powered data analysis tools are highly scalable, they are capable of handling large datasets with ease. As businesses generate increasingly large volumes of data, AI provides the scalability needed to analyze and handle the increased workload without a proportional increase in resources.
- **Predictive Analytics:** AI is capable of generating predictive models that forecast future trends, behaviors, and outcomes based on historical data. Businesses can anticipate customer needs, identify potential risks, and make proactive decisions with the help of predictive analytics.

ChatGPT Prompts for Data Analysis

Here are some ChatGPT prompts you can use to analyze data:

- Generate a summary of the key trends in the dataset provided.
- Provide insights into customer behavior based on the given dataset.
- Analyze the correlation between two specific variables in the dataset.
- Create visualizations (charts, graphs) to illustrate the patterns in the data.
- Identify outliers in the dataset and explain their potential impact on the analysis.
- Compare the performance of different product lines based on the sales data.

- Predict future trends based on historical data provided.
- Segment the customer base into distinct groups based on their purchasing behavior using the data provided.
- Evaluate the effectiveness of a marketing campaign using the available data.
- Recommend personalized product offerings based on customer preferences.
- Identify factors that influence customer satisfaction using survey data.
- Analyze the impact of pricing changes on sales volume.
- Predict customer churn based on historical customer data.
- Determine the optimal pricing strategy for a new product based on market research data.
- Analyze website traffic data to identify opportunities for improving user experience.
- Evaluate the performance of different advertising channels based on conversion rates.
- Identify trends in social media engagement that can inform content strategy.
- Analyze product reviews to identify common themes and sentiments.
- Forecast demand for a product based on historical sales data.
- Provide recommendations for inventory management based on sales forecasting data.

Wrap-Up

As we conclude our exploration of AI-driven data analysis, it is important to recognize the broader implications of these capabilities. The use of AI in data-driven decision-making extends far beyond improving operational efficiencies; it has the potential to increase sales and lead generation strategies. Leveraging AI analysis can help businesses directly improve their sales strategies and lead generation. As we move forward, we will look at how AI technologies can boost sales and increase success in your business.

7. Sales and Lead Generation

.

Sales are the stronghold of many businesses, and entrepreneurs are looking for better and new ways to drive sales and increase profits. According to Ringover Statistics, businesses could save an estimated $89.07 billion per year if salespeople used AI to complete data entry and non-sales-related tasks, which currently take up 70% of their time. Moreover, integrating AI tools into the sales process has led to a 50% increase in sales leads for many companies. This means that businesses that use AI tools in their sales strategies and lead-generation processes stand to gain significant advantages in today's competitive marketplace.

In this chapter, we will explore in detail how AI and ChatGPT offer substantial advantages in sales strategies and lead generation processes. These tools have the potential to transform sales operations and increase profit, from automating routine tasks to enhancing customer interactions. We will show you how to leverage AI tools to identify and connect with highly qualified prospects.

Using ChatGPT in Sales

ChatGPT in sales processes marks a significant change in how businesses engage with customers and drive revenue. Gone are the days of cold calls and generic pitches. Today, savvy salespeople use AI tools to gain a competitive edge. ChatGPT isn't just about efficiency; although it excels at automating tedious tasks, it is also about using AI insights to make smarter decisions, develop winning strategies, and close more deals.

With ChatGPT, you can tap into a wealth of information to magnify sales success, from personalized customer interactions to predictive analytics. This tool can help your sales teams in various ways to improve efficiency and effectiveness and ultimately sell more. Here are some key use cases:

Sales Forecasting

AI algorithms can predict sales by ingesting data from your CRM (customer relationship management) system, marketing automation platform, and even social media interactions. They then analyze factors like sales stage, customer demographics, past buying behavior, and economic indicators. Based on this analysis, the AI generates a forecast that predicts the likelihood of closing each deal in your pipeline. Your sales team can focus their energy on the most promising opportunities by prioritizing leads based on their predicted closing probability, leading to a more efficient allocation of resources and time.

Summarize and Provide Action Items

Sales calls and meetings are crucial for building relationships and understanding customer needs. However, capturing key takeaways and outlining the next steps can be time-consuming. AI steps in as your virtual assistant, summarizing these interactions and providing clear action items. You can integrate AI-powered tools with your calendar and recording software.

After each call or meeting, the AI analyzes the recorded audio or video, extracting key points, decisions made, and next steps. This information is then presented in a concise and easily digestible format, often within your CRM system. With clear action items readily available, you are held accountable for moving the sales process forward. This promotes a sense of urgency and ensures tasks don't slip through the cracks.

Analyze Sales Calls

Every sales call holds valuable insights, but sometimes, these insights can be buried beneath layers of conversation. AI-powered sales call analysis tools help you unearth these hidden gems, highlighting strengths and weaknesses in your sales conversations. Similar to call summarization, these tools analyze recordings, focusing on factors like word choice, tonality, and objection handling. The AI then provides insights into how well salespeople are communicating value propositions, handling objections, and building rapport. By identifying areas for improvement, you can develop more effective communication strategies for a more persuasive and engaging sales pitch.

Recommending Next Actions for Sales Reps

AI tools like Algolia and Userbot.ai can act as coaches, whispering sales strategies in your ear. With AI-powered recommendation tools, you analyze large amounts of data, and, based on this analysis, they can recommend the most effective next steps after every customer touchpoint. AI considers the specific context of each interaction. Did the customer express concerns about the price? The AI might suggest offering a discount or financing option. Did they mention a specific product feature? The AI could recommend tailoring the pitch to highlight that feature's benefits. This ensures you are putting your efforts where they will yield the highest return and increase your efficiency.

Generating Sales Emails and Subject Lines That Convert

Crafting compelling email copy can be time-consuming, and, let's be honest, sometimes inspiration runs dry. But AI can step in and become your email writing partner. It can help you write compelling subject lines. Subject lines are the first impression—they determine whether your email gets opened or relegated to the trash.

AI can analyze proven subject line structures and high-performing email campaigns to generate attention-grabbing subject lines that entice customers to click. It can also personalize email content beyond simply inserting a name and suggesting email copy that speaks directly to the customer's needs and interests. This personalization can significantly increase open rates and engagement.

Identifying New In-Market Leads

Prospecting—finding new potential customers—is a fundamental aspect of sales. However, traditional methods can be time-consuming and yield mixed results. AI tools like Salesloft, HubSpot, Outreach.oi, etc., can help you with lead generation by monitoring social media conversations and spotting potential customers who are expressing needs or frustrations that your product or service can address. These tools constantly scan social media platforms like a hawk, looking for conversations relevant to your business and picking out keywords and phrases related to your industry, products, or services, especially those that signal a problem or need.

It then analyzes the tone of a post, recognizing frustration or a desire for solutions—prime lead territory and identifies specific users who might be interested in your offerings based on keywords, brand, or product category mentions. AI assigns "scores" to potential leads based on their engagement and fits with your ideal customer profile, helping your sales team prioritize their efforts. With AI predictive modeling abilities, it can use historical sales data and customer behavior to predict which leads are most likely to convert, with the highest potential for closing a deal.

Predicting Likelihood to Close

AI-powered sales tools like Salesforce Einstein, Clari, Drift, etc., can help predict the probability of a prospect becoming a customer by analyzing historical sales data and buyer interactions. AI tools use information from various sources, including customer demographics, past interactions (emails, calls, website visits), and industry trends, then search for patterns and correlations between past customer behavior and successful deals.

These patterns might include specific buying signals, response times to emails, or website pages visited. Based on the discovered patterns, a model that assigns a "score" to each lead is created, indicating the likelihood of closing the deal. This score is a powerful tool for prioritizing your efforts and resources and identifying leads with the highest closing probability. This ensures you are spending more time nurturing the most promising opportunities.

Predicting Readiness to Buy

Timing is everything in sales. Reaching out to a prospect who isn't ready to buy can backfire. AI can help you predict a prospect's readiness to buy, ensuring your approach is well-timed and impactful. It works by analyzing a prospect's online behavior, social media activity, and interactions with your brand to identify buying signals.

These signals might include downloading white papers, attending webinars, or visiting specific product pages on your website. When AI detects a prospect nearing their buying window, it can trigger automated outreach or send you an alert to initiate a conversation. Reaching out at the right time when a prospect is actively considering a purchase can significantly increase your chances of closing the deal.

Automatic Lead Scoring

AI-powered lead scoring helps you reduce time spent chasing unqualified leads. AI algorithms use the data of your existing customers and past sales to check for patterns and characteristics that are common among successful conversions. Once these patterns are established, the AI assigns a score to each new lead.

This score reflects the likelihood that the lead will convert into a sale. Leads with high scores are likely your ideal customers, the ones who are most interested in your product or service. With leads ranked by their conversion potential, you can use fewer resources and waste less time on clients. Low-scoring leads aren't ignored; they can be nurtured with targeted campaigns or passed on to a different sales team.

AI-Powered Competitive Intelligence

Staying ahead of the competition is important in sales. However, manually monitoring competitor activity can be a daunting task. AI tools like Kompyte, G2Crowd, Craft, Wappalyzer, etc., can offer you real-time information about what your competitors are up to. AI tools can crawl the web, social media platforms, and industry publications to gather information about your competitors. They analyze news articles, press releases, product launches, and marketing campaigns, building a comprehensive picture of your competitor's activities.

This information is then processed by AI algorithms to reveal a competitor's focus on a specific product line, a new marketing campaign they have launched, or even changes in their pricing structure. This helps you to make informed decisions, identify areas where your product or service excels compared to the competition, develop targeted marketing campaigns to counter their strategies and adjust your pricing strategy to remain competitive.

Leveraging ChatGPT for Lead Generation

Generating leads is the lifeblood of any business. Using ChatGPT for lead generation offers a unique approach to nurturing potential customers. It helps you engage with leads conversationally, providing personalized interactions that fit individual needs and preferences. However, let's look at how ChatGPT can play a role in each stage of lead generation.

Website Chatbots

Gone are the days of limited-hour lead capture. ChatGPT chatbots can act as virtual salespersons, engaging website visitors in conversations, qualifying leads, and scheduling appointments—even while you sleep. ChatGPT Zapier allows you to create chatbots that can hold natural conversations, understand visitor intent, and respond with relevant information. With ChatGPT chatbots integrated into your website, you will never miss a potential lead again. It can answer questions and capture leads even outside of business hours, keeping your lead generation engine running around the clock.

Social Media Management

Social media is a gold mine for leads, but managing multiple platforms and creating engaging content can be overwhelming. If you are struggling with writer's block, ChatGPT can help you generate engaging social media posts, captions, and even scripts for video content. When you identify relevant conversations and potential leads on social media platforms, you can paste them on ChatGPT to craft personalized messages to initiate conversations and nurture leads further down the funnel. It also makes responding to social media comments and messages easier by assisting you in handling basic inquiries and promoting positive interactions with potential customers.

Email Campaigns

Crafting personalized email campaigns that resonate with your audience is very important for lead nurturing. ChatGPT can streamline your email marketing efforts by creating attention-grabbing subject lines and tailoring email content to specific segments of your audience, increasing open rates and engagement. If you are unsure of which email format or call to action works best, ChatGPT can help you generate variations and run A/B tests to optimize your email campaigns for maximum lead conversion.

Content Creation

High-quality content is a magnet for leads. However, consistently generating informative and engaging content can be a challenge. ChatGPT can help in generating informative blog posts and articles on topics relevant to your target audience. It can assist you with research, outlining, and even writing engaging content that positions you as an industry thought leader. Aside from website content and blog posts, it can aid in developing valuable lead magnets like ebooks and white papers to capture leads in exchange for their contact information.

Cold Outreach

Cold outreach, the art of contacting potential customers who haven't expressed initial interest, is often a numbers game. ChatGPT can transform this process from a monotonous chore into an easier process. To do this, you need to provide

ChatGPT with basic information about your ideal customer profile and target audience.

It can then generate personalized email templates or social media messages that resonate with their specific needs and pain points rather than generic pitches. It can also personalize greetings, insert relevant company details, and even tailor the tone of the message based on the recipient's demographics or online behavior. This level of personalization can significantly increase response rates and engagement.

Lead Qualification

Qualifying leads and identifying those with a genuine interest in your product or service is a critical aspect of your business. ChatGPT can help you develop a scoring system based on predefined criteria like industry, company size, and website behavior. ChatGPT makes chatbots feel more human, encouraging leads to share details. It can ask qualifying questions to identify promising leads based on their needs while tailoring responses and content based on the lead's interests, keeping them engaged. This allows you to focus your sales team's efforts on qualified leads most likely to convert.

CRM Integration

A well-maintained CRM (customer relationship management) system is vital for tracking leads and nurturing them through the sales funnel. ChatGPT can bridge the gap between your lead generation efforts and your CRM. Leads interact with a

ChatGPT-powered chatbot, sharing details and answers while key information like contact details, conversation history, and lead qualification responses are sent to your CRM. This saves time and minimizes the risk of errors. Based on the information in your CRM, ChatGPT can help you create targeted email sequences or social media campaigns tailored to each lead's specific needs and interests. This ensures your communication resonates with each lead and keeps them engaged throughout the sales cycle.

Prompts for Lead Generation

Here are a few ChatGPT prompts you can copy and paste into its chatbots for lead generation:

- Generate a list of potential leads for our new product launch in the healthcare industry.
- Craft an email template to engage potential leads and encourage them to sign up for a webinar.
- Create a social media post to promote our latest ebook and capture leads.
- Develop a lead magnet idea that will attract potential leads interested in our services.
- Write a blog post that addresses the common pain points of our target audience and includes a call-to-action to capture leads.
- Brainstorm creative ways to use interactive content, such as quizzes or assessments, to capture leads.
- Draft a series of follow-up emails to nurture leads who have shown interest but have not yet converted.

- Create a landing page that highlights the benefits of our product or service and encourages visitors to provide their contact information.
- Design a lead capture form for our website that is simple, user-friendly, and optimized for conversions.
- Develop a content calendar that includes lead generation-focused content to attract and engage potential leads.
- Write a script for a cold outreach campaign to reach out to potential leads via email or LinkedIn.
- Create a lead scoring system to prioritize and qualify leads based on their level of engagement and interest.
- Optimize our website's SEO in the article provided to attract organic traffic and generate more leads.
- Design a social media advertising campaign targeting our ideal customer profile to generate leads.
- Create a webinar or virtual event that provides valuable information to our target audience and captures leads.
- Develop a referral program to incentivize existing customers to refer new leads to us.
- Write a case study showcasing how our product or service has helped a client, with a call-to-action to contact us for more information.
- Craft a series of lead nurturing emails to guide leads through the sales funnel and convert them into customers.
- Create a lead magnet that offers a free trial or demo of our product to capture leads' contact information.
- Develop a strategy to engage with leads on social media and build relationships that lead to conversions.

Wrap-Up

As we have explored the impact of AI on sales and lead generation, it's clear that these technologies are important in our day-to-day business activities. The information gained from effective sales and lead generation strategies can directly inform product development and design, creating a feedback loop that positively impacts business growth. Next, we will discuss how businesses can use AI tools to streamline the design process and create products that resonate with their target audience.

8. Product Development and Design

The success of a product relies not only on its functionality but also on its ability to relate to users and meet their needs. As businesses continue to grow and stay ahead of the competition, the role of artificial intelligence (AI) and ChatGPT in product development and design has become increasingly prominent.

According to Unbounce Statistics, more than 80% of businesses believe that AI tools will positively impact their business in three years or less. This explains the growing recognition among businesses of the potential of AI to improve designs and product development. Here, we will look at the role of AI and ChatGPT in product development and design, explaining how these technologies can ease the ideation process, enhance user-centric designs, and refine product functionality for market success.

AI's Role in Ideation and Conceptualization

The ideation stage of product development is often messy and unpredictable. Ideas come in fits and starts, leaving you struggling to find that "next big thing." But with AI, you can improve your ideation and conceptualization process, from sparking creative thinking to conducting market research. However, here's how AI can help in generating product ideas and conducting insightful market research:

Idea Generation

If you are feeling out of ideas, you can provide ChatGPT with a broad starting point related to your industry or target market. It can help you generate a list of random prompts or ideas to spark your creativity. What you need to do is feed ChatGPT data on current market trends, competitor analysis, and even social media conversations. It can then use this information to generate product ideas that directly address unmet needs and capitalize on emerging market opportunities. Don't let your initial ideas exist in a vacuum. Use ChatGPT to analyze your product concepts against market data, suggesting features that better align with customer preferences and buying habits.

Market Research

Don't just generate ideas; validate them with market research. ChatGPT's advanced data analysis can be used to analyze social media conversations and online reviews. It will help you understand customer pain points and desires, allowing you to tailor your product ideas to address market demands.

Also, if you are struggling to define your ideal customer profile, provide ChatGPT with demographic data and psychographic information to help you create detailed customer personas. This helps in generating product ideas that cater to their specific needs and preferences. Also, analyzing your competitor's market can help you understand the emotional triggers and values associated with your competitor's products to develop ideas that compete functionally.

Prototyping

While ChatGPT can't physically build prototypes, it can play a role in the pre-prototyping phase. Once you have a promising idea, ChatGPT can assist you in prototyping. You need to describe your idea to ChatGPT and let it generate basic sketches, wireframes, or even user interface mockups for quick testing of the functionality and user experience without extensive design resources.

It can also check for potential design flaws before any physical prototypes are built. When ChatGPT analyzes the technical aspects of your product concept, it might flag potential hurdles related to feasibility or integration with existing technologies. This foresight allows you to address these challenges early on to simplify the prototyping process.

Testing and Gathering Feedback

Before a full-fledged launch, testing and gathering user feedback are important. If you have multiple design variations for your product concept, ChatGPT can help you create A/B testing scenarios, presenting different versions and analyzing their preferences, which allows you to identify the most appealing features. You can also use ChatGPT to analyze market research data and generate detailed user personas.

These detailed profiles of your ideal customers can guide your user testing by ensuring you recruit participants who accurately represent your target audience. This allows you to develop a comprehensive set of user testing questions that target specific aspects of your product concept and user experience. This ensures you gather valuable data during the testing phase.

Marketing and Launch

The final stretch is bringing your product to market. As you prepare for launch, ChatGPT can assist in crafting a compelling marketing strategy. Don't settle for generic marketing messages; use ChatGPT's ability to understand user needs and generate persuasive language to create targeted marketing copy that resonates with your audience.

To do this, you need to provide it with your target audience demographics, online behavior, and product information to recognize the most effective marketing channels for reaching your ideal customers. It can also generate creative social media post ideas, captions, and even hashtags tailored to your target audience for maximum reach.

Why AI Is Important in Identifying Unmet Customer Needs

Understanding your customers' needs is paramount. However, traditional methods of customer feedback, like surveys and focus groups, can be limited. This is where AI steps in to help identify unmet customer needs you might have otherwise missed.

Customers don't always explicitly state their needs, especially negative ones. AI, particularly tools like sentiment analysis, can analyze customer data to pick out underlying frustrations and desires, even if they are not directly expressed. Traditional feedback methods often attract a specific demographic or those with strong opinions. AI can analyze data from a wider range of sources and reveal needs from diverse customer segments you might not have reached.

Social media platforms are a gold mine for customer sentiment. AI can help analyze the tone of social media posts and comments to sieve through positive and negative sentiments toward your brand, products, or services. Negative sentiment often highlights areas where customer needs are not being met.

Understanding your customers' needs allows you to develop products and services that directly address their pain points and desires, which eventually improve customer satisfaction and loyalty. Being at the forefront of customer needs allows you to differentiate yourself from competitors and capture a larger market share.

Enhancing Design with AI Insights

Before technology, design relied heavily on human creativity and intuition. While this approach has produced countless successful products and experiences, AI helps to enhance the design process. Let's look at how AI simulates and tests design concepts.

Step 1: Feeding the Machine

The first step involves equipping your AI tool with the necessary knowledge. This includes:

- **Design Concepts:** Provide high-fidelity mockups or detailed descriptions of the design concepts you plan to test.
- **Target Audience Data:** The more AI knows about your target user base, the better. Share demographics, online behavior patterns, and any relevant psychological insights about your audience.
- **Competitor Analysis:** Give AI a glimpse into the competitive landscape. Share information about existing products or similar designs to help it understand the context and identify potential differentiators for your concept.

Step 2: AI in Action

Once fed with this information, AI steps into action.

- **Simulating User Behavior:** AI tools can use advanced algorithms to create virtual users that interact with your design concepts. These simulations mimic real-world user behavior, allowing you to observe how users navigate the design, sort out areas of confusion, and assess overall usability.
- **Data-Driven Analysis:** AI doesn't just simulate; it analyzes. It tracks user interactions, clicks, time spent on specific elements, and even eye movements to spot patterns and areas of strength or weakness in your design.
- **A/B Testing on Steroids:** Imagine testing multiple variations of your design concept simultaneously. AI can facilitate A/B testing so you can compare different design elements and pick the version that performs best with your target audience.

Step 3: Human and Machine Synergy

As much as AI provides invaluable data and insights, it cannot replace human intuition. Here's how it happens:

- **Interpreting the Results:** AI-generated data requires human interpretation. Designers and marketing professionals will use their expertise to analyze the data and identify and make informed decisions about refining their design concepts based on AI's feedback.

- **Refining the Design:** With AI insights, you can choose concepts, address usability issues, optimize user experience, and create a design that fits with the target audience.

How to Use ChatGPT for Product Design

Using ChatGPT for product design can ease the design process and enhance creativity. Here's how you can use it for various aspects of product design:

Finding Feature-Specific Inspiration

ChatGPT can help generate ideas for specific features of your product. Describe the functionality or purpose you are looking for, and it will provide you with fresh, creative ideas. For example, if you are designing a new mobile app and need ideas for a unique onboarding process, you can describe the app's target audience, goals, and desired user experience to ChatGPT, and it will suggest new onboarding approaches.

Creating Feature Flow

A smooth feature flow is important for a positive user experience. ChatGPT can assist in designing the flow of features within your product. You can describe the user journey, interactions, and desired outcomes, and it will help map out the feature flow. For instance, if you are designing an e-commerce website and want to optimize the checkout process, you can describe the current flow and ask ChatGPT for suggestions on how to simplify and improve it.

Explaining Complex Terms

Great design often involves effectively communicating complex ideas to users. ChatGPT can simplify complex terms and concepts related to product design. If you are discussing technical details with stakeholders or team members who may not be familiar with design terminology, it can help you explain these concepts in plain language. For example, if you need to explain the concept of "user persona" to a non-designer, you can ask ChatGPT to provide a simple explanation that anyone can understand.

Understanding User Requirements

Understanding your target audience is the foundation of successful product design. ChatGPT can help designers understand user requirements by generating responses based on user input. By interacting with ChatGPT, you can gather insights into user preferences, frustrations, and expectations, which can inform the design process. For example, you can ask ChatGPT questions like, "What features would you like to see in a new smartphone?" or "How do you envision using this product in your daily life?" to gather user feedback.

Discovering Tools and Websites

The design world is a large ecosystem. ChatGPT can help you navigate it by discovering new tools and websites related to product design. You can ask ChatGPT for recommendations and help you find tools for prototyping, 3D modeling, graphic design, and other aspects of product design. Designers can ask ChatGPT, "Can you suggest any websites for finding inspiration for product design?" or "What tools do you recommend for creating interactive prototypes?"

Creating Better Prompts for AI Image Generators

AI image generators are becoming increasingly popular in the design process. Vague prompts lead to vague results. Use ChatGPT to refine your descriptions for AI image generators. It helps you create better prompts for AI image generators.

So, provide detailed information about color palettes, layouts, user interface elements, and overall design aesthetic to get the most out of your AI-generated visuals. Don't settle for the first version. Use the ChatGPT Plus subscription to analyze the AI-generated images and suggest refinements. Ask it to generate variations based on specific feedback, allowing you to explore different design directions and arrive at the optimal concept.

Create Design System Documentation

ChatGPT can assist in creating design system documentation, which includes guidelines, principles, and components used in a design project. You can ask ChatGPT to generate descriptions, explanations, or examples for design components, layouts, color schemes, typography, and more. If you are worried about inconsistencies creeping into your design system, ChatGPT can analyze your existing documentation and pick up any discrepancies to ensure your design language remains uniform across all projects.

Get Ideas for Design-Related Tasks

If you ever feel stuck, ChatGPT can be a valuable resource for generating ideas for design projects. By describing your project requirements or goals, you can suggest design concepts, layouts, color schemes, and visual styles. You can also use it to brainstorm creative solutions for specific design challenges or to explore new design directions.

Ask ChatGPT How It May Help You

Don't underestimate the power of a simple question. If you are unsure about the best approach for a specific design element, ask ChatGPT. It will provide insights and recommendations based on established design principles. It can also analyze your ideas and suggest potential solutions or any limitations to consider. Whether you are looking for design inspiration, advice on design tools and techniques, or tips on improving your design workflow, ChatGPT can offer great assistance.

Upskill

ChatGPT can be your design coach, helping you to expand your design skill set. Ask ChatGPT to explain specific design trends, software functionalities, or design principles that you don't understand. You can ask for learning resources, tutorials, or examples to improve your understanding of design concepts and practices. For example, you can ask for recommendations on books, courses, or workshops to expand your design expertise. This can help you stay updated with the latest developments in the field of design and enhance your design skills.

Prompts for Product Development

Here are some simple ChatGPT prompts you can use to guide your design process:

- Can you suggest innovative features for a fitness-tracking app aimed at improving user engagement?
- What are some design trends in e-commerce websites that can enhance the shopping experience?
- How can we improve the user interface of our mobile banking app to make it more intuitive for customers?
- Can you provide ideas for eco-friendly packaging designs for a new line of skincare products?
- What are some ways to incorporate gamification into a productivity app to motivate users?
- How can we redesign our website to increase conversion rates for our online store?

- Can you suggest improvements to the user onboarding process for a social networking app?
- What are some effective strategies for creating a cohesive brand identity across different products and platforms?
- How can we design a more user-friendly interface for our smart home device?
- What are the key elements to consider when designing a mobile game for a specific target audience?
- Can you provide examples of successful product launches and the strategies they used for market penetration?
- How can we use storytelling in our product packaging to create a stronger emotional connection with customers?
- What are some best practices for designing a mobile app that caters to users with accessibility needs?
- Can you suggest ways to incorporate user feedback into the iterative design process for a software application?
- What are some cost-effective materials and manufacturing methods for prototyping a new consumer electronics device?
- How can we optimize the user interface of our website for better performance on mobile devices?
- Can you provide examples of successful rebranding efforts and the impact they had on customer perception?
- What are some emerging technologies that could disrupt the market, and how can we prepare for them in our product development?

- How can we use data analytics to inform our product design decisions and improve user engagement?
- Can you suggest strategies for creating a seamless omnichannel experience for customers interacting with our brand across different platforms?

Wrap-Up

The role of AI and ChatGPT in product development and design cannot be overstated. These technologies can help streamline the ideation process and improve and enhance user-centric designs for market success. As businesses continue to use AI in their product development efforts, we can expect to see a wave of inventions that will reshape industries.

The efficiencies gained in product development can be amplified by improving how teams collaborate and manage projects using AI tools. Businesses can ensure that the ideas generated during the ideation phase are brought to market efficiently by enhancing team collaboration. In the next chapter, we will discuss the role of AI in team collaboration and project management. We will discuss how AI tools can improve communication, task management, and productivity.

9. Team Collaboration and Project Management

Team collaboration and project management are important for business success. Teams are becoming more diverse and distributed, and the need for solutions to enhance collaboration and optimize project workflows has never been greater.

As businesses strive to float, more and more are turning to artificial intelligence (AI) to optimize their team's performance and project outcomes. A recent survey by beautiful.ai indicates that 95% of managers already utilize AI tools to heighten productivity levels within their teams. This shows how important AI tools are and will be in a few years to come.

However, we will explore how AI and ChatGPT can help improve team collaboration and optimize project management processes. From streamlining workflows to improving communication and ensuring projects are completed efficiently and effectively, these tools are helping teams work together to achieve their goals.

AI's Role in Facilitating Team Collaboration

Building strong teams requires more than just individual skills —it demands effective communication, collaboration, and cohesion. However, achieving this can be challenging, especially in diverse or remote teams. ChatGPT can help teams overcome communication barriers by providing real-time language translation to enable seamless interaction among team members who speak different languages. This capability promotes inclusivity and ensures that everyone's voice is heard, regardless of their linguistic background.

ChatGPT also enhances remote collaboration by acting as a virtual meeting assistant. It can help generate agendas and even provide summaries, making it easier for team members to collaborate effectively across different time zones and locations. Decision-making becomes easier with AI tools. It can improve the decision-making process within teams by analyzing data, providing useful information, and offering recommendations. This enables teams to make informed decisions on time, leading to more efficient workflows and better outcomes.

They say, "Knowledge is power." AI tools can help in facilitating knowledge sharing by acting as a repository of information. Team members can ask ChatGPT for information on specific topics or processes, helping to disseminate knowledge and best practices across the team.

Benefits of AI-Powered Collaboration Tools

The way we work is constantly changing, and collaboration is more important than ever before. However, old methods of teamwork can be hindered by communication barriers, geographical separation, and repetitive tasks. AI-powered collaboration tools offer many benefits to improve the ideation process, help team members, and promote creativity. Here are some benefits:

Boosting the Ideation Process with AI Generation

AI tools are great for sparking new ideas and overcoming creative roadblocks. It can generate variations on existing concepts or even create visual prototypes based on preliminary ideas. This infuses fresh perspectives into the process, encouraging teams to think outside the box and explore new possibilities. For instance, AI can generate basic wireframes for web applications, create rough drafts of marketing copy, or even develop simple 3D models based on team descriptions. This allows teams to test and refine concepts without needing extensive technical expertise, leading to faster decision-making.

Empowering Team Members through Automation

Many collaboration tools incorporate AI-powered automation features that can handle repetitive tasks such as scheduling meetings, taking notes, generating reports, or managing data. It allows time for team members to focus on higher-level cognitive tasks like strategic planning, creative problem-solving, and building strong relationships with colleagues. AI can also analyze team communication patterns and identify areas where individual members might benefit from additional training or skill development. This allows for personalized learning recommendations to ensure that each team member is equipped with the necessary skills and knowledge to contribute effectively.

Enhancing Engagement and Fostering Creativity

AI tools can analyze communication patterns and sieve out potential conflicts or areas of tension within a team for early intervention and proactive measures to address issues before they escalate. It can analyze communication styles and tailor its interactions as required. This can be particularly helpful for managing remote teams or working with individuals from diverse backgrounds. Certain AI tools can incorporate gamification elements into the collaboration process to make tasks more engaging and encourage friendly competition among team members.

Reducing Time Wasting

Misunderstandings and a lack of clarity can waste significant time in team settings. AI tools can translate languages and summarize complex information into clear takeaways. This ensures everyone is on the same page, eliminates the need for repetitive clarification requests, and allows for a smoother communication flow. It can also be used to automate the creation and assignment of action items following meetings or discussions.

This provides a clear record of the next steps, removes the ambiguity of "who's responsible for what," and allows for easy tracking of progress. With clear ownership and automated reminders, your team members can hold each other accountable.

Providing Clarity on Next Steps

AI-powered project management tools can provide daily insights into project progress, identify potential roadblocks, and suggest alternative courses of action. This allows for proactive decision-making and ensures that teams are always aware of the necessary steps and adjustments. It can also analyze meeting recordings or transcripts and generate summaries that highlight key decisions, action items, and deadlines to ensure everyone has a clear understanding of the next steps and eliminate the need for lengthy recap emails or follow-up meetings. With clear and concise summaries, teams can quickly get back to work without wasting time trying to piece together the details of previous discussions.

Strengthening Human Skills

Some AI tools can analyze team communication patterns and check for areas where individual members might benefit from additional training or skill development. This allows for the creation of personalized learning pathways, ensuring that everyone on the team continues to develop their skills and contribute to their full potential. It can also suggest targeted resources, helping your team become better collaborators.

Also, by automating repetitive tasks, AI frees up brainpower for teams to focus on higher-level tasks that involve creative problem-solving and developing solutions. You no longer spend hours on administrative tasks but can dedicate that time to developing long-term plans.

Balancing Workloads and Working Hours

With AI tools, you can analyze team skill sets, workload capacity, and project deadlines. This allows for intelligent task distribution so that tasks are assigned to the most suitable team member based on their expertise and current workload. This optimizes project outcomes and prevents situations where certain individuals are overloaded while others are underutilized.

It can use historical data and project requirements to predict potential workload bottlenecks to allow for proactive workload management, enabling teams to adjust project timelines, delegate tasks strategically, or even use opportunities for automation to prevent burnout.

Promoting Independence and Confidence

You can use AI tools to analyze team communication patterns and look out for areas where individual members might benefit from additional training or skill development. These insights can be used to curate personalized learning recommendations, which help you focus on areas that will enhance your skills and contribute more effectively to the team. AI tools that act as virtual mentors can give feedback on tasks, suggest best practices, and give guidance on overcoming challenges. This support helps you tackle tasks independently, promoting a sense of self-reliance and boosting confidence in your abilities.

ChatGPT Prompts for Team Collaboration

Here are twenty ChatGPT prompts you can try as a team to improve collaboration and communication patterns:

- **Brainstorming Boost**: We are facing a creative block on (project name). Generate ten unexpected ideas related to (key challenge) to spark a brainstorming session.
- **Meeting Magician**: Craft an engaging agenda for a (meeting type) meeting focused on (meeting objective). Include discussion prompts and icebreaker activities for a geographically dispersed team.
- **Task Delegation Dynamo**: Considering team skill sets and the current workload, suggest an optimal way to distribute tasks for the upcoming (project name) project.
- **Knowledge Navigator**: Our team is working on (topic). Generate a concise summary of the key points and insights from the top three relevant research articles.

- **Action Item Architect**: Based on our meeting discussion, create a clear and actionable list of the next steps with assigned owners and deadlines for each task.
- **Meeting Recap Maestro**: Summarize the key decisions and action items from our recent meeting on (topic) in a clear and concise format for easy reference. (Provide ChatGPT with the details of the meeting.)
- **Conflict Calmer**: Two team members seem to have differing viewpoints on (issue). Generate a list of open-ended questions to facilitate a productive and respectful discussion.
- **Feedback Facilitator**: We are conducting peer reviews for (project type). Craft a set of unbiased questions to guide team members in providing constructive and actionable feedback.
- **Icebreaker Improviser**: The team is feeling a bit disconnected working remotely. Suggest a fun and engaging virtual icebreaker activity to promote team bonding.
- **Presentation Polisher**: We are finalizing a presentation for (audience). Analyze the content and suggest improvements for clarity, flow, and audience engagement. (Provide ChatGPT with the content.)
- **Diversity and Inclusion Detective:** Review our current team communication style and identify potential areas where we can improve inclusivity for diverse team members. (Provide ChatGPT with details on the communication style.)

- **Meeting Minutes Marvel**: "Based on the audio recording of our meeting, generate a comprehensive set of meeting minutes with timestamps for key points.
- **Gamification Guru**: We are looking for ways to make our weekly team meetings more engaging. Suggest a gamified approach that incentivizes participation and knowledge sharing.
- **Brainstorming Buddy**: We need to develop a marketing strategy for (product/service). Generate a mind map outlining potential target audiences, messaging ideas, and promotional channels.
- **Decision-Making Dynamo**: The team is divided (decision point). Analyze the pros and cons of each option based on available data and suggest a data-driven approach to reach a consensus.
- **Project Planner Pro**: Outline a detailed project plan for (project name), including milestones, deadlines, resource allocation, and potential risk factors.
- **Meeting Mood Meter**: Analyze the sentiment of our last team meeting based on transcripts. Identify areas for improvement in fostering a positive and collaborative atmosphere.
- **Knowledge Repository**: Create a searchable knowledge base for our team, summarizing key takeaways from past projects, best practices documents, and frequently asked questions.
- **Meeting Role Randomizer**: We typically have the same team members take on specific roles in meetings. Randomly assign roles (facilitator, timekeeper, and

notetaker) for the next meeting to encourage
participation from all members.

- **Teamwork Translator**: Our team includes members
from different cultural backgrounds. Help us identify
potential communication gaps and suggest strategies
for effective cross-cultural collaboration.

Using AI for Project Management Optimization

Project management is a delicate dance—juggling tasks,
resources, and deadlines while keeping everything on track.
However, with artificial intelligence (AI), you can optimize
every stage of the project lifecycle, from planning and execution to monitoring and completion. Here's how AI helps in
project management:

- **Planning with Foresight:** No more endless
spreadsheets and manual calculations. AI can analyze
historical project data, including task durations,
resource dependencies, and potential roadblocks. This
allows it to generate intelligent and realistic project
schedules to help you start your project on the right
foot.
- **Resource Allocation Redefined:** You no longer need to
do guesswork about who should be assigned to which
task. AI takes your team's strengths, skills, and current
workloads into account to make optimal resource
allocation. The right person gets the right job at the
right time, every time.

- **Risk Management on Autopilot:** Project risks are like uninvited guests at a party—they can derail everything. AI acts as your security guard to analyze past project data and predict potential risks before they crash the party. It will then suggest preventative measures and contingency plans to be prepared for the unexpected.

- **Automating the Mundane:** Let AI handle the repetitive tasks that bog down your team, like automatic progress reports, scheduling meetings, and data entry. This task automation allows your team to have valuable time and mental space for more strategic work and to focus on what truly matters.

- **Real-Time Progress Tracking:** Gone are the days of scrambling for updates. AI provides live project monitoring, gathering data from various sources and presenting a clear picture of your project's progress. It does this by analyzing your data in real-time, spotting risks and roadblocks before they become disasters, and then predicting future issues based on past projects and current trends for proactive solutions. Tools like Otus can give off alerts to warn of potential problems, while ChatGPT helps generate reports and suggest solutions to keep everyone informed.

- **Predictive Power for Course Correction:** AI is your proactive partner. It processes progress data and singles out potential deviations from the plan. Before minor issues creep into major problems, it will suggest course corrections or resource adjustments so your project stays on track.

- **Communication and Collaboration on Steroids:** Communication breakdowns can cripple a project. Different AI tools can step in as your communication facilitator, automatically generating status reports with ChatGPT, distributing task updates with Trello, and translating languages with EdApp. This promotes collaboration within your team and ensures that everyone is on the same page all the time.
- **Data-Driven Decisions, Every Time:** Stop relying on gut feelings. AI helps you make informed decisions accurately and effectively with its data-driven insights. Real-time data and project performance metrics will help guide your choices for better outcomes.
- **Reduced Costs and Boosted Efficiency:** Optimizing resource allocation, automating mundane tasks, and minimizing rework through risk mitigation—these all add up to one thing: reduced project costs. This translates to increased efficiency across the board and a significant productivity boost for your team.

ChatGPT Prompts for Project Management

Here are a few ChatGPT prompts to boost project management:

- **Project Kickoff Canvas:** We are kicking off a new project called (project name). Generate a comprehensive project charter outlining goals, stakeholders, deadlines, and success metrics.

- **WBS Wizard**: Help us create a detailed Work Breakdown Structure (WBS) for (project name), breaking down the project into manageable tasks and subtasks.
- **Schedule Sensei**: Based on task dependencies and resource availability, create a realistic project schedule using Gantt chart format, highlighting critical paths and potential milestones.
- **Risk Radar**: Identify the top five potential risks associated with (project name) and suggest corresponding mitigation strategies for each.
- **Budget Blueprint**: Develop a comprehensive project budget outlining estimated costs for labor, materials, and any potential contingencies.
- **Communication Calendar Composer**: Craft a communication plan for (project name) that outlines communication channels, frequency, and key information to be shared with stakeholders.
- **Meeting**: Generate an engaging agenda for a project kickoff meeting, including introductions, project overview, and opportunities for team members to ask questions.
- **Meeting Minutes**: Summarize the key decisions, action items, and next steps from our recent project meeting on (topic) in a clear and concise format for easy reference.
- **Progress Tracker Pro**: Provide tips to design a user-friendly dashboard to track project progress visually, including key metrics like task completion rates, budget

adherence, and deadline milestones. (Use ChatGPT premium.)

- **Collaboration Catalyst**: The team seems to be struggling with collaboration on a specific task. Suggest strategies and tools to improve communication and information sharing within the team.
- **Issue Identifier**: Analyze project data and identify potential roadblocks or areas where the project is falling behind schedule.
- **Change Management Champion**: We need to communicate a significant change to the project scope with stakeholders. Craft a clear and concise message that outlines the rationale for the change and its impact on the project.
- **Meeting Energizer**: The team's energy seems low during project meetings. Engaging activities or icebreakers are recommended to boost morale and participation.
- **Lessons Learned Log**: Help us capture key takeaways and lessons learned from (project name) to inform future project management decisions.
- **Risk Re-Assessment Radar**: The project has progressed significantly since the initial risk assessment. Re-evaluate potential risks and adjust mitigation strategies accordingly.
- **Budget Variance Analyst**: Project costs are exceeding the original budget. Analyze the reasons for the variance and suggest cost-saving measures to stay within budget.

- **Stakeholder Satisfaction Surveyor**: Develop a survey to collect feedback from stakeholders on their satisfaction with the project's progress and communication.
- **Project Post-Mortem Mastermind**: Facilitate a team discussion to analyze the successes and challenges of (project name). Identify areas for improvement for future projects.
- **Teamwork Trainer**: The project team is encountering communication challenges due to cultural differences. Recommend strategies and resources to foster a more inclusive and collaborative team environment.

Wrap-Up

While AI offers tremendous benefits for team collaboration and project management, it is important to acknowledge the ethical and privacy concerns that come with its implementation. Businesses are embracing AI technologies to improve productivity and efficiency, but they must also be aware of ethical considerations surrounding data privacy, algorithm bias, and transparency. The next chapter will look into these critical issues, guiding ethical AI use and data protection. Addressing these concerns will help to ensure that AI initiatives align with ethical principles and respect the rights and privacy of individuals.

10. Ethics, Privacy, and the Future

As AI becomes a staple in business, 90% of shoppers believe retailers should be required to openly disclose how they use customer data in applying AI usage (TalkDesk Stats). This striking statement gives a glimpse into a growing awareness and concern among consumers regarding the ethical implications of AI integration in business operations. AI technologies, especially ChatGPT, are becoming increasingly popular, and businesses need to understand the principles of ethics and privacy.

Businesses that continue to use AI in their daily operations must answer questions of transparency, fairness, and accountability. How should AI algorithms be trained and deployed to minimize bias and discrimination? What measures should be put in place to protect consumer privacy and data security in an increasingly connected world? These are just a few of the pressing ethical considerations that businesses must address as they leverage AI technology.

Also, staying abreast of future ethical directions and regulatory expectations is important to maintain trust and credibility with consumers and stakeholders. This chapter will confront the ethical dilemmas and privacy challenges posed by the integration of AI and ChatGPT in business operations. It will equip you with the knowledge and tools needed to implement AI solutions responsibly, safeguard data privacy, and adhere to ethical standards.

Understanding Ethical Considerations

AI offers much potential for improving efficiency and decision-making in the workplace; however, its implementation raises critical questions about responsible and ethical use. Ethical AI goes beyond simply complying with legal regulations. It's about establishing a strong ethical framework that guides the development, deployment, and use of AI within a business. This framework centers around core values that ensure AI benefits society and avoids causing harm. Here's a breakdown of some key ethical considerations for businesses:

- **Nondiscrimination:** AI algorithms can perpetuate biases present in the data they are trained on. This can lead to discriminatory outcomes in areas like hiring, loan approvals, or even facial recognition software. Businesses must ensure their AI is developed and used in a way that treats everyone fairly and avoids perpetuating existing societal inequalities.

- **Privacy:** AI systems often rely on data, raising concerns about user privacy. Businesses must be transparent about how they collect, store, and use customer data. They also need safeguards in place to prevent unauthorized access or misuse of personal information.

- **Individual Rights:** The increasing use of AI in decision-making processes can raise concerns about individual rights. For instance, AI-powered hiring algorithms could unfairly disadvantage certain candidates. Businesses need to ensure individuals have the right to understand how AI is being used to make decisions about them and have avenues to appeal or rectify any potential biases.

- **Nonmanipulation:** AI can be used for manipulative purposes, such as creating deepfakes or crafting targeted advertising that exploits user vulnerabilities. Businesses must ensure their AI is used responsibly and ethically, avoiding practices that deceive or manipulate consumers.

Why Prioritize Ethical AI?

Why prioritizing ethical AI goes beyond just being the "right thing to do":

- **Reduces Risk:** Unethical AI practices can lead to legal repercussions, reputational damage, and consumer backlash. Businesses that proactively address ethical considerations can mitigate these risks.

- **Builds Trust:** Consumers are increasingly concerned about how their data is used. You can build trust with customers, employees, and stakeholders by demonstrating a commitment to ethical AI practices. This promotes a positive brand image and leads to a competitive advantage.
- **Sustainable Growth:** Long-term success hinges on responsible AI development and use. Ethical AI ensures that AI technology benefits all of society, not just a select few, and that it aligns with positive societal values, contributing to a responsible and ethical future.

How to Operationalize Data and AI Ethics

Operationalizing data and AI ethics requires a multi-faceted approach that goes beyond having good intentions. Here's a breakdown of key steps to translate ethical principles into concrete actions within your organization:

Establish a Strong Foundation

The AI framework should clearly outline your organization's values and principles regarding data and AI use. It should address issues like fairness, transparency, accountability, and privacy. Organize training sessions and workshops to educate employees about ethical considerations surrounding data and AI. This builds a culture of ethical responsibility and helps employees flag potential issues.

Integrate Ethics into the AI Lifecycle

Clearly define the purpose of data collection, ensure user consent, and establish procedures for data anonymization and security. You should also scrutinize the data used to train AI models to mitigate potential biases while employing techniques like fairness checks and bias mitigation algorithms to ensure fair and nondiscriminatory outcomes. Continuously monitor the performance of deployed AI models to detect and address any unintended consequences or biases that may occur over time.

Promote Transparency and Accountability

Whenever possible, strive to develop AI models that are explainable and interpretable. This allows humans to understand how the AI arrives at its decisions and potential biases. Also, consider offering users the right to request an explanation for AI-driven decisions that impact them to promote trust and allow for potential redress if an AI decision seems unfair. Regular auditing and reporting are also important; conduct regular audits to assess your organization's adherence to ethical AI principles and develop clear reporting mechanisms to communicate ethical considerations and potential risks to stakeholders.

Embrace Continuous Improvement

The regulatory landscape surrounding AI is changing every day. You should stay up-to-date on new regulations, adapt your practices accordingly, and encourage open communication within your organization about ethical concerns related to data and AI. Provide clear channels for employees to report potential issues without fear of reprisal and actively participate in industry discussions while collaborating with other organizations to share best practices and learn from each other's experiences in operationalizing data and AI ethics.

Common Ethical Concerns Related to AI

Here are common ethical concerns businesses should look for when using AI:

Unjustified Actions

One of the primary ethical concerns with AI is the potential for unjustified actions or decisions. AI systems, particularly those based on machine learning algorithms, make decisions based on patterns in data. However, these decisions may not always align with ethical or moral principles. For example, an AI-powered recruitment system may mistakenly discriminate against certain demographics, leading to unfair hiring practices. Unjustified actions can also arise when AI systems lack proper oversight or fail to consider the broader societal implications of their decisions.

Opacity

Opacity refers to the lack of transparency and explainability in AI systems. Many AI algorithms operate as "black boxes," meaning that their decision-making processes are not easily understandable or explainable to humans. This lack of transparency can lead to distrust and uncertainty, especially when AI systems are used in critical applications such as healthcare or criminal justice. Without transparency, it's challenging to address biases or errors in AI systems, potentially causing unintended consequences or harm.

Bias

Bias in AI systems occurs when the algorithms produce results that systematically favor or disadvantage certain groups of people. It can arise from various sources, including biased training data, flawed algorithms, or unintentional biases in the design or implementation of AI systems. If historical data used to train a predictive policing algorithm reflects existing biases in law enforcement practices, the algorithm may perpetuate or even exacerbate these biases. Bias in AI systems can lead to unfair treatment, discrimination, and social inequality.

Discrimination

Discrimination is the risk of AI systems exhibiting bias or making decisions that disproportionately impact certain individuals or groups based on factors such as race, gender, age, or socioeconomic status. This bias can arise from prejudiced training data or unintended correlations in the data. Discriminatory AI systems can perpetuate or worsen existing societal inequalities and injustices.

To address this concern, it is important to implement measures to mitigate bias in AI systems. This includes using diverse and representative training data, conducting bias assessments and audits, and developing fairness-aware algorithms that prioritize equitable outcomes. Also, transparency and accountability mechanisms should be in place to ensure that AI decisions are explainable and auditable.

Autonomy

The increasing autonomy of AI systems raises ethical concerns regarding accountability, responsibility, and control. As AI systems become more autonomous and capable of making decisions without human intervention, questions arise about who should be held accountable for the actions and decisions of these systems. There is also concern about the potential loss of human agency and control over AI systems, especially in critical domains such as healthcare, criminal justice, and autonomous vehicles.

To address these concerns, there is a need to establish clear lines of accountability and responsibility for AI systems. This includes defining the roles and responsibilities of developers, operators, and users of AI systems and establishing mechanisms for oversight, transparency, and recourse in case of errors or failures. Also, human oversight and intervention should be incorporated into AI systems to ensure that they operate within ethical and legal boundaries.

Informational Privacy and Group Privacy

Informational privacy refers to the right of individuals to control their data and how it is collected, used, and shared by AI systems. Ethical concerns arise when AI systems collect and process large amounts of personal data without individuals' consent or awareness, causing privacy breaches, surveillance, and exploitation.

To protect informational and group privacy, businesses must enforce data protection measures and privacy-enhancing technologies. This includes obtaining informed consent from individuals for data collection and processing, implementing data anonymization and encryption techniques to protect sensitive information, and establishing clear data governance policies and procedures. Also, regulatory frameworks such as the General Data Protection Regulation (GDPR) provide guidelines for the responsible use of personal data and impose penalties for noncompliance.

Moral Responsibility and Distributed Responsibility

Another major ethical concern is the allocation of moral responsibility for the actions of AI systems. As AI becomes more independent, questions regarding who should be held accountable for the decisions and actions of AI systems should be discussed. This concept of "distributed responsibility" challenges traditional notions of accountability and raises questions about the ethical implications of AI systems acting independently of human control.

Automation Bias

Automation bias refers to the tendency of individuals to favor information or decisions made by automated systems, even when they conflict with their judgment or expertise. This can lead to over-reliance on AI systems, causing errors or ethical issues. Addressing automation bias requires careful consideration of how AI systems are designed and implemented to ensure that they augment human decision-making rather than replace it entirely.

Safety and Resilience

Safety and resilience are important ethical concerns in high-stakes domains such as healthcare, autonomous vehicles, and finance. Ensuring the safety of AI systems involves designing rugged systems that can detect and recover from errors or unexpected situations. Also, ethical considerations around safety include minimizing the potential harm caused by AI systems and ensuring that they do not pose a risk to individuals or society.

Ethical Auditing

Ethical auditing involves assessing the ethical implications of AI systems throughout their lifecycle. This includes evaluating the design, development, deployment, and use of AI systems to ensure that they align with ethical principles and values. Ethical auditing helps point out and mitigate potential ethical risks associated with AI systems and ensures that they are used in a responsible and ethical manner.

Addressing Privacy Concerns in AI

The use of AI presents significant privacy implications due to its remarkable capacity to analyze data. AI algorithms process data from various sources, including personal information, and infer sensitive information about individuals, such as their location, preferences, habits, and even health status. For instance, AI systems can analyze browsing history, social media activity, and online purchases to make predictions about an individual's interests, behavior, and lifestyle. This capability raises concerns about the privacy of personal data and the potential for unauthorized access or misuse.

The use of AI increases the risk of unauthorized data distribution, where sensitive information is shared or accessed without consent. AI systems may disclose personal data through data breaches, hacking attacks, or unauthorized access by third parties. This can lead to privacy violations, identity theft, and other forms of harm to individuals. It can also manipulate personal data to create detailed profiles of individuals, increasing the risk of theft and fraud. Cybercriminals can use AI to automate the process of gathering and analyzing personal information, making it easier to impersonate individuals or access their accounts. This poses a significant threat to individuals' privacy and security.

Also, AI-powered surveillance systems can monitor individuals' activities in public spaces, workplaces, and online environments, leading to increased scrutiny and violations of privacy rights. Moreover, the deployment of facial recognition technology and other biometric identification systems raises concerns about mass surveillance and the reduction in privacy.

Best Practices for Data Privacy When Using AI

As the use of AI continues to become prevalent among industries, ensuring data privacy remains an important aspect of its use. However, here's a breakdown of best practices for data governance when implementing AI solutions:

Understanding AI Laws and Regulation

Research and understand relevant regional and national data privacy regulations, such as GDPR (General Data Protection Regulation) and CCPA (California Consumer Privacy Act). These regulations outline guidelines for data collection, storage, usage, and user consent. Familiarize yourself with relevant regulations applicable to your location and industry. Consult with legal professionals specializing in data privacy to ensure your AI practices comply with current regulations. They can advise on specific steps to take to mitigate legal risks.

Establishing a Data Governance Framework

Develop a clear framework outlining data collection practices for AI applications. This includes obtaining informed user consent, minimizing data collection to vital elements, and adhering to data minimization principles. Whenever possible, anonymize data to protect individual identities. Use techniques like differential privacy that use only the minimum data points necessary for AI functionality.

Make privacy concerns important and implement cybersecurity protocols to safeguard sensitive data. This includes encryption techniques, access controls, and regular security audits. You also need to define your data retention policies, outlining how long data is stored and the procedures for secure disposal after its designated purpose is fulfilled.

Assessing Ethical Implications

Thoroughly assess the ethical implications of AI technologies before deployment. Consider potential biases in the training data and how the AI might affect individuals or groups. You should also integrate diverse perspectives into the development process. This includes ethicists, lawyers, and individuals from varied backgrounds to ensure inclusive AI development.

Providing Transparency and Awareness

Be transparent about how user data is collected, used, and shared for AI applications, and give clear and accessible privacy policies that users can understand. You should also offer users control over their data by providing the right to access, rectify, or erase their data upon request.

Conduct a Privacy Impact Assessment (PIA)

Before deploying any AI system, a privacy impact assessment (PIA) is essential. This approach helps pinpoint likely privacy risks. A PIA involves identifying all the data points collected, how they are used by the AI system, and with whom they might be shared, analyzing the risks associated with each data point, and formulating strategies to minimize the impact of each specified risk. This might involve anonymization techniques, data minimization practices, or enforcing security measures.

Implement Data Retention and Minimization Policies

Data collection for AI applications should be a targeted exercise. The principle of data minimization dictates that only the data essential for the AI's functionality should be collected. Avoid collecting extraneous information that doesn't directly contribute to the AI's purpose. Establish clear guidelines on how long data is stored. Once the data has fulfilled its purpose for the AI system, it should be securely disposed of following established protocols.

Introduce Robust Data Security Measures

Since AI systems often handle sensitive data, cybersecurity measures are paramount. Implement encryption techniques to protect data at rest and in transit, reducing the risk of unauthorized access in the event of a breach. You also need to establish clear access control protocols, granting access to data only to authorized personnel who require it for their specific roles.

Conduct regular security audits to check for vulnerabilities in your systems and execute necessary security patches promptly.

Develop a Breach Response Plan

Despite the best precautions, data breaches can still occur. Having a well-defined breach response plan in place helps you deal with such situations better. You should start by establishing procedures for promptly detecting a data breach and reporting it to the relevant authorities and affected individuals, as mandated by law. Develop strategies to contain the breach, minimize damage, and remediate the vulnerability that led to the incident, and define a clear communication strategy for informing affected individuals and stakeholders about the breach, its impact, and the steps being taken to address it.

Guidelines for Responsible AI Implementation

The use of AI goes hand-in-hand with a great responsibility: ensuring its ethical and responsible use. This guide provides a roadmap for businesses to understand AI ethical implementation, promote trust, and achieve long-term success.

Anchoring AI in Ethical Values

A strong ethical framework is the cornerstone of responsible AI. Here's how to establish one:

- **Identify Core Values:** Define the core values that will guide your organization's AI development and use.

These values should reflect your commitment to fairness, transparency, privacy, and accountability. Examples include nondiscrimination, data security, and human oversight.

- **Develop AI Principles:** Translate your core values into specific AI principles. This could include ensuring unbiased decision-making, respecting user privacy, and maintaining human control over AI systems.
- **Embed AI Principles in Culture:** Integrate your AI principles into your company culture. Educate employees about ethical AI practices and create an environment where responsible AI development is championed.

Establishing Accountability through Structure

Clear lines of responsibility are important for ethical AI. Here's how to achieve that:

- **Form an AI Governance Board:** Create a dedicated body responsible for overseeing the ethical development and deployment of AI within your organization. This board should include representatives from various departments (engineering, legal, ethics, etc.) for a well-rounded perspective.
- **Define Roles and Responsibilities:** Clearly define roles and responsibilities for all stakeholders involved in AI development and use. This includes data scientists, engineers, project managers, and executives.

Everyone should understand their part in maintaining ethical principles.

- **Implement Oversight Mechanisms:** Establish clear oversight mechanisms to monitor AI systems for potential biases, fairness issues, and security vulnerabilities. Regular audits and reporting can help address problems faster.

Mitigating Risk and Building Resilience

AI systems are not without risks. Here's how to curb them:

- **Conduct Bias Audits:** Regularly assess your AI systems for potential biases in the data, algorithms, and decision-making processes. Identify and address any biases found through bias mitigation techniques or data cleansing.
- **Prioritize Data Privacy:** Implement data security measures to protect user privacy and ensure data is collected and used in accordance with ethical guidelines and regulations (refer to data privacy best practices for specifics).
- **Build Explainable AI Systems:** Strive to create AI systems that are transparent and explainable. This allows for human oversight and intervention when necessary. Explainable AI techniques can help understand how AI arrives at decisions.
- **Develop Robust Testing Processes:** Implement thorough testing procedures throughout the AI development lifecycle to recognize and address possible

risks and vulnerabilities before deployment. Testing should include edge cases and real-world scenarios.

Detecting and Remediating Bias

AI systems are susceptible to biases that can lead to unfair or discriminatory outcomes. Here's how to combat them:

- **Identify Biases in Data:** Analyze your data sets for potential biases. Look for imbalances in demographics, historical trends, or how data is collected. Consider using bias detection tools like IBM AI Fairness 360, Microsoft's Fairlearn, and What-If Tool to help identify potential issues.
- **De-bias Training Data:** If biases are found in your training data, take steps to reduce them. This could involve data augmentation (adding data points to underrepresented groups) or data cleansing (removing biased data).
- **Fairness Testing:** Incorporate fairness testing throughout the AI development lifecycle. Test your AI system against diverse datasets to ensure it delivers fair and unbiased results across different demographics.

Ensuring Human Oversight

AI is powerful, but it shouldn't replace human judgment entirely. Here's why human oversight matters:

- **Ethical Decision-Making:** Humans can provide crucial ethical considerations that AI systems may lack. Maintain human oversight for pressing decisions made by AI systems, especially those with more social or legal implications.
- **Accountability and Transparency:** Human oversight ensures clear lines of accountability. If an AI system makes a mistake, it's clear who is responsible for addressing it.
- **Maintaining Control:** Humans should maintain control over AI systems to ensure they are used for their intended purposes and can be deactivated or adjusted if necessary.

Ensuring Transparency and Explainability

Without understanding how AI systems arrive at their decisions, it's difficult to trust them. Here's how to promote transparency:

- **Explainable AI (XAI) Techniques:** Use XAI techniques to make AI decision-making processes more transparent. This allows humans to understand the factors influencing the AI's outputs.
- **Documenting AI Development:** Maintain clear documentation of the AI development process, including data selection, algorithm design, and testing procedures. This transparency builds trust and facilitates future audits.

- **Communicating with Stakeholders:** Communicate how AI systems work to stakeholders, including users, regulators, and the public. Explain the limitations of AI and the safeguards in place to reduce risks.

How to Educate Your Employees Involved in AI Development and Deployment

Integrating AI successfully into your business requires not just technology but also a workforce equipped with the knowledge and skills to use AI responsibly and effectively. Let's look at ways you can educate your employees on the right implementation of AI.

Establishing an AI Usage Policy

Develop a comprehensive AI usage policy that outlines your organization's commitment to ethical AI principles. This policy should cover data privacy, bias mitigation, human oversight, and transparency. You should also communicate the AI usage policy widely throughout your organization. Organize town halls, Q&A sessions, or internal communication campaigns to ensure all employees understand the policy and its implications.

Providing Ethical AI Training

Go beyond traditional lectures. Combine interactive elements like case studies, simulations, and role-playing exercises to make learning engaging and practical. Develop training programs specific to different employee roles. For example, engineers might need in-depth training on bias detection in data sets, while marketing personnel might benefit from understanding how AI can be used ethically in customer interactions. Make this an ongoing process. Integrating AI training modules into existing learning and development programs can help ensure employees stay up-to-date with the latest advancements and best practices.

Building Organizational and Departmental Plans

Appoint AI champions within each department. These champions can act as internal resources, answering questions, providing guidance, and promoting ethical AI practices among their colleagues. Work with each department to create specific plans for integrating AI into their workflows. These plans should consider ethical considerations, potential risks, and solution strategies. Also, cross-departmental collaboration on AI projects should be encouraged. This promotes knowledge sharing and ensures a holistic approach to ethical AI implementation across the organization.

Training Employees on Effective AI Use

Don't just teach the theory behind AI. Train employees on how to use AI tools in their specific roles. This could include data analysis techniques, model interpretation, or responsible AI communication strategies. Encourage employees to ask questions, raise concerns, and report possible ethical issues related to AI while creating a safe space for open dialogue about responsible AI implementation.

Setting Goals and Optimizing

Set clear learning objectives for your AI education programs. This helps measure the effectiveness of your training and specify areas for improvement. Gather feedback from employees, adjust your training strategies based on their needs and the AI landscape, and embrace a culture of continuous improvement in your AI education efforts. As AI technologies and regulations expand, so, too, should your approach to employee training.

Future Trends

AI is constantly growing with daily improvements in its capabilities. Here, we will explore some of the most exciting trends that promise to reshape our interactions with technology and the world around us:

Beyond the Keyboard: The Rise of Voice-Centric AI

Text-based interfaces are becoming a thing of the past. With NLP, expect AI to become more adept at understanding the nuances of human speech, accents, and slang. Seamless voice interactions will become the norm, adjusting how we search for information, control smart devices, and interact with digital assistants. It can act as a personal trainer guiding you through a workout routine with voice commands or a doctor conducting a virtual consultation entirely through voice interaction.

Breaking the Modality Barrier

AI is no longer confined to a single data type—the future is multimodal. AI models are being trained to process information from different sources at the same time. Multimodal AI will create richer and more intuitive user experiences. For example, an AI assistant might use a combination of voice commands, facial recognition, and contextual awareness to predict your needs and offer help.

AI Planners

AI can become your ultimate productivity tool. It will automate more than just repetitive tasks. Expect AI planners to suggest relevant articles to read based on your interests, schedule meetings with the right people, or even book travel arrangements based on your preferences and budget. It will analyze your emails, calendar appointments, and even weather forecasts to suggest the most efficient schedule for your day. AI planners will learn your preferences and adjust schedules to stay on top of your tasks.

The Rise of Autonomous Agents

AI assistants are taking on a life of their own—in a good way. Autonomous AI agents won't just wait for instructions. They will proactively monitor situations, identify potential problems, and suggest solutions before they escalate. This could help in areas like network security or industrial process management. AI agents will be able to navigate a physical environment, interact with objects, and complete tasks independently. This paves the way for robots that can perform tasks in dangerous environments, assist with elderly care, or even provide companionship.

Vector Databases and Embeddings

Behind the scenes, the way AI processes information is under-going a transformation. These databases store information as vectors (multidimensional points) in a high-dimensional space. This allows AI to identify relationships and similarities between data points more subtly. The process of transforming data (text, images, etc.) into vectors is known as embedding. Vector databases and embeddings will play a vital role in enabling AI to perform complex tasks like natural language translation, image recognition, and recommendation systems.

How to Stay Ahead with AI News

The world of AI is a fast-paced one. New developments and breakthroughs seem to arise daily. But fear not, here are some helpful tips to ensure you stay informed and updated on the latest AI news and trends:

Follow the Right Online Resources

Subscribe to newsletters from reputable AI news sources. These newsletters will deliver the latest headlines and information straight to your inbox. You can also check out prominent AI blogs and websites like MIT Technology Review, AI Today, and VentureBeat. These platforms offer in-depth articles, interviews with experts, and analysis of the latest advancements. Join AI-focused groups on LinkedIn, Reddit, or Facebook. These groups promote discussions, allow you to connect with other AI enthusiasts, and provide access to shared resources.

Attend Events and Webinars

Engage yourself in the AI community by attending industry conferences and workshops. These events offer opportunities to learn from leading experts, network with peers, and discover emerging trends firsthand. Many organizations and institutions host free or paid webinars on various AI topics. Take advantage of these online learning opportunities to broaden your knowledge base.

Sharpen Your Skill Set

Enroll in online courses offered by platforms like Coursera, edX, or Udacity. These courses can teach you valuable skills in AI, machine learning, data science, or specific AI applications relevant to your field. Consider intensive coding boot camps to gain hands-on experience with AI tools and libraries. Learning to code will help you understand AI and potentially build your own AI applications.

Network with Peers and Experts

Follow prominent AI researchers, developers, and thought leaders on social media platforms like Twitter or LinkedIn. Engage in discussions, ask questions, and learn from their insights. Look for local AI meetups or events in your area. These gatherings provide a platform to connect with other AI enthusiasts, share knowledge, and collaborate on potential projects.

Experiment and Innovate

The best way to truly understand AI is to get your hands dirty. Explore open-source AI tools and experiment with building your own small-scale AI projects. This practical experience will solidify your understanding and spark your creativity. Consider contributing to open-source AI projects to allow you to learn from experienced developers, stay at the forefront of inventions, and give back to the AI community.

Embrace Curiosity and Open-Mindedness

The key to staying ahead in AI is a genuine curiosity about the technology and its prospects. Ask questions, explore diverse perspectives, and challenge your assumptions. The field of AI is constantly growing; be open to new ideas, technologies, and the impact of AI on various aspects of life.

Wrap-Up

We have explored the potential of AI for optimizing productivity, from planning and execution to monitoring and completion. However, this comes with a responsibility—ensuring the ethical and responsible development and implementation of AI. As we discussed, ethical concerns like bias and lack of transparency can cause discriminatory outcomes and break trust in AI systems. Similarly, failing to prioritize data privacy can turn away users and expose your business to legal risks.

As you move forward with AI in your business, remember that AI is the future of businesses and the world around us. Adopting ethical principles, prioritizing data privacy, and promoting a culture of responsible AI development can help you achieve sustainable success while leaving a positive impact on society.

One More Thing...

AI is now a tool in your toolkit, ready to enhance what you already do and help you reach new levels – and now you have a chance to do that for someone else too.

Simply by sharing your honest opinion of this book, you'll show new readers where they can find all the information they need to sharpen their own skills and use AI to make their natural talents shine.

Thank you so much for your support. It's more powerful than you realize.

Conclusion

Throughout this book, we have explored the wonders of AI—that is, how business decisions are backed by data insights, repetitive tasks are automated, and marketing campaigns generate leads with better precision. This is the reality within reach for businesses that leverage artificial intelligence (AI)'s potential at all levels of their operation.

However, AI is not a luxury reserved for tech giants; it is a toolkit accessible to businesses of all sizes. You no longer need to spend excess time over endless spreadsheets and struggle to gain information from mountains of data. AI-powered analytics tools can now crunch those numbers in seconds, revealing hidden patterns that inform smarter decision-making. Content creation, once a time-consuming effort, can be easy with AI that generates targeted marketing copy, product descriptions, or even personalized social media posts. The repetitive tasks that bog down your team's productivity—

data entry, scheduling meetings, or generating reports—can be automated with AI, allowing your employees to concentrate on what they do best: strategic thinking, creative problem-solving, and building meaningful customer relationships.

The impact of AI extends far beyond the back office. Your marketing campaigns can now target demographics, specific customer behaviors, and interests. Personalized product recommendations based on past purchases, customer service powered by AI chatbots that understand natural language, and pricing strategies that adjust based on market demand—these are just a few ways AI can transform the way you interact with your customers. A more personalized and effortless experience can help build customer loyalty and trust, leading to long-term business success.

However, with great power comes great responsibility. As we have discussed in the later chapter of this book, ethical considerations, and data privacy are paramount when implementing AI. Building trust with your customers and stakeholders requires a commitment to responsible AI practices. This means ensuring fairness and transparency in AI decisions, prioritizing data security, and remaining mindful of the potential impact of AI on society.

Remember Amazon? This e-commerce giant has leveraged AI not just for product recommendations but also for logistics and inventory management. It processes its data to predict customer demand and optimize inventory levels, ensuring products are readily available when customers need them. This translates into a smoother customer experience, reduces waste, and optimizes costs for Amazon.

The success story of Amazon is just one example of the benefits of AI for retail giants, businesses of all sizes, and across all industries. Whether you are a healthcare provider using AI to analyze patient data for faster diagnoses, a manufacturer using AI to predict equipment failure and prevent downtime, or a financial institution using AI to facilitate loan applications, the opportunities are endless.

Start the journey of integrating AI into every aspect of your business today. Let this book be your guide to implementing AI in a way that propels your business forward and does so with ethical integrity and respect for privacy—the true markers of lasting success. The future is bright for businesses that use AI responsibly, and I hope this book has equipped you with the knowledge and confidence to be a part of it.

AI has been a tremendous benefit to my business and me; however, there's one thing that AI cannot replace: genuine human interaction. With that being said, can I ask you a personal favor? You can make a real difference by sharing your review on Amazon. I am deeply touched by the kindness of my readers and would love to hear your experiences, too. Genuine reviews left by real people sharing real experiences help ensure trustworthiness to prospective readers. AI is a fantastic tool, but it can't replace human insight. But we can leverage it tremendously to build your business. Thank you for your support—it means a lot.

References

"541+ Top ChatGPT Prompts for Content Creation for Best Result," September 16, 2023. https://chatgptaihub.com/chatgpt-prompts-for-content-creation/.

"70 Useful ChatGPT Prompts for Marketing." Rodeo Software B.V., September 25, 2023. https://www.getrodeo.io/blog/chatgpt-prompts-for-marketing.

"The Rise of AI Content Creation: What It Means for Writers." AIContentfy, May 26, 2023. https://aicontentfy.com/en/blog/rise-of-ai-content-creation-what-it-means-for-writers.

"What Is Artificial Intelligence (AI)? | IBM," March 19, 2024. https://www.ibm.com/topics/artificial-intelligence.

AIContenfy Team. "The Benefits of AI in Content Creation: Enhancing Efficiency and Quality." AIContentfy, September 18, 2023. https://aicontentfy.com/en/blog/benefits-of-ai-in-content-creation-enhancing-efficiency-and-quality.

AIContenfyTeam. "ChatGPT and the Future of Customer Service." AIContentfy, January 27, 2023. https://aicontentfy.com/en/blog/chatgpt-and-future-of-customer-service.

AIContentfy Team. "The Future of Content Collaboration with AI-Powered Tools." AIContentfy, February 18, 2023. https://aicontentfy.com/en/blog/future-of-content-collaboration-with-ai-powered-tools.

Akshita. "100+ ChatGPT Prompts to Elevate Your Content Game," January 11, 2024. https://narrato.io/blog/100-chatgpt-prompts-for-content-creation-to-get-the-best-outputs/.

Alloba. "The Benefits of Using AI in Data Analysis," n.d. https://www.alooba.com/articles/benefits-of-using-ai-in-data-analysis/.

Alston, Elena. "How to Automate ChatGPT," April 8, 2024. https://zapier.com/blog/automate-chatgpt/.

Arshad, Umar. "49+ Best ChatGPT Prompts for Leads Generation in 2024 (Boost Conversion)," October 8, 2023. https://chatgptaihub.com/chatgpt-prompts-for-leads-generation/.

avcontentteam. "Top 20 AI and Machine Learning Trends to Watch in

2024." *Analytics Vidhya* (blog), May 1, 2023. https://www.analyticsvidhya.com/blog/2023/05/emerging-trends-in-ai-and-machine-learning/.

Babich, Nick. "How to Use ChatGPT in Product Design: 8 Practical Examples." Medium, January 4, 2023. https://uxplanet.org/how-to-use-chatgpt-in-product-design-8-practical-examples-a6135308b9b2.

Baker, Kristen. "10 Proven Ways to Use ChatGPT for Business for Growth." Podium, October 19, 2023. https://www.podium.com/article/ways-to-use-chatgpt-for-business/.

Bashir, Iman. "8 Reasons Using AI Will Improve Your Content Creation Process." Entrepreneur, June 15, 2022. https://www.entrepreneur.com/leadership/8-reasons-using-ai-will-improve-your-content-creation/426695.

Bhanu Teja, P. "How To Set Up A Customer Service Chatbot ChatGPT." SiteGPT, October 28, 2023. https://sitegpt.ai/blog/customer-service-chatbot-chatgpt.

Blackman, Reid. "A Practical Guide to Building Ethical AI." *Harvard Business Review*, October 15, 2020. https://hbr.org/2020/10/a-practical-guide-to-building-ethical-ai.

Bossmann, Julia. "Top 9 Ethical Issues in Artificial Intelligence." World Economic Forum, October 21, 2016. https://www.weforum.org/agenda/2016/10/top-10-ethical-issues-in-artificial-intelligence/.

Bowman, Jeremy. "10 Top Companies Using AI." The Motley Fool, n.d. https://www.fool.com/investing/stock-market/market-sectors/information-technology/ai-stocks/companies-that-use-ai/.

Brandon, Samantha. "5 Ways to Power Up Your Content Marketing With AI." StoryChief - Content Marketing Blog, n.d. https://storychief.io/blog/power-up-content-marketing-with-ai.

Bungsy, Agnes. "ChatGPT Prompts for Data Analysis." AnalyticsHacker, n.d. https://www.analyticshacker.com/analytics-resources/ai-prompts-for-data-analysis.

Calzon, Bernardita. "The Importance of Data Driven Decision Making for Business," November 17, 2022. https://www.datapine.com/blog/data-driven-decision-making-in-businesses/.

ClickUp. "ChatGPT Prompts For Data Analysis," n.d. https://clickup.com/templates/ai-prompts/data-analysis.

ClickUp. "ChatGPT Prompts For Lead Generation," n.d. https://clickup.com/templates/ai-prompts/lead-generation.

ClickUp. "ChatGPT Prompts For Project Scheduling," n.d. https://clickup.com/templates/ai-prompts/project-scheduling.

ClickUp. "ChatGPT Prompts For Team Meetings," n.d. https://clickup.com/templates/ai-prompts/team-meetings.

Copeland, B.J. "Artificial Intelligence (AI) | Definition, Examples, Types, Applications, Companies, & Facts | Britannica," April 29, 2024. https://www.britannica.com/technology/artificial-intelligence.

Council of Europe: Artificial Intelligence. "History of Artificial Intelligence - Artificial Intelligence," n.d. https://www.coe.int/en/web/artificial-intelligence/history-of-ai.

Council of Europe: Human Rights and Biomedicine. "Common Ethical Challenges in AI," n.d. https://www.coe.int/en/web/bioethics/common-ethical-challenges-in-ai.

Crabtree, Matt. "How to Use ChatGPT for Sales." Datacamp, June 2023. https://www.datacamp.com/tutorial/how-to-use-chat-gpt-for-sales.

Craig, Lindsay. "How to Use ChatGPT to Generate Product Ideas & Marketing Campaigns." *Medium* (blog), December 15, 2022. https://lindsay-craig.medium.com/how-to-use-chatgpt-3-to-generate-product-ideas-marketing-campaigns-204dee40ab1d.

Dasha. "Why Understanding Customer Needs Through AI Is Crucial," December 7, 2023. https://dasha.ai/en-us/blog/why-understanding-customer-needs-through-ai-is-crucial.

dealcode. "ChatGPT for Sales: 7 Ways to Boost Your Sales Process | Dealcode," May 11, 2023. https://www.dealcode.ai/blog/chatgpt-for-sales-7-ways-to-boost-your-sales-process.

Derungs, Amy. "ChatGPT for Copywriting: 10 Easy Ways To Boost Conversions in 2024." Niche Pursuits, April 27, 2023. https://www.nichepursuits.com/chatgpt-for-copywriting/.

Describely. "Free Resource: 30+ Time Saving Ecommerce ChatGPT Prompts." Describely, October 11, 2023. https://describely.ai/blog/chatgpt-ecommerce-prompts/.

Document360 Team. "8 Use Cases of ChatGPT for Customer Service." Document360, May 19, 2023. https://document360.com/blog/chatgpt-for-customer-service/.

Dr Mark van Rijmenam, CSP | Strategic Futurist Speaker. "Privacy in the Age of AI: Risks, Challenges and Solutions," February 16, 2023. https://www.thedigitalspeaker.com/privacy-age-ai-risks-challenges-solutions/.

Dragonfly AI. "How to Use AI in Graphic Design," n.d. https://dragonflyai.co/resources/blog/how-to-use-ai-to-inform-design.

Dutta, DataStax, Deb. "Unlocking the Power of Data Analysis with ChatGPT." CDO Trends, September 18, 2023. https://www.cdotrends.com/story/18409/unlocking-power-data-analysis-chatgpt.

Ecommerce Prompts. "ChatGPT Prompts for the Ultimate Ecommerce Marketer," n.d. https://www.ecommerceprompts.com/.

Editorial Team. "How to Use ChatGPT to Write Marketing Copy," March 20, 2024. https://dorik.com/blog/how-to-use-chatgpt-to-write-marketing-copy.

Fitzpatrick, Klarissa. "AI in Sales and Marketing: What Is It?" Ringover, June 26, 2023. https://www.ringover.com/blog/ai-in-sales-marketing.

Five Star Visibility. "How to Use an AI Chatbot to Increase Customer Satisfaction for Your Small Business." LinkedIn, January 5, 2024. https://www.linkedin.com/pulse/how-use-ai-chatbot-increase-customer-satisfaction-your-ldkke.

Flores, Brian. "5 Ways Generative AI Fosters and Improves Team Collaboration." Agility PR Solutions, October 18, 2023. https://www.agilitypr.com/pr-news/public-relations/5-ways-generative-ai-fosters-and-improves-team-collaboration/.

Gandía, Rafa. "10 Ways to Generate Leads with ChatGPT in Seconds." *FindThatLead* (blog), January 31, 2023. https://blog.findthatlead.com/en/generate-leads-with-chatgpt.

Georgiou, Michael. "30+ Key Business Automation Statistics You Should Know." Imaginovation | Top Web & Mobile App Development Company Raleigh, n.d. https://imaginovation.net/blog/business-automation-statistics/.

Gerrard + Bizway AI Assistant. "11 Helpful ChatGPT Prompts for Report Writing (December 2023)," December 18, 2023. https://www.bizway.io/blog/chatgpt-prompts-for-report-writing.

Greenan, Richard. "ChatGPT for UX Design: The Top 15 Prompts," July 25, 2023. https://careerfoundry.com/en/blog/ux-design/chatgpt-for-ux-design/.

Guest Author. "8 Surprising Benefits of AI in Team Collaboration You Might Not Realize." Stormboard, August 4, 2023. https://stormboard.com/blog/8-surprising-benefits-of-ai-in-team-collaboration.

Guinness, Harry. "How to Use ChatGPT for Copywriting and Content Ideation," May 31, 2023. https://zapier.com/blog/chatgpt-marketing-writing/.

Gunn, Elliot. "11 of the Best ChatGPT Data Analysis Prompts You Should Know," July 28, 2023. https://careerfoundry.com/en/blog/data-analytics/data-analysis-prompts/.

Gupta, Pragati. "ChatGPT Prompts for E-Commerce That You Can Check out in 2023." The Writesonic Blog - Making Content Your Superpower, April 29, 2023. https://writesonic.com/blog/chatgpt-prompts-ecommerce/.

Hari, Jishnu. "10 Powerful Ways to Use ChatGPT as a Product Designer." Medium, April 18, 2023. https://uxdesign.cc/10-powerful-ways-to-use-chatgpt-as-a-product-designer-b3c395d20a00.

Hariri, Farah. "20 Ingenuis ChatGPT Prompts for UX & Product Designers." Medium, February 3, 2023. https://bootcamp.uxdesign.cc/20-ingenuis-chatgpt-prompts-for-ux-product-designers-1ffca0b451fa.

Harry's Blockchain Blog. "Unlocking the Potential of ChatGPT for Inventory Management: Our Roadmap with ChatGPT." Medium (blog), February 3, 2023. https://medium.com/gearchain/unlocking-the-potential-of-chatgpt-for-inventory-management-our-roadmap-with-chatgpt-9a5071cb1bbe.

Helpwise. "50 Expert-Approved ChatGPT Prompts For Customer Service Challenges," May 22, 2023. https://helpwise.io/blog/chatgpt-prompts-for-customer-service.

Helpwise. "The Complete Guide to Using ChatGPT for Customer Service," May 5, 2023. https://helpwise.io/blog/how-to-use-chatgpt-for-customer-service.

Hines, Kristi. "History Of ChatGPT: A Timeline Of The Meteoric Rise Of Generative AI Chatbots." Search Engine Journal, June 4, 2023. https://www.searchenginejournal.com/history-of-chatgpt-timeline/488370/.

Hirsch, Dennis, and Piers Norris Turner. "What Is 'Ethical AI' and How Can Companies Achieve It?" The Conversation, May 25, 2023. http://theconversation.com/what-is-ethical-ai-and-how-can-companies-achieve-it-204349.

Howarth, John. "57 NEW AI Statistics (Apr 2024)." Exploding Topics, August 17, 2021. https://explodingtopics.com/blog/ai-statistics.

Inclusion Digital Engineering. "10 Steps to More Ethical Artificial Intelligence," March 17, 2023. https://inclusioncloud.com/insights/blog/ethical-artificial-intelligence/.

Innovation at Work. "Three Ways To Prepare Your Workforce for Artificial Intelligence." IEEE Innovation at Work (blog), September 8, 2021. https://innovationatwork.ieee.org/three-ways-to-prepare-your-workforce-for-artificial-intelligence/.

Ipsen, Adam. "ChatGPT's Code Interpreter Is Now Advanced Data Analysis," September 20, 2023. https://www.pluralsight.com/resources/blog/data/ChatGPT-Advanced-Data-Analytics.

James. "10 ChatGPT Email Prompts to Boost Your Email Performance." Mailbutler, May 19, 2023. https://www.mailbutler.io/blog/email/chatgpt-email-prompts/.

Jasaitis, Algirdas. "Top 10 Best Business Report Chatgpt Prompt Example 2024." WPS Blog, August 3, 2023. https://www.wps.com/blog/top-10-best-business-report-chatgpt-prompt-example-2023-1/.

Jenni. "Chat GPT in Data Analysis: Unlocking the Future of Research," October 30, 2023. https://jenni.ai/chat-gpt/research-data-analysis-uses.

Joy, F. "40 ChatGPT AI Prompts for Stellar Lead Generation," September 7, 2023. https://themarketinghustle.com/ai-marketing/40-chatgpt-ai-prompts-for-stellar-lead-generation/.

Kanev, Kal. "Responsible AI: How to Make Your Enterprise Ethical, so That Your AI Is Too." DXC Technology, n.d. https://dxc.com/us/en/insights/perspectives/paper/responsible-ai.

Karp, Ethan. "ChatGPT Swears It Can Optimize Your Inventory. Let's Examine." Forbes, March 1, 2023. https://www.forbes.com/sites/ethankarp/2023/03/01/chatgpt-swears-it-can-optimize-your-inventory-lets-examine/.

Kempton, Beth. "How Is AI Used in Business? 10 Ways It Can Help." Upwork, August 11, 2023. https://www.upwork.com/resources/how-is-ai-used-in-business.

Kleinings, Hanna. "How to Get the Most out of AI in 2023: 7 Applications of Artificial Intelligence in Business." Levity, January 18, 2023. https://levity.ai/blog/8-uses-ai-business.

Lazarevikj, Oliver. "10 Powerful Ways to Use ChatGPT as a Product Designer." *Visual Side* (blog), March 20, 2023. https://medium.com/visual-side/10-powerful-ways-to-use-chatgpt-as-a-product-designer-caee567d9dcb.

Leadership AI. "20 Ultimate ChatGPT Prompts for Team Leaders." Spinach.io, October 25, 2023. https://www.spinach.io/blog/best-chatgpt-prompts-for-team-leaders.

Lee, Alvin. "How to Protect Data Privacy When Using AI." Twilio, November 13, 2023. https://www.twilio.com/en-us/blog/ai-data-privacy.

LIGS University. "The Role of Artificial Intelligence in Improving Project

Management," August 6, 2020. https://ligsuniversity.com/blog/the-role-of-artificial-intelligence-in-improving-project-management.

Lile, Samantha. "50 Best ChatGPT Prompts for Communications Workflows." Simpplr, January 29, 2024. https://www.simpplr.com/blog/2024/chatgpt-communication-prompts/.

LinkedIn. "Essential Chat GPT Prompts for Designers," August 23, 2023. https://www.linkedin.com/pulse/essential-chat-gpt-prompts-design ers-designwithpro.

LinkedIn. "How Can Artificial Intelligence Enhance Conceptual Design Feedback?," December 6, 2023. https://www.linkedin.com/advice/0/how-can-artificial-intelligence-enhance-conceptual-design-h6a6e.

LinkedIn. "How Can You Stay Up-to-Date with the Latest Research in Artificial Intelligence?" n.d. https://www.linkedin.com/advice/3/how-can-you-stay-up-to-date-latest-research-1c.

LinkedIn. "How Do You Keep up with the Latest Trends and Innovations in AI?" January 17, 2024. https://www.linkedin.com/advice/3/how-do-you-keep-up-latest-trends-innovations-7041842070671556608.

Lundberg, Steph. "Benefits of AI in Customer Service: 4 Ways AI Can Help." Help Scout, n.d. https://www.helpscout.com/blog/benefits-of-ai-in-customer-service/.

Macready, Hannah. "65 ChatGPT Prompts for Marketing to Make Work Easier." Social Media Marketing & Management Dashboard, July 25, 2023. https://blog.hootsuite.com/chatgpt-prompts-for-marketing/.

Maderis, Giana. "Top 22 Benefits of Chatbots for Businesses and Customers." Zendesk, November 20, 2019. https://www.zendesk.com/blog/5-benefits-using-ai-bots-customer-service/.

Mailbutler. "ChatGPT Email Prompts," November 1, 2023. https://www.linkedin.com/pulse/chatgpt-email-prompts-mailbutler-gmbh-uhjze.

Majumder, Deepa. "Top Benefits of AI-Powered Service Desk." workativ.com, n.d. https://workativ.comfalse.

Mandula, Mark S. "What Kind of Training Could I Do for My Employees on AI/GenAI?" LinkedIn, September 14, 2023. https://www.linkedin.com/pulse/what-kind-training-could-i-do-my-employees-aigenai-mark-s-mandula.

Marr, Bernard. "The 10 Best Examples Of How Companies Use Artificial Intelligence In Practice." *Bernard Marr* (blog), July 2, 2021. https://bernardmarr.com/the-10-best-examples-of-how-companies-use-artificial-intelli

gence-in-practice/.

Martin, Michelle. "10 AI Content Creation Tools That Will Make Your Job Easier." Social Media Marketing & Management Dashboard, October 5, 2023. https://blog.hootsuite.com/ai-powered-content-creation/.

Maryville University. "AI in Business: Ethical Considerations," March 28, 2023. https://online.maryville.edu/blog/ai-ethical-issues/.

Mason, Scott. "4 Ways to Use AI in Content Marketing (Plus Examples)." GLC | Your Audience Awaits, September 16, 2022. https://glcdelivers.com/4-ways-to-use-ai-in-content-marketing-plus-examples/.

McKay, Sam. "ChatGPT Advanced Data Analysis: Explained | Master Data Skills + AI," September 26, 2023. https://blog.enterprisedna.co/chatgpt-advanced-data-analysis-explained/.

Medairy, Brad. "4 Ways to Preserve Privacy in Artificial Intelligence," n.d.   https://www.boozallen.com/s/solution/four-ways-to-preserve-privacy-in-ai.html.

Melara, Ale. "Exploring the Benefits and Limitations of Using AI for Content Creation." SmartBug., April 25, 2023. https://www.smartbugmedia.com/blog/benefits-and-limitations-of-ai-for-content-creation.

Mike Paul. "How to Stay Up-to-Date on the Latest AI Trends," May 14, 2023. https://techpilot.ai/how-to-stay-up-to-date-on-the-latest-ai-trends/.

MIT Management. "How to Use ChatGPT's Advanced Data Analysis Feature." MIT Sloan Teaching & Learning Technologies (blog), n.d. https://mitsloanedtech.mit.edu/ai/tools/data-analysis/how-to-use-chatgpts-advanced-data-analysis-feature/.

MonkeyLearn. "What Is Data Analysis and How Can You Get Started?" MonkeyLearn, n.d. https://monkeylearn.com/data-analysis/.

Moulton, Luke. "7 Ways ChatGPT Can Help with Lead Generation | LeadSync," March 24, 2023. https://leadsync.me/blog/chatgpt-lead-generation/.

Nawab, Alsabah. "How Can We Use ChatGPT to Automate Workflows?" n.d. https://www.linkedin.com/pulse/how-can-we-use-chatgpt-automate-workflows-alsabah-nawab.

Neher, Krista. "Council Post: Five Ways To Get Your Employees AI Ready." Forbes, January 9, 2024. https://www.forbes.com/sites/forbescoachescouncil/2024/01/09/five-ways-to-get-your-employees-ai-ready/.

Newberry, Christina. "74 Artificial Intelligence Statistics to Guide Your Marketing Plan." Social Media Marketing & Management Dashboard, August   16,   2023.   https://blog.hootsuite.com/artificial-intelligence-statistics/.

Nyman, Cheryl. "Launching Your AI Journey: Four Essential Steps to Success." BPM, November 7, 2023. https://www.bpm.com/insights/how-to-start-your-ai-journey/.

Oana. "10 Key Benefits of Business Process Automation." Penneo, February 10, 2021. https://penneo.com/blog/10-benefits-business-process-automation/.

Overvest, Marijn. "ChatGPT Inventory — Using AI to Optimize Stock Levels." *Procurement Tactics* (blog), November 27, 2023. https://procurement tactics.com/chatgpt-inventory/.

OVIC: Office of the Victorian Information Commissioner. "Artificial Intelligence and Privacy – Issues and Challenges," n.d. https://ovic.vic.gov. au/privacy/resources-for-organisations/artificial-intelligence-and-privacy-issues-and-challenges/.

Padmavati. "Building Stronger Teams With ChatGPT." Northwest Executive Education, June 13, 2023. https://northwest.education/insights/careers/building-stronger-teams-with-chatgpt/.

Pappas, Christopher. "The Role Of AI In The Future Of Project Management." eLearning Industry, October 2, 2023. https://elearningindustry.com/role-of-ai-in-the-future-of-project-management.

Petit, Maria. "AI Project Management: The Future of Efficient Project Execution." Monitask, November 21, 2023. https://www.monitask.com/en/blog/the-role-of-artificial-intelligence-in-improving-project-management-how-ai-can-help-make-projects-run-smoothly.

Podium Staff. "AI Chatbot for Customer Service: How To Do It Right With 10 Examples." Podium, n.d. https://www.podium.com/article/ai-chatbot-for-customer-service-how-to-do-it-right/.

Porter, Jon. "ChatGPT Continues to Be One of the Fastest-Growing Services Ever." The Verge, November 6, 2023. https://www.theverge.com/2023/11/6/23948386/chatgpt-active-user-count-openai-developer-conference.

PricewaterhouseCoopers. "6 Generative AI Business Myths That Will Make You Rethink Everything." PwC, n.d. https://www.pwc.com/us/en/tech-effect/ai-analytics/six-generative-ai-business-myths.html.

Pro AI Prompt. "Generating Team Collaboration Workflows ChatGPT Prompts - Pro AI Prompt," December 12, 2023. https://proaiprompt.com/generating-team-collaboration-workflows-chatgpt-prompts/.

process.st. "How to Automate Business Processes In 6 Simple Steps (+ Tools List)," July 13, 2023. https://www.process.st/how-to-automate-business-processes/.

Proprompter Editor. "ChatGPT Prompts for Report Writing ." *ProPromter* (blog), October 3, 2023. https://proprompter.com/chatgpt-prompts-for-report-writing/.

Randolph, Kevin. "AI for Sales: Benefits, Challenges, and How You Can Use It." Nutshell, May 11, 2023. https://www.nutshell.com/blog/ai-for-sales.

Repaka, Ram Sekhar. "How to Integrate ChatGPT with Ecommerce Website?" Ram Sekhar Repaka, March 4, 2023. https://www.ramsekharrepaka.com/post/how-to-integrate-chatgpt-with-ecommerce-website.

Repin, Stefan. "AI-Powered Forecasting: Use AI to Predict Future Market Trends, Sales Performance, and Customer Behavior." Platforce, November 23, 2023. https://platforce.io/ai-powered-forecasting-use-ai-to-predict-future-market-trends-sales-performance-and-customer-behavior/.

Roberti, Damian. "Implementing ChatGPT for Effective Inventory Management." Marketing Food Online, April 20, 2023. https://marketing foodonline.com/blogs/news/implementing-chatgpt-for-effective-inven tory-management.

Robinson, Ryan. "Content Marketing AI: How to Make the Most of It | Zapier," October 5, 2023. https://zapier.com/blog/content-marketing-ai/.

Rockwell, Anyoha. "The History of Artificial Intelligence." *Science in the News* (blog), August 28, 2017. https://sitn.hms.harvard.edu/flash/2017/history-artificial-intelligence/.

Samuel. "AI-Assisted Collaboration: Empower Your Team with ChatGPT!" *Collection Performance* (blog), April 17, 2023. https://collection performance.com/collaboration-with-chatgpt/.

SendBoard. "50 Useful ChatGPT Prompts To Boost Your Email Writing Productivity," n.d. https://www.sendboard.com/blog/chat-gpt-prompts.

Seth, Huang. "How ChatGPT Helps Teams Be Better Communicators - and Everyone Is Happier for It," March 8, 2023. https://www.linkedin.com/pulse/how-chatgpt-helps-teams-better-communicators-seth-huang-ph-d-.

Shivani, D. "How Do You Identify and Prioritize the Most Suitable Business Processes for Automation?" LinkedIn, n.d. https://www.linkedin.com/advice/0/how-do-you-identify-prioritize-most-suitable.

Sidor, Jonathan. "50+ Top Stats on AI in Customer Service for 2024," December 28, 2023. https://getzowie.com/blog/stats-ai-customer-service.

Simplilearn. "What Is Data Analysis: A Comprehensive Guide." Simplilearn.com, May 27, 2020. https://www.simplilearn.com/data-analy

sis-methods-process-types-article.

Singh, Dilip. "How to Use Chatgpt for Product Development." LinkedIn, April 16, 2023. https://www.linkedin.com/pulse/how-use-chatgpt-product-devel opment-dilip-singh.

Smarty, Ann. "ChatGPT Prompts for Customer Support." *Practical Ecommerce* (blog), May 30, 2023. https://www.practicalecommerce.com/ chatgpt-prompts-for-customer-support.

Smulders, Stefan. "Chat GPT For B2B Sales & Lead Generation: The Ultimate Guide." *Expandi* (blog), August 8, 2023. https://expandi.io/blog/use-chat gpt-for-lead-generation/.

Snook, Jason. "How Businesses Can Start Their AI Journey." CapTech, May 12, 2023. https://www.captechconsulting.com/articles/how-businesses-can start-on-their-ai-journey.

Spisak, Brian, Louis B. Rosenberg, and Max Beilby. "13 Principles for Using AI Responsibly." *Harvard Business Review*, June 30, 2023. https://hbr.org/2023/ 06/13-principles-for-using-ai-responsibly.

Stobierski, Tim. "The Advantages of Data-Driven Decision-Making." Business Insights Blog, August 26, 2019. https://online.hbs.edu/blog/post/data driven-decision-making.

Tamilore, June. "6 Applications of AI for Content Creation." Buffer: All-you-need social media toolkit for small businesses, June 4, 2023. https://buffer. com/resources/ai-content-creation/.

Team Kissflow. "20+ Key Business Process Automation Stats You Need To Know," April 8, 2024. https://kissflow.com/workflow/bpm/business-process-automation-statistics/.

Team, OTS Marketing. "Business for AI | Top 10 Steps to Prepare Your Business for AI." OTS Solutions, February 14, 2019. https://otssolutions.com/top-10-steps-to-prepare-your-business-for-ai/.

The Investopedia Team. "What Is Artificial Intelligence (AI)?" Investopedia, April 9, 2024. https://www.investopedia.com/terms/a/artificial-intelli gence-ai.asp.

The Upwork Team. "The Top 8 Benefits of Business Process Automation." Upwork, April 12, 2023. https://www.upwork.com/resources/business-process-automation-benefits.

todook. "AI Chatbot Implementation: Overcoming Challenges & Lessons," July 17, 2023. https://todook.io/overcoming-challenges-in-ai-chatbot-imple mentation-lessons-learned/.

Tsuei, Judy. "Optimize Your Calendar with ChatGPT." clockwise, May 31, 202AD. https://www.getclockwise.com/blog/chatgpt-calendar-optimiza tion.

Tully, Maggie. "50 Practical ChatGPT Prompts for Project Management." Rodeo Software B.V., May 30, 2023. https://www.getrodeo.io/blog/chatgpt-prompts-for-project-management.

Tushar, Jain. "10 Best Chatgpt Prompts For Customer Service-2024." *Enthu.Ai* (blog), June 26, 2023. https://enthu.ai/blog/chatgpt-prompts-for-customer-service/.

Unbounce. "Break Free: The State of AI Marketing for Small Business," September 23, 2023. https://unbounce.com/ai-for-small-business-report/.

Unity Group. "Uncover 9 Myths About AI in Business," April 18, 2023. https://www.unitygroup.com/blog/ai-in-business-most-common-myths-debunked/.

Valchanov, Iliya. "Best 25 ChatGPT Prompts for Marketing in 2024." *Team-GPT* (blog), September 15, 2023. https://team-gpt.com/blog/chatgpt-prompts-for-marketing/.

Venkateswaran, Hari Narayanan. "How to Utilize Chatbots to Improve Customer Satisfaction." Customer Service Blog from HappyFox – Improve Customer Service & Experience, October 22, 2020. https://blog.happyfox.com/how-to-utilize-chatbots-to-improve-customer-satisfaction/.

Vishal, Dave. "ChatGPT For Content Writing: 20+ Prompts To Try," February 6, 2023. https://meetanshi.com/blog/chatgpt-for-content/.

Watters, Ashley. "11 Common Ethical Issues in Artificial Intelligence." CompTIA Community, November 16, 2023. https://connect.comptia.org/blog/common-ethical-issues-in-artificial-intelligence.

Way, Paul. "Top 5 Trends to Look Forward to in 2024 for Generative AI." Hitachi Solutions, December 19, 2023. https://global.hitachi-solutions.com/blog/5-generative-ai-trends-2024/.

Webster, Mark. "149 AI Statistics: The Present and Future of AI [2024 Stats]," May 24, 2023. https://www.authorityhacker.com/ai-statistics/.

Wharton Online. "How Do Businesses Use Artificial Intelligence?," January 19, 2022. https://online.wharton.upenn.edu/blog/how-do-businesses-use-artifi cial-intelligence/.

Wren, Hannah. "ChatGPT for Customer Service: A Complete Guide." Zendesk, October 17, 2023. https://www.zendesk.com/blog/chatgpt-for-customer-service/.

Wright, Verrion. "8 Generative AI Best Practices for Privacy." *BigID* (blog), October 26, 2023. https://bigid.com/blog/8-generative-ai-best-practices-for-privacy/.

Xeven, S. E. O. "How to Integrate ChatGPT with an E-Commerce Website." Xeven Solutions, August 8, 2023. https://www.xevensolutions.com/blog/the-uses-of-chatgpt-integration-with-an-e-commerce-website/.Webster,

M. (2024, January 10). 149 AI Statistics: The Present and Future of AI [2024 stats]. Authority Hacker. https://www.authorityhacker.com/ai-statistics/

Made in United States
North Haven, CT
06 October 2024

58428160R00213